CW01401559

£1.50

TOOKEY'S TALKIES

CHRISTOPHER
TOOKEY

A61581

ARTS REVIEWER
OF THE YEAR
2013

TOOKEY'S
TALKIES

144 GREAT FILMS FROM
THE LAST 25 YEARS

Copyright © 2015 Christopher Tookey

The moral right of the author has been asserted.

Apart from any fair dealing for the purposes of research or private study,
or criticism or review, as permitted under the Copyright, Designs and Patents
Act 1988, this publication may only be reproduced, stored or transmitted, in
any form or by any means, with the prior permission in writing of the
publishers, or in the case of reprographic reproduction in accordance with
the terms of licences issued by the Copyright Licensing Agency. Enquiries
concerning reproduction outside those terms should be sent to the publishers.

Matador
9 Priory Business Park,
Wistow Road, Kibworth Beauchamp,
Leicestershire. LE8 0RX
Tel: (+44) 116 279 2299
Fax: (+44) 116 279 2277
Email: books@troubador.co.uk
Web: www.troubador.co.uk/matador

ISBN 978-1784621-988

British Library Cataloguing in Publication Data.
A catalogue record for this book is available from the British Library.

Typeset in Adobe Garamond Pro by Troubador Publishing Ltd, Leicester, UK
Printed and bound in the UK by TJ International, Padstow, Cornwall

Matador is an imprint of Troubador Publishing Ltd

MIX
Paper from
responsible sources
FSC
www.fsc.org   FSC° C013056

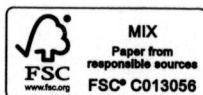

To all those critics who have lost their jobs

PREFACE

For eight years, I was TV and then film critic for the Sunday Telegraph. For twenty years after that, I was sole movie critic for the Daily Mail and the world's most popular internet newspaper, Mail Online. In 2013, I won the award Arts Reviewer of the Year from the London Press Club. I've seen at least 10,000 films.

Tookey's Talkies is a book celebrating 144 great movies of the last 25 years.

They range from movies which are generally accepted as great (from *The Artist* to *Toy Story*) through to films I liked much more than my colleagues. These include a very wide variety of films, from the memorably horrific Japanese film *Audition* to the courageous Chinese drama *To Live*, via Denmark's fine but little-seen political thriller, *King's Game*.

I also try to explain why I loved *Ed Wood, Isn't She Great?* and *Queen of Hearts* – all commercial flops – along with such critically underrated movies as *Cheri, Separate Lies* and *The Tourist*.

In a companion volume, *Tookey's Turkeys*, I have written about the 144 films that annoyed or angered me most over the same period.

The good ones collected in this volume are welcome evidence that quality has not yet been drowned out by quantity, and creativity has not been entirely destroyed by commerce. For me, film remains the most exciting and uplifting art form of our times.

If space had permitted, I could easily have come up with another 500 movies that are worth watching, but these are at least some of the very best. I hope you enjoy reading about them, and that my reviews will encourage you to see or resee them.

Versions of these reviews have appeared in the Daily Mail, in the Sunday Telegraph and on my website www.movie-film-review.com. I have modified them to remove topical references that have dated, although I haven't needed to revise my opinions.

Christopher Tookey,
London

A GROSS OF GOODIES

THE ACT OF KILLING *(2012)*

Many good films invite us to empathise with the persecuted. Hardly any try to get inside the minds of the persecutors. It's too dangerous, and besides most of them are ashamed, "in denial", or anxious not to sully their image.

Here is the notable exception, an astonishing documentary that's essential viewing for anyone wishing to understand the darker aspects of the human condition.

Film-maker Joshua Oppenheimer somehow managed to persuade various Indonesian mass killers – now middle-aged or elderly – to boast, justify and re-enact how they murdered more than a million alleged Communists, ethnic Chinese and intellectuals in 1965-6.

Unforgettable footage includes an old man gleefully imitating the sound of someone having his head sawn off, a younger man rhapsodising about the rape of 14 year-old girls, and a terrifyingly vacuous chat-show hostess treating mass murder as a fabulous means to achieve celebrity.

It presents the worst possible image of Indonesia, past and present, and offers an unsettlingly truthful account of how corrupt "democracy" can be. But by implication it explores the way oppressive regimes behave the world over.

Films as shocking could be made – if any film-maker were brave enough – in many parts of Africa, South America and even Europe. I imagine many citizens of Putin's Russia would watch this exposure of government by gangsters with more than one shiver of recognition.

In passing, the killers reveal how far film culture helped to influence them for the worse; just like the Krays in our own country, they watched gangster movies to inspire them and lend them a kind of spurious glamour.

So much for those who pretend that films have no harmful effects on society. And no, I'm not arguing that gangster movies should be banned; I'm saying that film-makers have social and moral responsibilities. Man is, for good and ill, an imitative species.

Technically the film isn't perfect and could have been more ruthlessly edited. However, it deserves to win awards, some of them for sheer bravery. No wonder most of the crew members are listed as "anonymous". Let us hope that this film will inspire more documentary-makers to reveal damning truths in their own countries. Needless to say, it is not an easy watch; but watch it, you should. Because of its revelatory honesty, this might be the most important documentary ever.

ADAPTATION *(2002)*

Adaptation is the eagerly awaited follow-up to director Spike Jonze and writer Charlie Kaufman's engagingly eccentric *Being John Malkovich*. Adaptation is even more bizarre, and in an age when most movies seem to have been made by and for the mentally challenged, it fizzes with joy in its own intelligence and creativity.

The story juggles playfully the real with the fictitious. The central character is screenwriter Charlie Kaufman (played by Nicolas Cage), who – in common with most writers – is self-obsessed, arrogant yet lacking in self-confidence. "Do I have an original thought in my head?" he worries.

He wonders if his time might not be better spent learning Chinese or playing the oboe – anything, in order to avoid having to write, or (worse still) suffer the embarrassment of having human relationships. He is especially mortified by his lack of status on the set of the movie he wrote, *Being John Malkovich*. None of the actors recognises him, and he is constantly in the way.

The fictitious Charlie, just like the one in real life, leaps at an offer made by a film producer (Jonathan Demme in real life, Tilda Swinton in the movie) to adapt a (real) non-fiction book, *The Orchid Thief*, by an equally real New Yorker journalist Susan Orlean (played by Meryl Streep).

As in real life, Charlie agonizes for months over how to adapt the book. The leading character is Florida orchid poacher John Laroche (another real person, here played by Chris Cooper), and the book attempts to understand the nature of his passion for orchids.

Both the real and fictitious Charlie do their research and come to the conclusion that the appeal of orchids has something to do with their inspiring ability to adapt in order to attract insects that will enable them to propagate.

Charlie also spots a hint of sexual attraction in Susan Orlean's attitude to her hygienically and dentally challenged anti-hero. She admires Laroche's passion for orchids and his adaptabilty. And she wishes she had more of those qualities herself.

But these ideas are hardly dramatic or gripping enough to sustain an entire screenplay, and the fictitious Charlie (like the real one) tries to back out of the project after six months, on the grounds that there's no character development, no action and no drama.

Early on, he has told Swinton's movie executive that he's attracted to the project because it doesn't involve sex, guns, conflict, chases or people overcoming terrible obstacles – in other words, the mainstays of Hollywood movies. Midway through the movie, Charlie realises that because his screenplay lacks all these things, it is unfilmable.

At this point, Charlie's twin brother, Donald (also played by Nicolas Cage), comes to the rescue. In real life, Charlie doesn't have a brother although he mischievously credits him with co-writing his screenplay, which means that for the first time an entirely imaginary person has been nominated for an Oscar.

For the first part of the movie, Donald acts as comic relief. He's all the things Charlie isn't – lithe, confident, attractive to women. He finds writing film scripts annoyingly easy, mainly because he hasn't an original thought in his head and adheres ruthlessly to the principles expounded by real-life screenwriting guru Robert McKee (wonderfully impersonated by Brian Cox).

There are several funny scenes where Donald tries to get creative help from a querulous Charlie, who can't believe how crass and derivative his twin brother's ideas are. Humiliatingly for Charlie, Donald's first screenplay is snapped up by Hollywood.

"It's *Silence of the Lambs* meets *Psycho*" says Donald.

"Oh," says Charlie, compressing a lifetime of anger, distaste and hopelessness into one syllable.

The ebulliently optimistic Donald encourages the creatively constipated Charlie to attend a three-day seminar by McKee. Slumped hopelessly in McKee's audience, Charlie loathes the tutor's attempt to reduce screenwriting to formula. Charlie points out to the great man that in real life nothing much happens, people don't have epiphanies, nothing changes. McKee tells him that if he doesn't put these things in his screenplay, "you'll bore the audience out of its mind".

"You can not have a protagonist without passion," McKee barks. "God help you if you use voice-over," he snarls, badmouthing one of Charlie's most treasured devices.

And McKee warns the desperate writer against resorting to plot mechanics in the final act that are too convenient to ring true: "Don't you dare bring in a *deus ex machina*!"

Perversely inspired by McKee's instructions and helped by his more intrepid twin Donald's investigative abilities, Charlie discovers a final act for his movie, which I shall not reveal, except to say that it has nothing to do with reality but involves sex, drugs, guns, a chase, and an alligator as *deus ex machina*.

Some people don't like the denouement and feel it's a

Hollywood cop-out, but I loved it. It brilliantly captures the ambivalence of most professional writers. You want to express yourself and put across your ideas, yet at the same time you want to reach an audience.

The real Susan Orlean is understandably pleased with Kaufman's adaptation, even though Kaufman has invented a very different Susan Orlean to suit his purposes. In one of the best performances of her career, Meryl Streep attacks the part with gusto, showing us an icily elegant, ruthless New York journalist discovering the sleazy swamp rat within her – adapting, in other words.

The whole film is a pun on its title. Charlie Kaufman has to adapt to being an adaptor. He even finds out, like the adaptable orchid, how to make contact with the opposite sex, thus turning the movie into, among many other things, a romantic comedy.

Adaptation communicates the central ideas of Orlean's book, but does so in a totally unconventional manner that both imitates and satirises Hollywood convention.

Adaptation is as funny as *Being John Malkovich*, but displays a deeper understanding of human nature, particularly about the way people accumulate emotional baggage as they get older, and become decreasingly willing or able to adapt.

This is a wise, entertaining, exquisitely crafted comedy, enlivened by consistently witty visuals by Kaufman's collaborator, Spike Jonze. Cage is hilarious in both roles, and Chris Cooper is marvellously charismatic as the orchid thief.

Adaptation will appeal especially, though not exclusively, to anyone who writes, or wishes to write. It is not for the stupid or humourless, and will strike some people as too clever by at least three-quarters. But I haven't emerged from a screening so uplifted and excited for a long time. This is a marvellously rich, original movie, with a screenplay of genius.

ALMOST FAMOUS *(2000)*

Expect a no-holds-barred account of a rock band on tour in 1973, and you may be disappointed. Virtually all the sex and drug-taking takes place behind closed doors, and life on the road is mostly bathed in the forgiving light of nostalgia. But that's not what this movie is about. It is a coming-of-age tragicomedy about a 15 year-old boy (Patrick Fugit), an aspiring rock journalist based on the teenage Crowe himself, discovering first love and first principles along the road to manhood.

Cameron Crowe's follow-up to *Jerry Maguire* is a lovely, sweet-natured movie – and a great one. It's enjoyable as a poignant love story, thanks to the wide-eyed gawkiness of young Fugit and a luminous portrayal of the groupie he loves, played with a delightful mixture of lewdness and naivety by Goldie Hawn's daughter Kate Hudson. Everything to do with their burgeoning relationship is beautifully done. Everyone who sees it will be reminded of his or her own first emotions on falling in love, both painful and sweet.

The film is even more astute, and far more unusual, as an account of the birth of a journalist and social commentator- one reason, I suspect, why the film has gone down better with critics than with the general public.

The title *Almost Famous* describes not only the fictitious rock band on view, but also the fate of every good writer. Even though he is at the peak of a successful career, Crowe must know that he is never going to be famous as, say, Tom Cruise, who starred in the last picture he created, *Jerry Maguire*.

Philip Seymour Hoffman isn't on screen for long, but he's central to the movie as real-life rock critic Lester Bangs, bemusedly finding himself an elder statesman while still in his twenties, and offering plenty of good advice to his young protégé.

Lester's counsel, delivered with an endearing air of "I can't believe I'm pontificating like this", is to be honest and merciless, not to try to be "cool" or fashionable, and not to let one's judgement be corrupted by friendship – sound advice for journalists in general, and critics in particular, assuming they have any judgement to start with.

In those days, of course, long before the current craze for "celebrity critics", it was unnecessary to advise that you should always write the copy that goes out under your own name.

One weakness of *Almost Famous* is that it doesn't delve deeply into the clash between rock celebrity ethics on the one hand, and middle-class, "respectable" values on the other.

Promiscuity is treated non-judgmentally, as a part of growing up, with no short-term or long-term ill effects. Drug abuse is played for laughs, and comically denounced by the older generation, represented by the hero's mum. It's a tribute to Frances McDormand that she stops this character from descending into caricature. She finds vast depths of maternal concern, and makes totally credible the young hero's love for her, as well as his horror at the way she keeps showing him up in front of his friends.

Two of the most telling moments occur when she confronts the group's far too easy-going lead guitarist (charmingly played by Billy Crudup) with his own bad behaviour.

Any film about a rock band on the road has to cope with comparisons to *This Is Spinal Tap*... And this band doesn't quite come alive. The squabbles about artistic integrity versus commercialism ring hollow, since the band palpably isn't all that good, or all that pretentious. Most of the music in the movie is disappointingly second-rate.

Perhaps this serves Crowe's purpose, which is partly to show that rock is (or was) not merely a form of cultural rebellion, but also an attempt by its practitioners and commentators to prolong adolescence beyond any known time-limit. Hence, I think, the barbed and apparently gratuitous reference to the unlikelihood of Mick Jagger still going on stage at the age of 50.

But *Almost Famous* mostly avoids the acerbic, and settles for being immensely likeable. It contains delightful scenes of drama and comedy, and it's especially attractive for the way it respects its characters and allows them to reveal themselves with looks and tiny actions, rather than through dialogue. But it's a bit too polite and ingratiating, slightly over-willing to take the easy, comic option. And the scenes at the Rolling Stone offices don't ring true: they're facile and savour of TV sitcom.

Crowe might have done better to have taken Bangs' advice and been more merciless. There's a flabbiness about the film – it feels ten minutes too long – and his affection for his characters means that he's never as hard on them as he might have been.

Kate Hudson's groupie tells our young hero "You're too sweet for rock'n'roll", and Lester Bangs complains "There's nothing controversial about you". Both comments apply equally to the movie. And though they don't diminish it too much as intelligent, humane entertainment, they do weaken it as art.

AMERICAN BEAUTY (1999)

Kevin Spacey gives an Oscar-worthy performance as Lester Burnham, a middle-aged man despised by his social-climbing wife (Annette Bening) and sullenly resentful teenage daughter (Thora Birch). "They think I'm this gigantic loser," he tells us, "And they're right. I have lost something. I didn't always feel this... sedated."

Into Lester's less than lively home-life gyrates one of his daughter's fellow-cheerleaders (Mena Suvari), a blonde, aspiring model and self-publicised sexual predator. Lester embarks on some embarrassingly corny fantasies about her, most of them involving petals from his wife's favourite rose, American Beauty. We know Lester's making a fool of himself, but we can sympathise with his search for beauty and physical intimacy.

Like Willy Loman in *Death of a Salesman*, Lester's career prospects are behind him. He's a second-rate journalist serving third-rate bosses. So when Lester is asked to draw up his own job description (one of those ploys that modern companies use to justify future redundancies) he bravely describes the hardest part of his work as "masking my contempt for the "assholes in charge". Then, when they fire him, he blackmails them into giving him a generous severance payment.

This is one of those scenes which will have virtually every wage-slave in the audience emitting a silent cheer.

Meanwhile Lester's wife is cracking up in her pursuit of success as an estate agent. She is falling into the arms of a professional rival (Peter Gallagher) whom she can look up to, literally and metaphorically. Lester is understanding when his taller, darker, more handsome rival seems unable to remember him from one social occasion to the next. "It's all right," Lester smiles encouragingly, "I wouldn't remember me either."

Nor does he care, even slightly, when he discovers they are having an affair (the scene in which he does is a hilarious cameo of other people's social embarrassment.) Lester's air of superior detachment makes his wife even madder – mad enough, perhaps, to kill him.

For, as we discover early on, Lester has only a year to live, and a growing queue of people willing to kill him. The first thing we see in the movie is his daughter suggesting to her boyfriend (Wes Bentley) that he murder her father, and the boyfriend – a voyeuristic variant on the traditional boy next door – looks quite weird and disturbed enough to carry out the contract.

Even more sinister is the boy's father (Chris Cooper), an authoritarian ex-Marine with a wife (Allison Janney) who's practically catatonic, and a cache of firearms and Nazi memorabilia locked up in his study.

Alan Ball's screenplay is skilful at keeping us guessing whodunit (or who's going to do it) right up to the end. It is not so successful at creating supporting characters that avoid cliché. Thora Birch's role looks like a retread of similar disaffected adolescents, usually played by Christina Ricci. Not even Chris Cooper, that fine actor from *Lone Star*, can prevent us from feeling a sense of *déjà vu* when his dirty little secret is revealed.

Annette Bening gives a bravura impression of a yuppie having a nervous breakdown, but her character is such an exaggerated caricature that it's hard to believe she is entirely real.

And there's something rather bland and superficial about Lester's rebellion. It takes the form of smoking pot, listening to Jimi Hendrix, ogling teenage girls and taking more exercise: not all that elevating or, indeed, revolutionary.

However, Spacey is marvellous at making us feel sympathy for Lester. Just like Edward Norton in *Fight Club*, he yearns to feel something again; and finding that ability to feel and see the beauty in things (which is paralleled in the emotional development of his daughter) means that at least he dies happy.

Lester's semi-detachment from his own problems has charm; the honesty of his self-criticism is refreshing; and even the potentially nauseating sequence of him seducing his daughter's friend is handled with taste.

Some moments are truly touching, such as the one towards the end when Lester hears that his own daughter is in love. He pauses, thinks, smiles and says simply "Good for her."

As social satire, *American Beauty* comes out snapping at familiar targets and proves itself fairly toothless – which may be one reason it has won such acclaim from the baby-boom generation. It's Clintonism made celulloid – Blairism plus a taste for illicit sex. Yet it has a warmth which saves it from being just another facile sideswipe at the American Dream.

The central reason for its appeal is that the fear of growing old and not being respected by one's nearest and dearest is a universal worry, and it's never been more deftly or humorously portrayed. The movie resembles Ang Lee's masterly *The Ice Storm* in the brilliance of its ensemble acting, the cool way it dissects middle-class, Me-generation angst and reaches a grand emotional climax on a dark and stormy night; but it's funnier and less judgmental, and will be accessible to a wider audience. It also resembles Todd Solondz's *Happiness* in its frankness on sexual matters – which is why a few people will dislike this movie intensely.

It lacks the visual originality of *Fight Club* and the willingness of *Happiness* to challenge its audience's assumptions. And director Sam Mendes's symbolism is a little too self-consciously arty, as is his sub-Antonioni use of red throughout, which will endear it to the incurably pretentious. But it's an auspicious debut by Mendes, who uses his theatrical background to good effect, trusting his actors and giving them space to work.

This is an intelligent, perceptive film for grown-ups – a treasurable rarity. And, though it's quintessentially American, it's sufficiently universal to cause many of us to make a few sharp, uneasy comparisons with our own lives.

ARGO *(2012)*

Ben Affleck's third film as director tells an amazing but true story set against the context of the Iranian hostage crisis. 52 Americans were held hostage for 444 days from November 1979 to January 1981, after a group of Islamist militants invaded the US Embassy in Tehran. Unknown to us all at the time, six Americans found sanctuary in the Canadian embassy.

A preposterous plot was then hatched to smuggle them out of Iran, disguised as Canadian film-makers researching locations for a tacky rip-off of *Star Wars* – named, you guessed it, *Argo*. It is a matter of some controversy how much of the escape was planned by the Canadian ambassador (played in the movie by Victor Garber) and how much was the brainchild of CIA operative Tony Mendez (Affleck), but for cinematic purposes we see events mainly through the eyes of the latter.

The story that unfolds is always gripping and often very funny, especially when a Hollywood producer (Alan Arkin) and make-up artist (John Goodman) become involved and cast a cynical eye over the scam. In a way, the film is all about the technique of movie-making, the spinning of stories that will persuade the audience that they're true.

Heist movies that combine comedy with thrills are notoriously difficult to pull off, as the one tends to detract from the other. And any movie that deals with modern political realities – the relationship between America and Iran is arguably even more troubled now than it was then – has to be handled with a tact and awareness not often found in Hollywood films. Affleck and screenwriter Chris Terrio surmount these problems with panache.

As an actor, Affleck has been guilty of some lazy performances that made him look lumpish and unintelligent. However, with his third picture behind the camera he shows – as he did with *Gone Baby Gone* and *The Town* – that he's the most talented actor-turned-director since Clint Eastwood.

THE ARTIST *(2011)*

The Artist is that rarest of phenomena: cinematic perfection. A French picture shot in Hollywood with a largely American cast, it deserves to win Best Film, Director, Writer, Actor and Actress at next year's Academy Awards, along with numerous technical prizes. If there were such an award, it would be a certainty to win Best Dog.

The Artist is a work of genius: witty, sophisticated and blessedly original. It is moving, charming and funny. It's one of the most touching, feelgood celebrations of love: love between the sexes, love between man and dog, and love of cinema.

Oh, and it's largely silent. And in black and white. Please don't let either of these eccentricities put you off.

The "silent" soundtrack has more than enough sound on it to keep anyone entertained. The witty, Oscar-worthy orchestral score is by Ludovic Bourse, mostly pastiche of the 20s and 30s but with an extract from Bernard Herrman's score for *Vertigo* and a nod to Franz Waxman's *Sunset Boulevard*.

There's clever use of sound effects, especially during a hilarious nightmare sequence in which a silent-movie star finds himself trapped in a world where everything emits sound except him. And a marvellously unexpected transition to sound should have you grinning from ear to ear as you leave the cinema.

The style is breathtaking. It actually improves on the harsh photography of the originals, and looks more like the sophisticated, glamorous black-and-white of the 40s golden era. To achieve this, cinematographer Guillaume Schiffman shot on colour stock with special diffusion filters, and then converted it to monochrome. The effect is uniquely magical.

The film is a masterpiece of Art Deco design. Colour would only have detracted from its astonishing beauty.

The Artist is a spinoff from the French series of *OSS 117* spy films. Successful in France but largely ignored abroad, these were James Bond parodies with the same two co-stars and writer-director. *The Artist* is, however, infinitely superior.

It takes us back to an era associated with another of cinema's greatest films, *Singin' In The Rain*: the moment when sound came to cinema, making and destroying many a career.

A star in France but internationally unknown, Jean Dujardin plays George Valentin, a silent movie star with the swashbuckling energy of Douglas Fairbanks Sr and the cheesy self-confidence of Gene Kelly.

We first meet George in 1927, hamming to the audience and hogging the limelight at a movie premiere, where he pays more attention to his pet Jack Russell terrier (played, brilliantly, by Uggy) than his disgruntled co-star and wife, played by Penelope Ann Miller as a glowering cross between Mary Astor and the middle-aged Joan Crawford.

We see that one of George's most devoted fans is Peppy Miller (Berenice Bejo), herself an aspiring actress but still only an extra. George resists the temptation of an extra-marital affair but gives Peppy her first big break in showbiz.

George finds his star waning with the arrival of sound, which he thinks is only a fad. He insists on his integrity as an artist, and refuses to bow to fashion.

As a result, he loses wife, house and even his loyal chauffeur (James Cromwell). George watches jealously as his former studio boss (John Goodman) turns Peppy into a talkies superstar, similar to the young Joan Crawford. All that the self-destructive, near-insane George has left is booze, some very flammable old films and his super-intelligent dog.

You may feel as though you've seen this film before, when it was called *A Star Is Born*. There are similarities, but the film is more than a parody.

It's a brilliant tribute to a past age of movies, including the elegant romantic comedies of Ernst Lubitsch, the silent thrillers of Fritz Lang and the movies of Fred Astaire and Ginger Rogers.

The film is an affectionate pastiche of all those and more, with its storytelling gusto, deliberate naivety and seemingly effortless charm. Cineastes will love the many references, but you won't need to be a movie buff to be captivated.

Dujardin is famous in France as a comic actor, but shows marvellous profundity here. He has an extraordinary ability to overact and play for real at the same time.

Berenice Bejo, a gorgeous Franco-Argentine actress married to the director, is a real find: a comedienne with the goofy charm of silent star Marion Davies.

This is a joyously entertaining movie, but also a potentially important one. It will, in our age of mindless action, 3D blockbusters and multi-million dollar budgets, remind film-makers and audiences alike of the many wonderful qualities that cinema has largely lost: elegance, beauty, heartfelt emotion.

I am sure this will be the surprise hit of the year. I hope

it will send audiences back to films by Frank Borzage, F.W. Murnau and Lubitsch – directors hugely well-known in their own time, but unjustly forgotten today. This is a sweet, poignant, very funny movie. It's also a great one.

AUDITION/ ODISHON *(1999)*

This weirdest of horror films starts off as a relatively conventional romance, with a middle-aged widower (Ryo Ishibashi) trying to find a second wife by auditioning actresses for a non-existent feature film. His eye alights on a slender, submissive ex-ballerina (Eihi Shiina), and he's not unduly worried when she turns out to have lied about her professional experience. They date, and seem attracted.

There's one great shot when the whole mood changes. She is sitting on the floor of her apartment with the phone a little way from her, and what looks like a pile of blankets in the background. We realise she's been waiting obsessively for his call, not moving, for days. The phone rings, and we see a sinister smile of sensual triumph through the dark curtain of her hair. And the blankets in the background move. They're not blankets but a canvas sack, and there's something or someone in it, writhing and moaning in physical and psychological torment.

From that creepy moment, it's downhill all the way. Just as you think it may be turning into a classy, female revenge movie (a Japanese version of Clint Eastwood's *Play Misty For Me*), the female character turns from abused innocent into gloating sadist, and from there into a kind of erotic demon.

The film becomes a series of degrading mutilations. Immensely talented, stylish and unpleasant, *Audition* marks a new low in sadistic torture and amputation, allowed by the censors presumably because the sick acts of violence are carried out by a woman, and in a foreign language. So that's all right, then. Or is it?

This is a film that is well nigh impossible to mark out of ten. The first time I saw it, I gave it 5/10, for it is both talented and repulsive.

However, the film has lingered in my mind ever since, and it would be churlish to deny its power to surprise and shock. There haven't been many parables about sexism that have had this kind of power. It's a genuine one-off and far creepier and more subtle than the torture porn films it has doubtless helped to inspire. The two leading actors are also extraordinary, and no other films by Takashi Miike that I have seen come close to it in terms of atmosphere or quality.

So, ten years on from when I first saw it, I'm upping my mark considerably to 9/10. It's still a disgusting, unpleasant film, and I can understand those who have walked out of it; but it is also a masterpiece of horror, one of the most terrifying films ever made. And that shot of the canvas sack is an all-time great, as is the sequence where we discover what's in it.

BABE *(1995)*

The hero of this movie may be a little swine, but he's more sympathetic than most leading actors, and a lot less hammy. He is also the most lovable orphan to hit the pictures since Oliver Twist. True, he's a pig – but a pig of rare character and breeding, with the cutest toupee since Sean Connery's in *Never Say Never Again*.

A young pig is won at a fair by lean, lanky Farmer Hoggett (James Cromwell) and brought up by a friendly family of border collies. Nurture prevails over nature, and our hero develops an unlikely aptitude for herding sheep, which he does with a charm and courtesy far beyond the average canine. Not surprisingly, this puts the head sheepdog's nose out of, if you'll pardon the expression, joint.

Babe is one of those movies which sets out with a determination to make you laugh and cry, and it could easily have been too cute for comfort. One of its many marvels is that it neatly avoids Disneyesque sentimentality and has an engaging sense of the absurd. Particularly funny are the fieldmice who act as a kind of Greek chorus, and fill in when nothing much else is happening with three-part-harmony variations on *Blue Moon*.

Just as magically, the script combines the lightness of touch you expect from classics by A.A. Milne or Kenneth

Grahame, with the toughness of George Orwell's *Animal Farm*. Death, inter-species rivalry and the fear of being slaughtered for food are never far away. One of the sweetest moments comes as Babe celebrates Christmas with a joyful rendition of *Jingle Bells*, blithely unaware that the farmer's wife has him earmarked as the main ingredient in Christmas lunch.

It's a timeless tale, but the technology is very much of the Nineties. The Australian film-makers daringly use a mixture of real and animatronic animals (from Jim Henson's and John Cox's workshops in London and Queensland) – with such skill that it's impossible to distinguish the real from the artificial. The visual effects won the film's lone Oscar.

Animal trainer Karl Lewis Miller (who trained the St Bernards for *Beethoven*) does terrific work as well – Babe himself is played by 48 different piglets, but you'd never know.

Documentary-maker Chris Noonan's first feature as writer-director is amazingly expert. He and cinematographer Andrew Lesnie use an ingenious array of filters and camera angles to create a totally original look. The sequence where the farmer dances a jig to cheer up his ailing pig is as weird and wonderful as anything dreamed up by Terry Gilliam for *Brazil*, or Jeunet and Caro for *Delicatessen*.

The whole film is gorgeous to look at, taking place in a golden, glowing Neverland (actually Australia, but it could be anywhere) where modern fax machines exist alongside old-fashioned farming methods.

Noonan's experienced producer and co-writer George Miller has been responsible for enjoyable movies in many different genres – from *Mad Max* to *Flirting* and *Lorenzo's Oil* – and he approaches his first family film without a hint of patronising the audience.

The latest in computer animation means that the animals' mouths move in perfect synch, and equally impeccable casting ensures that they speak with hilariously appropriate voices. The human actors (especially James Cromwell and Magda Szubanski as Farmer and Mrs Hoggett) couldn't be better, and are all the more refreshing for having unfamiliar faces.

The film shines with an obvious affection for animals, nostalgia for mixed farming, and distaste for factory food-production, but this is no animal-rights tract. Instead, it has a delightful and unfashionable message. Babe is lovable not only because he is the kind of underhog who dares to be unconventional, but also because he is unfailingly polite and considerate to every animal he meets. This was the first movie in years to celebrate courtesy.

Babe is so talented and imaginative that it's beyond criticism, and magical whether you're three or ninety-three. Ebernezer Scrooge at his grumpiest could be dragged into the cinema to watch *Babe* and would emerge with a soppy grin, cheerfully acknowledging this to be among the most charm-laden, uplifting movies ever made.

BEAUTY AND THE BEAST *(1991)*

What is the greatest cartoon of all time? For innovation, nothing will ever beat *Snow White and the Seven Dwarves*, a revelation on release in 1937. But Disney's most perfectly achieved combination of animation, story-telling and song must surely be this loving tribute to the old fairytale.

If you were ever baffled as to why the enjoyable but flawed *Aladdin* became a colossal hit in 1992/3, look no further than this, its immediate predecessor. If any film deserved five stars, it's this.

Twenty-one years on from the original release, the skilful but largely unnecessary addition of 3D adds a tiny amount to the sense of this being a pop-up storybook come to life, but the great pleasure is to see it again on a big screen.

There's plenty to experience that you may not have appreciated before – especially the cleverly foreshadowing underscore and witty lyrics. Howard Ashman, who wrote those words, died of Aids at the age of 40 before he could see the finished film, but it remains his most enduring legacy.

I'd certainly forgotten how hilariously servile the villainous Gaston's friend Philippe is, fawning over his meat-headed mate's muscular masculinity. These sequences seemed harmlessly camp in 1991, but take on a more subversive tone now – deliciously satirical on the narcissistic cult of the body beautiful, and the boorish, ego-driven, win-at-all-costs ethos repellently fashionable in our age of *The Apprentice*.

And the conflict between bookish, open-minded civilization and thuggish barbarism remains potent. The opening sequence looks dated now because it harks back to a time when even a small, provincial village might have a library.

I do have a few quibbles. If our heroine is so intellectually superior to the local villagers, how come she's reading only fairytales when she's grown up? Isn't our leading man more attractive as the reformed Beast than he is when transformed into ultra-conventional beefcake? And isn't it a bit tough on the Beast's servants that they all got cursed and transformed when their employer was punished for his arrogance? That aspect of the set-up is never explained.

But let's not complain too much about a film that sets out to be family-pleasing entertainment, and triumphantly achieves that aim.

No matter how many times you see it, the *Be Our Guest* production number has the power to bring tears to the eyes by virtue of its quality, as does the title song, exquisitely sung by Angela Lansbury. On every level, and for every age group, this movie's a masterpiece.

BEFORE SUNSET *(2004)*

In the cult hit *Before Sunrise* (1995), two twentysomethings, one American (Ethan Hawke), one French (Julie Delpy) met on a train in Europe, talked a very great deal, and made love. They parted, promising to meet each other in six months' time. Though no blockbuster, the film became a modest success, especially with those in their twenties, who found the characters a good deal less annoying and immature than I did.

Director Richard Linklater's sequel reunites the same characters nine years on. Both have been battered by life, and are a good deal less blasé about their ability to find true love. "We were young and stupid," admits one; "Hear hear" say I.

This makes them much more vulnerable and sympathetic; and even though they still talk a great deal about themselves in very long takes (one lasts 11 minutes), there is a much greater sense of forward momentum in the plot – plus a saving sense of humour.

The result is a film which won't have the same appeal to over-serious twentysomethings who dress entirely in black; but it should strike every older age-group as one of the most delightful, realistic and subtly subversive love stories in years.

The film is similar in its gently ironic approach to

veteran French director Eric Rohmer's best pictures, such as *Claire's Knee*, and is surprisingly cinematic given the smallness of its scale. This is not for those who require explosions and car chases in their movies, but it makes a pleasant change to see recognisable, likeable characters in a romantic drama.

With this and the hit comedy *School of Rock*, Linklater is maturing into an intelligent and versatile director who isn't afraid to be unobtrusive and serve his actors and script, which he co-wrote.

Neither actor has done anything better. It doubtless helps that both contributed to the screenplay, and have sunk a lot of their own identities into the characters. But it's Julie Delpy who is the revelation, giving the kind of lively, sensitive and utterly real performance that deserves to revive her flagging career.

Yes, the film is talky, but the talk is refreshingly articulate, and anything but inconsequential. The Me-generation values are suspect in the way they dress up selfishness to look like a disinterested search for self-fulfilment; but at least they're honestly and endearingly expressed.

Some men are bound to be deterred by the high romantic content, but *Before Sunset* delivers romance while managing also to be tough and refreshingly astute about male and female sexual differences.

This is that extreme rarity, a "chick flick" that men who can be bothered to think about relationships will also enjoy – an all-time-great dating movie for intelligent couples.

BEING JOHN MALKOVICH (1999)

Craig Schwartz (John Cusack) is a greasy-haired puppeteer. He has tremendous manipulative talent but no concept of how to market his darkly neurotic, sexually explicit street-theatre production of *Abelard and Heloise*. His mousy, frumpish wife (Cameron Diaz, so cleverly cast against type that she is almost unrecognisable) is more fond of her pet chimpanzee than her husband, and fed up with his whingeing self-pity. "Maybe you'd feel better if you got a job or something," she suggests.

A human puppet easily manipulated by his wife, he puts on a tie and jacket underneath his anorak and mooches off to find a job as a filing clerk – after all, he has nimble fingers – in a weird company on floor 7 and a half of an office block. It can be reached only by stopping the lift between floors and prising open the steel doors with a crowbar.

It's a firm which prides itself on low overheads, so the ceiling is only about four feet from the floor. Some employees are short, but most – including Craig – have to walk around in a perpetual crouch.

Craig does surprisingly well in his interview with the firm's carrot-juice-drinking, sex-obsessed, 105 year-old boss (Orson Bean). Craig falls hopelessly in love with one of his colleagues, a self-confident career-woman called Maxine

(Catherine Keener), who regards him as a loser. When he tries to seduce her in a bar by telling her he's a puppeteer, she asks for the bill.

Craig finds the metaphorical way into her heart, however. It's behind one of the office filing cabinets – a tunnel leading, quite literally, into the brain of the actor John Malkovich, where he spends exactly a quarter of an hour before being ejected out of the sky at the side of the New Jersey turnpike.

He regards the experience as mind-blowing. "Do you see what a metaphysical can of worms this is?" he asks Maxine. She, being less complicated, regards it as a business opportunity: "We'll sell tickets". They market 15 minutes in the brain of a celebrity, at 200 dollars a go. The idea takes off, but in unexpected direction.

One of the characters so likes it inside Malkovich's head that she decides to become a transexual. Another gets the idea of moving into John Malkovich's brain permanently and turning him into a lifesize puppet. And when Malkovich himself discovers what's going on, he tries potholing into his own brain with farcical and nightmarish results.

Being John Malkovich is probably the oddest mainstream movie ever, and there will be some who find it implausible and silly. These will probably be the same people who dislike Harry Potter books or were bored by the Alice adventures of Lewis Carroll. I loved it.

I loved its originality, its cynical take on modern celebrity, gender roles and the marketing of art. I loved John Malkovich's performance as a vainer, more actorish version of himself. I even loved Charlie Sheen sending himself up as John Malkovich's highly improbable best friend.

Being John Malkovich is hilariously funny, a wonderfully original piece of story-telling and a brilliantly sustained flight of imagination. This has to be the least predictable movie of the year, yet it has its own twisted logic and a level of inventiveness that every surrealist from Salvador Dali to the Monty Python team would have envied. You keep thinking it's going to run out of steam, but it never does.

And it has surprising depth. It poses disturbing questions about the extent to which we are all changed by our physical appearance, by our gender and by how others perceive us. It examines one of the reasons why people become actors – to explore their own personality by becoming others.

It's a comic meditation upon how modern women manipulate men, and how so much art nowadays is about personality, marketing and fashion. There are thoughts on identity and immortality that could set philosophers pondering for days. And it has genuine affection for its bizarre characters, each of them splendidly acted.

So many American films look as if they have come off a conveyor belt. This is one of a kind. It is a first feature for its writer and director (the latter of whom is to be seen playing a dumb redneck in *Three Kings*). It's a debut that's as audacious and revolutionary in its way as Orson Welles' *Citizen Kane* – and a lot funnier.

BILLY ELLIOT *(1999)*

Billy Elliot is an eleven year-old (played by newcomer Jamie Bell) whose mother has died and left him the son of one striking miner (Gary Lewis) and brother of another (Jamie Draven). Billy is mortified to discover that his talent lies not in the traditionally masculine directions favoured by his dad – boxing and football – but in ballet. With the surreptitious help of a local dance teacher (Julie Walters), he applies for an audition to the Royal Ballet School.

Billy Elliot is not merely the best British film in decades, superior even to those acknowledged classics about growing up, *Kes* and *Gregory's Girl*. It offers an emotional experience you'll never forget. It's a totally home-grown, British-financed triumph – and an even more brilliant debut for theatre director Stephen Daldry than *American Beauty* was for Sam Mendes. It's a *tour de force* of editing (by John Wilson), cinematography (Brian Tufano) and screenwriting (Lee Hall).

This first-time writer of unbelievable talent and maturity was himself a small boy growing up in Newcastle during the miners' strike in the Eighties; and the film has an authenticity that makes it as real and personal as one's own memories of childhood. Remarkably for someone who has emerged from radio, Hall appreciates that "writing" is not simply about dialogue; he creates memorable collages, juxtapositions of images that draw you into the narrative emotionally, however resistant you may be at first to having your tear-ducts pummelled.

This is the kind of story about a local boy trying to make good that you may feel you've seen many times before. It could easily have become a sad British rip-off of *Flashdance* or *Fame*. But there's a truthfulness about it, and a poetic quality, that elevate it far above its predecessors.

It's notable for what it doesn't do. It doesn't hector us – as most British films would – about the rights and wrongs of the miners' strike. Instead, it allows us to experience the human tragedy that the strike represented, feel its impact on individuals, families and communities. The ease with which dissidents were called "scabs" enables us to understand the fear that Billy has of being different. And, like *The Full Monty*, it shows that unemployment is not an experience confined to the working class.

It doesn't sneer at upward mobility. It doesn't espouse some trendy notion of "laddishness". Nor does it badmouth men. Instead of taking the line on fathers which has been routine in almost every British film since the Sixties – that we are feckless, boorish, drunken and often violent – this one celebrates the tenderness which is a far more common characteristic.

Gary Lewis presents a heart-breaking portrayal of a father battling with his own prejudices and financial limitations, struggling to do what is best for his son. It's an even more gut-wrenching portrait of fatherhood than Roberto Benigni's Oscar-winning turn in *Life Is Beautiful.*

But Lewis is never sentimental. He is tough, tragic and often very funny – as is Julie Walters, equally remarkable as an abrasive woman with a failed career and a failing marriage, not only inspiring Billy but also having to accept that he will soon outgrow her.

No father or mother will be able to watch these performances without weeping buckets. But the miracle of the movie is Jamie Bell from Billingham, who seems to be able to do everything – from scrunched-up defiance to mischievous grin, bitterness to compassion, rage to joy. Helped by Peter Darling's choreography – set to well-chosen rock music by T Rex, the Jam and the Clash – his dancing has a power and virility that totally justify the film's view of dance as self-expression and challenge the prejudice that dancing is a sign of effeminacy.

The practical impact of this film on boys will be tremendous – and would be even greater had it not been saddled with a "15" certificate. I'm especially pleased for my sister Jill, who founded the National Youth Ballet without any help from the Arts Council, and still manages it without receiving payment for her services. She has moaned to me for over a decade about our national shortage of boy dancers, and this movie will help to change that.

Because of my sister, I've long been aware how many "ordinary" parents undergo extraordinary inconvenience and hardship to give their children even a half-chance of fulfilling their dreams, and this film will be an inspiration – and a deserved tribute – to their efforts.

Billy Elliot reminds us of so many virtues which tend to be ignored altogether in British movies or treated with sugary sentimentality in American ones: parental self-sacrifice, the love between father and son, and caring for elderly relations.

One of the best things about Billy himself is his compassion for his grandmother (Jean Heywood), as she hovers in and out of senility.

And the film treats the awakening of Billy's sexuality with a taste and sensitivity that is especially welcome at a time when each new Hollywood movie seems intent on outdoing its predecessors in grossness.

So at last some British film-makers have got it right. Somehow, producers Greg Brenman and Jon Finn have survived the anti-creative bias of BBC bureaucracy and the albatross of Lottery funding, to make a cheap, British yet totally universal tale that deserves to take the world – if not by storm, by charm.

As a beacon to guide other film-makers, it's of far more value than *Lock, Stock and Two Smoking Barrels*. Its assured artistic and commercial success will cross all classes, ages and nationalities, and make clear the public's appetite for movies that offer emotive story-telling, positive human values and involving characters.

Billy Elliot is a joy, not least because it celebrates the kind of positive values that have been virtually missing from the cinema since the heyday of Frank Capra (with *It's a Wonderful Life* and *Mr Smith Goes To Washington*) in the Forties.

Indeed, it harks back further, to Dickens – the first great artist to spot that children can be wonderful protagonists because of their emotional rawness and intrinsic vulnerability. We care about Billy because we have all had dreams that our parents didn't understand, all felt frustration when success didn't come easily – or, in many cases, at all. That's why *Billy Elliot* is one of the most successful British films of all time.

BLACK SWAN *(2010)*

Black Swan is one of the finest movies of the last few years; it is also sure to be among the most unjustly vilified and misunderstood.

The most uncontroversial element, and the one that deserves to be praised unanimously, is Natalie Portman's performance. This is acting of extraordinary power, all the more astonishing from an actress whose performances in the *Star Wars* movies were ridiculed for their woodenness. There hasn't been a more empathetic portrayal of obsessive perfectionism. Her dancing is impressive, too – perhaps not prima ballerina standard, but good enough to pass muster with the general public, and shot sufficiently brilliantly – especially in the opening and closing scenes – to justify comparisons with Moira Shearer's bravura turn in *The Red Shoes*. At this year's Oscars, you need look no further for Best Actress.

Because the central character is a ballerina, both the Guardian and Radio 4's *Today Programme* sent ballet dancers to review it. Unsurprisingly, they achieved near-perfect, wrong-headed unanimity in condemning it as an outrageously over-the-top collection of clichés about the ballet world, and a foul libel on their profession. Such a response is understandable but sublimely irrelevant to the film's merits and comically blinkered as to the director's achievement.

Asking dance professionals to review *Black Swan* for its realism is like inviting motel-owners to judge whether Alfred Hitchcock's *Psycho* is an accurate portrait of their own occupation, or polling inhabitants of New York's Gothic apartment block, the Dakota (notoriously used as a location for Roman Polanski's *Rosemary's Baby*), as to whether its inhabitants are really all Satanists. *Black Swan* is not a drama-documentary about ballerinas, nor does it set out to be; it is a deliberately stylised view of artistic obsession and descent into madness.

It is expressionistic in the same way as *Shutter Island*, *Fight Club* and *Repulsion*. All are examinations of a soul in torment. None is a fair representation of police detectives, office workers or attractive blonde Parisiennes living alone.

I have also heard grumblings from critical colleagues that the film exhibits little sense of humour. This is true. However, it is not setting out to be *The Importance of Being Earnest*, nor indeed *The Hangover*. It is a depiction of serious mental illness. In such a context, I would be prepared to argue that levity is inappropriate. I remain unconvinced that *King Lear* would be improved by the insertion of a few "knock knock" jokes, or that *Hamlet* could usefully be enlivened by a couple of scenes in which the leading character's trousers fall down.

Others have muttered that the film is "hysterical". Since it is a portrait of a hysteric, that too is completely appropriate.

Darren Aronofsky's film opens with an anxiety dream. 'I had the craziest dream last night, about a girl who was turned into a swan," says Natalie Portman's voice-over. The whole movie is, in a sense, that nightmare.

The story is about an up-and-coming ballerina called Nina (Portman) who lives only for her art. She is technically proficient but has more than a hint of emotional coldness and sexual frigidity. Her pink, fluffy bedroom suggests that she has been infantilized by her sinister, domineering mother (Barbara Hershey), a frustrated ex-dancer who blames our heroine for scuppering her own hopes of stardom.

A new production of *Swan Lake* is in preparation, and the company's artistic director (Vincent Cassel) is looking for a new dancer to fill the ballet shoes of his ageing, neurotic prima ballerina (the gaunt and mad-looking Winona Ryder, a cruel but effective piece of casting). He sees that Nina has the technique to dance the white swan, but lacks the darkness and sensuality required to play her black doppelganger.

Nina discovers that she has a new, earthier, sexier rival, Lilly (Mila Kunis) from outside the company. Just like Bette Davis in *All About Eve*, Nina wonders if she is being undermined. Is Lilly genuinely friendly, or does she have lesbian tendencies? Is the artistic director trying to draw out Nina's sensuality for the sake of the production, or is he trying to seduce her? Is Nina's mother really sympathetic to her daughter's aspirations, or is she selfishly trying to live through her?

As in Aronofsky's last movie, *The Wrestler*, the central character suffers intense physical pain in order to please an audience; but is this a necessary price to pay, or born out of an obsessive need to self-harm?

Black Swan has overtones of many backstage musicals, most obviously *42nd Street, A Star Is Born* and (in its nightmarish aspects) *Cabaret*. Likewise, there are elements of paranoid Gothic horror, with many an echo of Roman Polanski's *Repulsion* and *Rosemary's Baby*.

But the film is much more than horror hokum or campy pastiche. It is a memorable depiction of creative obsession, and the overwhelming physical and psychological demands of creating and interpreting great art. Anyone who has ever been fully committed to an artistic project will recognise that the process almost invariably involves an element of self-torture.

Those who have not put themselves through such a process may sniff disapprovingly, and feel that *Black Swan* is a preposterous overcooking of familiar ingredients, or – worse still – a self-indulgent exercise in extreme luvvyism. But anyone who feels that will have missed the point, which is that high achievement – in the arts, sports or any other field – does require an element of masochism and sacrifice. Excellence is rarely achieved easily.

Black Swan was never intended to be a film that exposes sensational scandals about the cloistered world of ballet; it is a mesmerizing evocation and illumination of the quest for perfection, and the awful price that must sometimes be paid. Just as Aronofsky's previous masterpiece, *Requiem for a Dream*, captured the seductiveness and horror of drug addiction, this is a miraculous account of the quest for success, taken to destructive extremes. It's one of the bravest, most visceral and supremely talented movies I have ever seen.

BLAST FROM THE PAST *(1998)*

In 1962, a geeky, paranoid inventor (Christopher Walken) abandons a cocktail party at the height of the Cuban missile crisis and takes his pregnant, thoroughly suburban wife (Sissy Spacek) down to the wildly elaborate bunker he has built below their unprepossesing home. A plane crashing into their house persuades them that the Commies have bombed America, and they stay below ground for 35 years, until they imagine the radioactive fall-out will have subsided.

When the paranoid Walken ventures above ground in the mid-Nineties, he is so appalled by the transvestite hookers, thugs brandishing guns, "adult" video stores and homeless people living off garbage that he is convinced America has been taken over by genetic mutants.

But his thirtysomething son Adam (Brendan Fraser) – innocent in the ways of the modern world but also intelligent, well-educated and unfailingly gentlemanly – volunteers to venture out in search of supplies and, if possible, a nice wife. His demands are simple, if unusual: a non-mutant who doesn't glow in the dark.

Adam meets sharp-tongued, aggressive Eve (Alicia Silverstone) who thinks at first that he's a stalker with excruciating dress-sense and a pitiable liking for the songs of Perry Como and. She's the kind of girl who acts the part of a tough, cynical bitch but only because she's been hurt too many times. Silverstone, in her best performance since *Clueless*, makes her such a sad and vulnerable lonely-heart that you want her to loosen up and warm to Adam's old-world charm, as of course she does.

Blast From The Past did no more than moderately well at the box office, but only because it was too original and confounded audience expectations. Misleadingly sold to the public as a romantic comedy starring Brendan Fraser and Alicia Silverstone, it was much more than that – the cleverest American comedy since *Groundhog Day*, *Forrest Gump* with brains.

Most of the fun in the second half of the movie comes from the arrogant superiority with which Nineties city-dwellers treat the anachronistic politeness of Adam, as he holds doors open for women, says grace before meals, and is offended at even mild profanities. It is a charming parable about the extent to which modern progress is really cultural regression. In the potentially cliched role of Eve's gay best friend, Dave Foley (who voiced the lead in *A Bug's Life*) is delightfully understated, and gets some cracking one-liners as he recognises the goodness in Adam and the shortcomings of modern life.

Some American critics felt that the first half-hour inside the bunker was too long, and it certainly breaks one of the conventions of cinematic story-telling – we don't get to see either of the top-billed actors inside 40 minutes. But it is also extremely funny, and essential to an understanding of the hero. Its affectionate satire on Sixties America takes the time to recognise its strengths as well as its weaknesses, and is much sharper yet less patronising than in the more acclaimed *Pleasantville*.

Walken gives a fine comedy performance as a completely humourless, scientific genius who has replicated every aspect of his normal existence but rendered it utterly crazed, putting lawn furniture on non-existent grass, and stocking his bookshelves with condensed Reader's Digest versions of literary classics, when he and his family have all the time in the world to read the real thing.

This is a surreal echo of normal bourgeois practices, reminiscent of the grotesque universes that the British playwright N.F. Simpson created in *A Resounding Tinkle* and *One Way Pendulum*.

Another of America's great screen actors, Sissy Spacek, is hilarious in her first comedy, turning her son into a wizard ballroom-dancer as she ages disgracefully from meek housewife to wacko alcoholic. Five times an Oscar nominee, Spacek here gives the performance of her life, as funny and touching in its presentation of motherliness as Brenda Blethyn's was in *Secrets and Lies*. It's absurd that Spacek failed to receive at least a nomination for Best Supporting Actress.

Blast From The Past is the best romantic allegory about innocence since *Big*, which won Tom Hanks an Oscar nomination. This film should have done the same for Brendan Fraser. He has much in common with the young Hanks – an easy charm and a guileless joy at being alive that is truly heart-warming. I can think of no other actor who could get belly laughs with lines such as : "Hot diggity dog! Thank you for calling me on my telephone!" and (admiringly, to a black woman) "Oh my stars – a Negro!"

Fraser proves himself as a physical comedian in a great scene where Eve instructs him on how to walk in a convincingly Nineties fashion. But he's a marvellously subtle, reactive actor beneath the apparent broadness.

Like every good comedy, *Blast From The Past* owes its greatest debt to its screenwriters, first-timer Bill Kelly and director Hugh Wilson. Wilson has had a couple of big hits with less-than-terrific screenplays (*The First Wives' Club* and *Police Academy*) and little recognition for a really good one (his underrated comedy, *Guarding Tess*). This is his best work.

THE CABIN IN THE WOODS *(2012)*

Ads make *The Cabin in the Woods* look like a cliched exploitation film, with good-looking young people murdered one-by-one in a spooky forest cabin by, as one of the characters says with understandable resentment, "zombified pain-worshipping backwoods redneck idiots". But don't worry, it's anything but conventional in where it goes from there.

Those directions are hinted at by the opening titles. They depict ancient scenes of ritual sacrifice. Then there's the first scene, which shows two middle-aged technicians (well played by Richard Jenkins and Bradley Whitford) swapping banalities as they prepare for a normal day at the office, or wherever it is they work.

Their cheery badinage, jokily reminiscent of Ricky Gervais' *The Office*, is interrupted by more menacing titles, which drip blood in a way that clash with the tone of the opening.

The endearingly playful, dazzlingly unpredictable movie that follows – and I'm not going to spoil it by telling you too much – shows Hollywood at its best. This is a hugely entertaining, brilliantly crafted entertainment that's witty, ground-breaking, and – most important of all – fun.

The actors, inspired by a screenplay that miraculously

bothers to give them funny things to say, hang around long enough to suggest they are capable of more than the necessarily stereotypical characters they have to play here.

Two make a particular impression: the more-or-less virginal heroine – the Neve Campbell/ Jamie Lee Curtis role – is engagingly played by Kristen Connolly, a redhead who's the spitting image of the young Shirley Anne Field.

Fran Kranz, looking like a youthful, even more frazzled Owen Wilson, is a hoot as a young man whose cannabis intake has unexpectedly revelatory side-effects.

The first picture to be written and directed by the co-writer of *Cloverfield,* Drew Goddard, *Cabin* is a personal triumph for him, but also recognisably the work of his co-writer Joss Whedon, who helped give us *Buffy The Vampire Slayer, Angel* and (a credit less well known) *Toy Story.*

Both men deserve credit for artistic integrity. *The Cabin in the Woods* was shot three years ago, in 2009. The delay came about because Joss Whedon and Drew Goddard objected to the studio Lionsgate's plans (later shelved, thank goodness) to convert it to 3D.

The creative influences upon Goddard and Whedon are clear. The scarily effective mixture of black comedy and horror is reminiscent of Sam Raimi's first two *Evil Dead* movies, and of Wes Craven, who gave us three of the other most memorably innovative achievements in the genre, *Scream, Scream 2 and Wes Craven's New Nightmare.*

The plot is also indebted to Welsh director Mark Evans' intelligent horror movie of 2002, *My Little Eye,* sadly underestimated by most critics at the time. The spooky corridors, chilly vision of the future and skilful blending of horror with social comment recall Stanley Kubrick's *The Shining, 2001* and *Dr Strangelove.*

Less obvious influences are two British authors, Clive Barker and Douglas Adams, both of them always keen to deconstruct the appeal of horror and science fiction, and reveal why they're important to so many of us. Their ideas underpin the entire movie.

Add to these ingredients five charming performances by the doomed college kids (you're actually sorry to see them die), and an unexpectedly lavish special effects extravaganza for a finale, and you have an innovative mixture of at least three genres: horror, science fiction and black comedy.

It's much cleverer and more mature than *The Hunger Games*, but it's about very similar things. *The Cabin in the Woods* ends up as the more biting satire on the entertainment industry, man's appetite for violence and older people's love-hate relationship with youth.

And don't worry, I'm not spoiling anything by saying that. It's clear from very early on that our two boffins are desensitised workers in an entertainment machine that regards human life as something that can be cavalierly ended in order to appease the audience.

Who and what that audience is, the movie leaves teasingly uncertain until a big guest star cameo reveals all, but it may not be the answer you're expecting.

If you wanted to be hyper-critical, you could argue that *Cabin* is guilty of the sins that it condemns. It values narrative ingenuity over genuine horror and treats with flippant callousness the characters it slaughters for our gruesome scary-movie delectation.

But I'm happy to swallow a small amount of hypocrisy in exchange for the pleasures this movie gave me. This is easily the best fun I've ever had watching a slasher movie.

CALENDAR GIRLS *(2003)*

This is the real-life story of those Yorkshire members of a Women's Institute who had the bright idea of posing naked for their annual fund-raising calendar. It was all in the best possible taste, of course; but the fact that they were aged between 50 and 70, and that they managed to raise half a million pounds for the hospital where one of their husbands had died of leukaemia, made them overnight celebrities.

Three cheers for everyone involved in *Calendar Girls*. This very funny, profoundly moving film shows what wonderful British actresses can do given a splendid script and sensitive direction. Not only is it a sure-fire hit, it's a revolutionary one – highly professional but quirky, crowd-pleasing entertainment yet with striking touches of originality and a real flair for the unexpected.

You know you're in good hands straight away as you see the fictionalised guiding lights behind the calendar (beautifully played by Helen Mirren, as the flamboyant but flaky one, and Julie Walters, as the quieter, more common-sensical one) giggling like naughty schoolgirls at a boring lecture. And we come to care about them, especially when Walters' husband (marvellously played by John Alderton) succumbs to the illness that inspired the calendar.

There are echoes of *The Full Monty* as the two friends

drum up support for their idea, and win over the doubters, including their nearest and dearest. Then, in the final and most original section of the movie, we see what happened after the calendar came out – how celebrity affected the women, their friendships and their marriages.

It's this darker side to this film that makes it truly memorable, and draws sensational performances from Walters and Mirren.

It's a tough job mixing comedy with tragedy, and most films that attempt it come unstuck. But when everything works, as it does here, the results can be spectacular.

There isn't a dud performance, and Nigel Cole (who directed *Saving Grace* and the first series of *Cold Feet*) makes the most of his terrific ensemble cast, including the redoubtable Annette Crosbie, Celia Imrie, Penelope Wilton and Linda Bassett.

Writers Tim Firth and Juliette Towhidi skilfully embroider upon real life, to build some dramatic and comic conflict. They invent a tyrannical head of the WI branch (Geraldine James), where none existed, and they build up the opposition to the calendar within the WI movement. In real life, just about everyone thought the idea was a hoot.

The writers do stray dangerously close to cliche when they give one of the women an erring husband who's a nasty male chauvinist. On the whole, though, the film avoids the trap of turning into a female empowerment fantasy. As in real life, most of the women's menfolk are sympathetic and supportive, if slightly anxious. Ciaran Hinds, playing Mirren's husband, is outstanding.

The result is a movie which has the unmistakable texture of real life. You feel you know these women and many like them. They are about as far as you can get from Lara Croft and Charlie's Angels. These are living, breathing people – not cartoon characters.

For far too long, real women have been barred from the big screen. Where are the women who gave up careers in order to spend time nurturing their children or looking after their husbands? I can't recall one movie character answering that description in the past 12 months. Yet the homes of Britain are full of them.

Where are the women who devote their lives to caring for the elderly? Where are the women who work unpaid for charities? Where are the women who enable the smooth running of the churches and political parties? Where are the women who make our homes and gardens beautiful, welcoming places? Where are the women who still cook most of our food and do most of the laundry?

Entire generations of women have disappeared, or – on the rare occasions they have been allowed on screen, as in Willy Russell's hugely popular *Shirley Valentine* – they are simply there to preach dissatisfaction with husbands, marriage and family relationships.

Film-makers might argue that the silenced majority of women don't lead interesting lives, that they want ass-kicking, man-hating escapism like the adolescent Americans who dictate so much – too much – of what we see in the cinema. But *Calendar Girls* proves them wrong. It's the kind of film that a lot of people, and not only women, will want to watch again and again, because it speaks to them in ways they're simply not used to experiencing. This is among the most heart-warming movies of many years, because it tackles issues such as middle age, bereavement and female friendship with a humour and depth that are not so much rare in modern cinema, as non-existent.

Instead of pretending to empower women by making them unrealistic, ambition-crazed man-haters, this film reflects the power that real women actually do have. Without even a hint of piety, it celebrates marriage, hearth and home, nurturing, working for the community – all the things that millions of real women take for granted (thank goodness) as part of their identities as women.

And, wonder of wonders, the movie doesn't portray men as feeble or violent. Overwhelmingly these women are supported by their husbands. They love each other; they respect each other's differences; they are even heart-broken when one partner dies.

How refreshing, and how unique! Seeing recognisably human behaviour on screen come as a culture shock after the fake-feminism that has distorted our movie viewing for too long.

I only hope that the success of this movie with critics and audiences alike will transform the way women are portrayed in the cinema. My intuition is that the public is fed up with the shrieking, anorexic harpies that Hollywood moguls think we want to watch. Thanks to *Calendar Girls*, real women are back.

CAPE FEAR *(1991)*

A lawyer (Nick Nolte) and his family are threatened by a
madman (Robert de Niro) in one of the most controversial
films of the Nineties. Technically – as even Scorsese's most
scathing critics admitted – his direction, Thelma
Schoonmaker's editing and Freddie Francis's cinematography
are spectacular. The film is an even more stunning succession
of images and visual pyrotechnics than *GoodFellas*. Scorsese
is a director who can turn a teddy-bear into a symbol of evil,
and an ordinary staircase into a vision of Dante's Inferno.

There's an unforgettable shot, for example, of the villain
(Robert De Niro) seducing the hero's daughter (Juliette
Lewis) over her pink little bedroom phone: De Niro's silky,
reasonable voice contrasts with the camera's serpentine slide
past his hard, black, fetishistic body-building equipment to
reveal the man himself. Only then do we find he's hanging
upside down, like a tattooed, muscular bat. And the camera
itself turns through 180 degrees, to show De Niro's unearthly
grin, with gravity standing his hair on end, as if he's a demon
from *Struwwelpeter*. Scorsese transforms a small, functional
scene into a masterpiece of menace.

But the best thrillers are more than well-crafted: they
bring us face to face with our deepest fears. De Niro's
bogeyman, Max Cady, is a wonderfully complex nightmare

figure, the unconscious wish-fulfilment of every main character. To his rape victim (Illeana Douglas), he's a piece of rough whom she picks up in a bar, to express her independence from the lover who's stood her up (Nick Nolte). She's turned on by Cady's boast that "I'm just one hell of an animal"; she even giggles in bed when he handcuffs her. Cady is an embodiment of her sexual fantasies, taken just that one horrible step further into nightmare.

Cady appeals to the hero's 15 year-old daughter by voicing her adolescent sense of injustice. He echoes the marital resentments of his wife (Jessica Lange), with whom Cady shares a sense of betrayal and a history of mental illness. To our lawyer hero (Nick Nolte), Cady represents his own guilty conscience – Cady has a perfectly reasonable legal grievance against him. Cady is also an unpleasant reminder to our hero of his own violent side. From the start, Nolte is a mass of sublimated aggression: his squash defeat of his mistress is as violent in its way as Cady's rape of her, only a few scenes later. Nolte hires men to beat up Cady and – another hint of suppressed sadism – goes to watch. Under stress, Nolte even comes close to striking his wife and daughter.

In the first *Cape Fear*, Gregory Peck played the hero as a pillar of family rectitude: Nolte is an altogether more flawed, Scorsesian and believable character.

Here, as in *Taxi Driver,* Scorsese is fascinated by the violence which exists below the surface of respectable society. The first attack we see in the picture is performed not by the psychopathic villain, but by Nolte on Cady – and the setting is highly significant. The 4th July parade featuring soldiers carrying an American flag, is a reminder that America is a society founded not only on legal rights, but also on the threat of institutionalised violence.

This most Hobbesian of films also exploits our unconscious fears about the rule of law. Nolte's original betrayal of Cady, by not revealing the sexual past of his last rape victim, reflects our hero's belief that the law doesn't protect a promiscuous woman who has been raped. Nolte's girl-friend, the rape victim, knows for the same reason that the law won't protect her and refuses to press charges.

And it's a film which strikes to the heart of middle-class anxieties about materialism. Cady expresses Nolte's unconscious fear that he has lost his sense of values. "I'm gonna teach you the meaning of commitment," Cady tells him, in a friendly moment. "You could say I'm here to save you". Nolte and his family pass through a Hell where they are tested by fire and water, and end up baptized and "born again". It's a story of guilt and redemption. Scorsese once studied to become a Catholic priest, and his religious theme places *Cape Fear* in the mainstream of his work.

The acting throughout is of a high standard. Juliette Lewis is sensational in her one-take scene with De Niro in an empty theatre, and Robert De Niro makes seamless transitions from sly comedy to the grandest of grand guignol. It's not hard to see why De Niro likes appearing in Scorsese movies (*Cape Fear* is his seventh). He is wonderfully served by the visuals: one of the most terrifying shots is almost before he's had to start acting. Cady leaves jail with storm clouds and lightning flickering overhead, walks expressionlessly towards camera and never stops coming until his face is distorted by the anamorphic lens. You can actually feel the audience flinch and pull back.

The serious aspects of the film are, to some extent, victims of its success as a thriller: you can enjoy *Cape Fear* merely as the Rolls Royce of slasher movies, a two-hour anxiety attack, without bothering to look far into its murky depths. But that is only to say that it repays being seen more than once. Okay, it is a genre piece – but *Cape Fear* is one of the most undervalued films in recent history.

CAPTURING THE FRIEDMANS
(2003)

First-time director Andrew Jarecki set out to make a documentary about Silly Billy, the number one children's birthday clown in New York City. But he ended up making one of the darkest and most upsetting films of all time.

Silly Billy (real name David Friedman) is a living showbiz cliché: he's a clown wearing a smile that masks a seething maelstrom of pain. He is one of the most obviously disturbed characters ever to appear on celluloid, as – surrounded by magic tricks and a comedy rubber chicken – he rails against the police and his own mother, whom he blames irrationally for the crimes that his father committed.

For David is the oldest son of Arnold Friedman, a respected, popular high school science teacher and pillar of his suburban community in Great Neck, Long Island, until 1987 – when Arnold was discovered in possession of paedophile magazines. Worse was to follow: he was found guilty of using a computer class he ran in his own house, to abuse and sodomise boys between 9 and 11 years old. Arnold pled guilty and committed suicide in prison.

And that's not all. David the children's clown is also the elder brother of Jesse Friedman, youngest of Arnold's three sons, who was found guilty of assisting in the rape of these boys. Faced with more than 200 criminal accusations ranging from sodomy to child endangerment, he too pled guilty, and received a prison sentence of 13 years.

The clichéd, psychobabble response to David's anger would be that he is "in denial", that he can't come to terms with the truth. And to some extent that's right. He still finds it impossible to associate the loving father he knew with the cunning paedophile presented in court. Small wonder, then, that David clings on for comfort to his father's admission that he did indeed interfere with two small boys – but not in his own house.

That defence may not mitigate Arnold's guilt much to an outsider; but with regard to Jesse's guilt, it is crucial. Of course there remains the possibility that Arnold lied about never interfering with children in his own home in order to protect Jesse; but director Andrew Jarecki makes a very strong case for the alleged misconducts with the computer class never taking place at all, or becoming wildly exaggerated.

No medical or physical evidence of abuse was ever produced; and the police investigation methods were highly questionable for the way they led and browbeat child witnesses, some of whom clearly invented stories – as one prosecution witness confesses on camera – "to get them off my back".

Another supposed victim "recalled" the molestation only after being placed under hypnosis (a means of therapy during which, as we now know, suggestions can be placed in a subject's mind to induce a false memory). And within the Great Neck community such hysteria spread about Arnold Friedman's paedophilia that parents actually started indulging in one-upmanship about the number of times their children had been abused.

As the film progresses, it becomes clear that both the accused were forced into making plea bargains of "guilty" because of evidence from a small minority of children involved in the computer classes, that was contradictory, confused and in all probability invented to please their interrogators.

Among the most incredible aspects of the accusations is that children who had allegedly been abused over several months took a break and then came back for more, and that none of the parents – most of them intelligent professionals – ever noticed anything wrong with their allegedly sodomised and severely beaten children until after Arnold had been found in possession of child pornography.

Perhaps the most devastating revelation within this movie is the fallibility of human memory. Arnold freely confesses to having sodomised his own brother Howard when Arnold was 13 and Howard was 8, but Howard – though now in a happy, longterm homosexual relationship – can remember nothing about it.

Frances Galasso, the chief detective who led the police effort and is now retired, says at one point that child pornography was openly on display throughout the Friedmans' house – clearly a false memory, since Arnold's wife Elaine was patently unaware of his tastes, and everyone else's testimony suggests that Arnold hid his pornography behind a piano in his study.

One of the weirdest aspects of *Capturing the Friedmans* is that the family gave Jarecki free access to their home movies. They make creepy but utterly compulsive viewing. First they capture the Friedmans when they were, to all appearances, happy and normal.

But, astonishingly, David carries on filming even after

Arnold and Jesse have been indicted. We witness the family falling apart, in searing sequences of sullen silences, angry outbursts and gallows humour, as the Friedman males attempt to see the ironic side of their predicament and their mother Elaine (not blessed with a sense of humour, but who can blame her?) looks on appalled.

The film doesn't offer easy answers, but it does offer important insights. One is that child abusers are people too. Like the father in Todd Solondz's fictional film *Happiness,* Arnold Friedman was a loving father to his boys and, initially at least, a fond if emotionally distant husband to Elaine. Arnold did some monstrous things, but he wasn't a monster at all times. After he has been indicted, he wanders through his oldest son's home movies, looking numb, ashamed and desperately unhappy. And 15 years on from his crimes, we know that there are many thousands, perhaps millions, of men like him.

Another insight is that the gathering of evidence in such highly-charged cases is fraught with danger. It may be that Jesse was guilty of some of the crimes for which he was sentenced; but the film makes a plausible case for thinking that he wasn't. He comes across as a genuinely tragic figure, with the sins of his father – and the hatred of the community – visited upon him.

For the victims of child abuse are not only the children who have been raped. When Arnold gave in to temptation, he deeply wounded his wife and three sons. The middle one, Seth, who's moved west, married and had a daughter, allowed use of his image in the home movies but wouldn't be interviewed, believing it better to cut himself off entirely from the past – and you can see his point.

Everyone professionally involved in that most emotive

area of criminality, child abuse, should see this film – and so should every parent. This is a documentary that leaves a few questions of guilt or innocence hanging in the air, but it will open your eyes not only to the darkest, ugliest aspects of human nature, but also to the extraordinary selectiveness of memory.

This is not merely a unique documentary, it is a great film which will never be bettered in its area. Watch it, and I guarantee that it will move you deeply, and then have you talking and thinking for days.

THE CASTLE *(1998)*

The Castle comes from the sunny land that brought us *Strictly Ballroom* and *Muriel's Wedding*, and it's a ripper. It made me weep with laughter.

Darrel Kerrigan (Michael Caton) is one of life's optimists, and a firm believer in family values. His home may be a shack situated ear-splittingly close to an airport runway, but to him it's an enchanted castle.

He is often to be found making lovingly botched home improvements or gazing at the electricity pylon which dwarfs his humble abode, an awesome reminder – as he tells his dim-witted sons – of man's ability to generate electricity.

Darrel is grateful for the life he leads. He is especially admiring of his wife's culinary genius. "What do you call this?" he gasps, as some new mouth-watering delicacy is brought before him. "Sponge cike," she announces proudly.

The Castle is a bizarre cross between *The Simpsons* and *The Brady Bunch*, but funnier than either. It celebrates family life, even as it spoofs it.

Like the best of Mike Leigh, the film is wonderfully observant about the way ordinary people behave and the banalities of everyday speech. But it also communicates a delight in the commonplace, an infectious faith in human goodness. There's no snobbery about the Kerrigans' vulgarity, poverty and ignorance.

We laugh at their pride in the daughter being the first in the family to receive a tertiary education – a diploma in hairdressing – yet there's something sweet about their supportiveness, enchanting about their optimism.

The story is a simple one, of how Dad and his dopey family take on big business when the powers-that-be attempt to make a compulsory purchase of their much-loved home.

The hilarity lies in the detail – in the way, for example, their extravagantly incompetent solicitor (Tiriel Mora) fights a losing battle with everything, from roman numerals to his copying machine, from old judges to new technology. He dictates letters imperiously into a dictaphone, but then has to sit down and type them out himself.

The message of the film is familiar but powerful, and patently sincere – that the common people frequently exhibit deeper wisdom and sounder values than the rich and powerful. The spirit of Dickens and Capra is alive and well, and living down under.

Staggeringly, the picture was shot in only ten days by first-time director Rob Stich. The ensemble cast is faultless, and Michael Caton gives a miraculously comic performance. This being an Australian comedy, the F-word abounds, but it's used to genuinely comic effect. *The Castle* is on a par with those small but perfectly formed films (*Gregory's Girl*, *Local Hero*) that Bill Forsyth used to make, up in Scotland.

CHANGELING *(2008)*

Do you want some news to cheer you up? Clint Eastwood is making the best movies of his life right now, and he's 78 years old. His latest is not only among the finest pictures of 2008; *Changeling* is right up there with the big emotional experiences that cinema has to offer.

It contains a wonderfully passionate, sometimes ferocious leading performance by Angelina Jolie. The ensemble cast – packed with little-known character actors – is among the strongest ever assembled.

Huge credit should also go to journalist and screenwriter J. Michael Straczynski, who makes an astonishing big-screen debut at the age of 54. Not only did he discover the story and research it. He has organised it into a film that abandons the tyranny of the conventional Hollywood three-act structure – for the extremely good reason that it ain't the way it happened – and fashioned a true story so fascinating that it should hold you gripped for every one of its 141 minutes.

In 1928 Los Angeles, single mother Christine Collins (Jolie) returned home to discover that her nine year-old son Walter had vanished. After months of searching, a boy calling himself Walter Collins turned up in Illinois, and his relieved mother scraped together the cash to bring him home.

The trouble was that the boy wasn't Walter Collins at all. He was three inches shorter, he was circumcised, his dental records didn't match, and he didn't recognise his former schoolfriends or teachers. Amazingly, none of these revelations deterred the LAPD Police Chief James E. "Two Guns" Davis (Colm Feore) and the head of his juvenile investigation unit Captain J.J. Jones (Jeffrey Donovan), who declared the case closed.

The more Christine Collins protested that the child wasn't hers, the more mentally unstable she appeared to the male authorities. When she engaged the help of outspoken pastor Gustav A. Briegleb (John Malkovich, interestingly odd), whose sermons and radio broadcasts declared the LAPD guilty of longtime corruption, she was arrested and taken to a psychiatric ward.

I won't tell you more, except that the story takes us into areas evocative of such memorable psychological melodramas as *The Snake Pit* and *One Flew Over The Cuckoo's Nest*, and then into an even more nightmarish world.

Jason Butler Harner gives a memorably creepy performance as Gordon Northcott, a farmer with something to hide. Michael Kelly is equally outstanding as Detective Lester Ybarra, whose discoveries blew the Christine Collins case wide open, while Geoff Pierson radiates decency and determination as S.S.Hahn, the mother's crusading "pro bono" lawyer.

There is the sense throughout of a film that refuses to pull its punches. Eastwood has clearly reached the age when he does as he damn well likes. He's interested in telling the truth and making classic films, not merely turning a profit.

As a riveting picture of the Los Angeles underbelly, this is on a par with *LA Confidential*. It also develops into a coruscating critique of male sexism. All the same, it's not too tough a watch, for there are elements of black humour in the bone-headedness of men unwilling to countenance the possibility that a woman might know her own child better than they do.

Changeling is among the finest films Eastwood has made, and an all too rare example of a Hollywood film that's been made for grown-ups. It is remarkably craftsmanlike in its evocation of period, with few verbal infelicities – though someone's reference to serial-killing is an anachronism, for the term was coined in the 1970s by FBI man Robert Ressler.

The story-telling is consummate, and what a mind-bogglng story it is. It unfolds in constantly unexpected ways, which gives it the feeling of real life; and the explanations – such as the false Walter's excuse for his behaviour – are so crazy that they could only be the truth.

There isn't a weak performance, but Jolie is the revelation. She shows miraculous depth as an ordinary mother who doesn't want to make waves, but is then forced into situations where she has to make a stand. She's only Eastwood's second heroine in the whole of his directing career, but this is a landmark female performance to rank alongside Hilary Swank's in *Million Dollar Baby*.

The film is also a splendid expose of political corruption. Though male chauvinism isn't as toxic today, much of the subject-matter, including its warning against allowing those in power to cover up mistakes, establish a police state and spin the "news" against anyone who crosses them, remains as powerful and relevant as ever.

I'm always wary of using that overused word "masterpiece", but this is one film that deserves the accolade.

I urge you to see it, if only to remind yourself that cinema doesn't have to be the artistic equivalent of junk food. This is *haute cuisine*, served to perfection by an all-time-great.

A final note on the facts behind the movie, which I would advise you not to read until after you have seen it:

Possibly in order for *Changeling* not to be too depressing to bear, or to avoid accusations of homophobia, Eastwood soft-pedals some of the details concerning murderous paedophilia. He prefers not to delve into Gordon Northcott's revealing family background.

His mother, who doesn't appear in the movie, helped him with his crimes, for which she received a life sentence, and his father (who died in a lunatic asylum) sodomized him since the age of ten. Another indication that this was far from a normal family is that one of Northcott's uncles was also found guilty of murder years later, and died in San Quentin Prison while serving a life term.

Eastwood also ignores the probability that the kidnappings were, in part, financially motivated. Part of Northcott's confession was that he hired his victims out to wealthy Californian perverts, whom he named. The film-makers choose to ignore the fact that they were never brought to justice.

I imagine that Eastwood left out these details because he wished to keep the focus of his movie on Christine Collins, bring some kind of closure to his film, and leave us in a comparatively hopeful frame of mind. But I thought you might like to know the truth.

CHERI *(2009)*

The premise behind this tragi-comedy, based on two novels by Colette, may seem unpromising and even distasteful. It's about a veteran Parisian courtesan of the early twentieth century (Michelle Pfeiffer) who embarks on a scandalous, six-year affair with a young man of eighteen (Rupert Friend).

Eventually his mother (Kathy Bates), herself a former courtesan, marries him off to a pretty, rich but inexperienced girl (the exquisite young actress Felicity Jones), with disastrous consequences.

Screenwriter Christopher Hampton and director Stephen Frears, together for the first time since *Dangerous Liaisons* 20 years ago, cleverly negotiate the pitfalls of the scenario.

They are helped by the wit of Colette and the physical charms of their leading actors. There's extraordinary sexual chemistry between Pfeiffer and Friend, which neatly overcomes the age difference.

Her lust for a lithe body and handsome face turns into gut-twisting vulnerability, offset by a determination that she shall not become an object of pity, or a laughing stock.

His youthful self-centredness matures into an awareness that he has obligations to his young wife, and can not be a toy boy all his life. And yet… doesn't he love his old flame, despite her age?

Early on as I was watching, I wrote down grumpily that Cheri was "like *Gigi* without the songs", that Stephen Frears' omniscient narration seemed unnecessary, and that audiences would come out whistling the sets. But gradually I fell in love with it; and even the seemingly redundant narration comes into its own in the final moments.

There won't be a more visually seductive picture this year, with gorgeous *art nouveau* design by Alan MacDonald and Denis Schnegg, flamboyant costumes by Consolata Boyle and superb cinematography by Darius Khondji, but its beauty is more than skin deep.

It appears at first to be a brittle, escapist costume comedy, but it deepens to become the film that *Benjamin Button* aspired to be: a moving tragedy about the passing of time.

Michelle Pfeiffer has been Oscar-worthy before, notably in Frears' *Dangerous Liaisons* and Scorsese's *The Age of Innocence*, but this is the performance of her life. Now in her fifties, she looks more stunning than ever, and her mesmerising performance combines comedic charm, tragic depth and that never-to-be-underrated ingredient, sex appeal.

Kathy Bates is hilariously bitchy in a variety of outrageously bosomy outfits. She gives top-quality comic support as she pursues her selfish agenda while dispensing unwanted advice to all around her, like the *belle epoque*'s answer to Edna Everage.

There's a cavalcade of British talent in smaller roles, with such fine but undervalued actresses as Frances Tomelty, Nichola McAuliffe and Gaye Brown all memorable in different ways.

However, the revelation, even after his promising performances as Mr Wickham in *Pride and Prejudice* and Prince Albert in *The Young Victoria*, is Rupert Friend.

Emerging from the shadow of his real-life amour Keira Knightley and defying those who dismiss him as an Orlando Bloom lookalike, he delivers a nuanced, sensitive performance which confirms he is an extremely gifted actor.

Frears has always been skilful at eliciting terrific performances from actors, from Daniel Day Lewis in *My Beautiful Laundrette* through to Helen Mirren in *The Queen*. But this is his most stylish and cinematic film yet, and in his late sixties he's revealing a wisdom and relaxed maturity that put most directors to shame.

And let's not forget one more up-and-comer. The film is immaculately produced by someone not normally associated with cinema, Bill Kenwright, who should have been knighted years ago for his services to theatre. Over the past ten years, he's cleverly adapted his talents to the cinema. *Cheri* radiates quality in every department, and – whether it's a popular success or not – this splendid achievement establishes him as one of Britain's very best film producers.

CHICAGO *(2002)*

This deliciously witty black comedy tells the story of Roxie Hart, a blonde flapper who kills her lover and becomes a celebrity, thanks to her unscrupulous lawyer (Richard Gere) and a jealous fellow murderess Velma Kelly (Catherine Zeta Jones), whose help to Roxie is less than intentional.

We have had to wait far too long for *Chicago* to reach the screen. It first hit Broadway in 1975, the same year as *A Chorus Line*, filmed 17 years ago. Pretty obviously, *Chicago* has gone into production now only because of the unexpected success last year of *Moulin Rouge*.

And what a pleasure it is to experience once again a colourful, well-written, imaginatively staged, superbly performed musical on the big screen! Will it be a hit with a modern cinema audience? That's hard to predict, but it certainly deserves to be. I, for one, was razzle-dazzled.

The ever-photogenic Catherine Zeta-Jones certainly looks the part of the luscious but hard-bitten Velma, and can do Velma's silky bitchiness standing on her head – or a table.

She has all the dancing skills required, great legs and a strong (if not particularly expressive) singing voice. But everything she does looks choreographed. She reminded me of Jane Russell struggling not to be eclipsed by Marilyn Monroe's star quality in *Gentlemen Prefer Blondes*. There's nothing wrong with Zeta-Jones's performance; it's just that whenever Zellweger is on with her, it's Zellweger you watch.

Renee has the knack of making every choreographed move look as if she's only just thought of it. It's this spontaneity and joy in her own naughtiness that makes Roxie more than just another not-so-dumb blonde. This is easily the funniest, most charismatic performance by any actress this year.

Renee first caught the public eye with her portrayal of nice girls in *Jerry Maguire* and *Bridget Jones's Diary*. It's a shock at first to see her playing a murderous floozie with few scruples and tons of iron-clad ambition.

Wisely, Renee doesn't soften the character or sentimentalise her. Just as Nicole Kidman did in the black comedy *To Die For*, she makes her anti-heroine so energetic, sexy and outrageously lacking in shame that you can't help but extend your grudging admiration. If ever they want to make a new version of Thackeray's masterpiece *Vanity Fair*, she'd be the perfect Becky Sharp.

The first time I noticed the talent of Richard Gere was when he played the lead in a West End show – *Grease* in 1973 – so it's good to see him returning to his musical roots with so much enthusiasm.

His singing voice isn't the greatest – it's a bit thin and reedy – and his tap-dancing is efficient rather than remarkable; but he has no problem playing an egocentric, cheerfully hypocritical lawyer. Gere looks as if he's enjoying himself, and that makes the audience enjoy him too.

Director Rob Marshall occasionally betrays a lack of experience in the cinema – this is his debut and he's come up from being a choreographer on American TV. His biggest fault lies in being over-busy. Some numbers would have benefited from less frenetic editing and a greater willingness to allow the dancers to show off their paces.

However, Marshall's staging of the songs is done with high style. His pacy storytelling moves cleverly – and seamlessly – between the naturalism of old-fashioned prison movies and the stylised presentation of a musical cabaret. If the whole thing has echoes of Bob Fosse, that's appropriate in a film which owes its genesis to Fosse's original Broadway staging of the show.

A few of the best numbers, regrettably, have been dropped for the movie, notably *When Velma Takes the Stand* and *Class*; but I hope they'll surface on the DVD.

Most of my doubts about *Chicago* are really reservations about the musical itself. It's so totally heartless that it doesn't really involve the emotions; and any musical that tries to exist without at least one romantic ballad can certainly be accused of superficiality and a lack of warmth.

The film pretends to have something to say about the fickle nature of celebrity and the public's amoral appetite for it, but as social satire it lacks the bite of Andrew Niccol's *S1mone*.

Nor are the songs particularly memorable. The best ones are *All That Jazz, Cell Block Tango* and *Razzle Dazzle*, all production numbers rather than standards. The score is skilful pastiche, rather than anything strikingly original.

The best thing about the movie is that it stages these numbers with an enormous amount of flair and showmanship. *Chicago*'s basic deficiencies mean that it may not quite rank up there in the top ten classic musicals, but it still manages to offer 107 minutes of thoroughly enjoyable entertainment.

THE CHRONICLES OF NARNIA: THE LION, THE WITCH AND THE WARDROBE (2005)

This is a wonderful, colossal, stupendous film. Not only does it miraculously do full justice to C.S. Lewis's classic 1950 fantasy. It improves upon it, giving it a more sophisticated sense of humour and a spectacular sense of scale (using yet more of the natural beauty of New Zealand) that turns the Narnia saga from a children's series on a relatively modest scale into a worthy successor to *The Lord of the Rings* as an epic piece of storytelling.

Just as miraculously, it achieves all this without sacrificing the much loved qualities of the original novel, including its charm, sense of wonder and feeling for myth.

Even the Christian subtext of Lewis's book is handled with taste and sensitivity. It's there, but never laboured. And – with one tiny exception, the actor voicing the wolf Maugrim – the cast is British. Though shot in New Zealand by an American production company (Disney) it remains lovingly true to its original cultural background – which has not always been the case with Disney films, and is particularly welcome in the context of so British a book.

The script sticks amazingly – you could say "religiously" – close to Lewis's novel. Four Pevensie children are sent from London as evacuees during the Blitz to the huge, rambling country house of the mysterious, eccentric but twinklingly benevolent Professor Kirke (played by the great Jim Broadbent).

Peter (played by Prince William lookalike William Moseley) is the oldest of the children, but his authority is disputed by his stroppy younger brother Edmund (Skandar Keynes). Peter's somewhat priggish sister Susan (Anna Popplewell) regards herself as a more responsible guardian of their small sister Lucy (Georgie Henley).

It is, of course, Lucy who, during a game of hide and seek, discovers that a huge Jacobean wardrobe on the top floor contains more than just coats and mothballs. "It's an awfully big wardrobe," she comments in a masterpiece of English understatement as she stumbles out of its back and into the enchanted (and fabulously large) landscape of Narnia, where she is invited to tea by a faun Mr Tumnus (James McAvoy) and first hears of the White Witch (Tilda Swinton) who has ruled the land for a hundred years of winter.

Director Andrew Adamson proves himself not only a master of effects and animation, which might be expected of the director of *Shrek* and *Shrek 2*, but an extraordinarily accomplished director of children.

The quality of the four young leading actors is exceptional – light years ahead of the Harry Potter cast, even on a first attempt. They make an utterly convincing and captivating family, and provide marvellous depth to characters which were fairly sketchy in Lewis's original. As in all the best action films, every sequence leads to a telling character development, and each gradation in the development of the children and their family relationships is captured by the young actors with terrific intelligence and wit.

Even their comic timing is impeccable, as when Peter resists the responsibility of saving Narnia from the White Witch by objecting "We're not heroes". And Susan amplifies this by adding bathetically "We're from Finchley".

The direction is a constant delight in both its sweep and its detail, as when the White Witch casually torches a passing butterfly and turns it to stone without even bothering to watch it plummet to earth. The costume department has a whale of a time with Swinton's dresses, which give a whole new meaning to the term "power dressing".

The adult supporting cast is faultless throughout, but Tilda Swinton must be singled out for her cold, cruel and commanding performance as the Witch; Ray Winstone and Dawn French are delightfully funny as the voices of Mr and Mrs Beaver (just two of many animated triumphs); James McAvoy is a subtle, sprightly and enormously charming Mr Tumnus (with extraordinary CGI effects providing his lower half); and, perhaps best of all, Liam Neeson is impeccably leonine as the voice of the kind but powerful Aslan.

We have grown accustomed to brilliant special effects in the past few years, but even by modern standards these are breathtaking. Armies of Minotaurs, Centaurs, Gryphons, Giants – you imagine it, they're all here, along with talking animals of astonishing verisimilitude. The final battle scene is truly amazing, and in some ways even improves upon *The Return of the King* in its grandeur and inventiveness.

Despite the long running time (over two hours) I would recommend this even to small children. Whatever your age, this is a magical movie, and far classier and more imaginative than I ever dared to hope. The Narnian books were my boyhood favourites, and I read them again and again – especially *The Voyage of the Dawn Treader* and *The Silver Chair*. It's a relief to see the books in hands that are not merely safe, but inspired.

The Narnian novels have already sold 85 million copies in 29 languages, and now they are all going to have to be reprinted. In the face of Philip Pullman's spirited attacks on them from an atheistic standpoint, the Narnia books were in danger of becoming regarded as old-fashioned and irrelevant. No longer.

CRAZY, STUPID, LOVE (2011)

Delightful, intelligent romantic comedies are few and far between, as are entertaining movies starring Steve Carell. *Crazy, Stupid, Love* is both of these things, and it's blessed with one of the most adroit comedy scripts since Richard Curtis burst upon the romcom scene with *Four Weddings and a Funeral.*

Not everyone loves this kind of movie, as is proved by the chequered critical reaction to one of the finest pictures in this genre, *Love Actually*, but if you enjoy sophisticated romcoms like *The Kids Are All Right, Up In The Air* and *An Education*, you're going to want to see this film more than once.

It's the most ambitious Hollywood comedy in a decade, skilfully weaving together three plot strands and steering an enjoyable route through comedy and drama. It culminates in two classic scenes that perfectly blend comedy and romance.

Steve Carell, back on form after the demeaning *Dinner For Schmucks*, plays Cal Weaver, a nice husband and doting father who discovers that even his wife for a quarter-century (Julianne Moore) thinks he's boring. She's had a fling with an accountant (Kevin Bacon) and wants a divorce.

Accepting her request without putting up a fight, Cal moves to a small flat, hangs out in a singles bar and gets drunk on alcohol and self-pity. Here, twentysomething lounge lizard Jacob (Ryan Gosling) takes pity on him, with the memorable line "I don't know whether I should help you or euthanise you".

In a fresh, funny buddy-buddy relationship across the generations, Jacob teaches Cal to dress better, improve his conversational skills and rebuild his sex life. Previously a one-woman guy, Cal embarks on a series of flings with attractive singles, one of them played with ferocious sexuality by the reliably marvellous Marisa Tomei.

There are two subplots. In one, Cal's thirteen year-old son (Jonah Bobo) wrestles with being in love with his 17 year-old babysitter (Analeigh Tipton), while she has equally unrequited feelings for Cal, who's sublimely oblivious.

The other, superior strand features the lovely Emma Stone, as funny and charming here as she was in *Easy A*. Like Lucille Ball, she's attractively willing to appear ugly, and she's sparky and fresh as Hannah, a trainee lawyer with an inexplicable crush on her nerdy boss.

When the scales of injustice fall from her eyes, she returns for uncomplicated sex to the lounge lizard who once chatted her up in a local bar. That's Jacob, of course, played by Gosling. This gives rise to a seduction scene of pure genius, where Jacob uses his can't-fail seduction technique on the cynical Hannah, with ridiculous but romantic consequences.

All three plot strands come together in a garden scene so farcical that Alan Ayckbourn might have written it in his prime. So brilliant is it that the twenty minutes that follow, in which all the plot lines are tidied up, complete with life-lessons, are a bit of an anti-climax. But hey, not even five-star films are perfect.

Dan Fogelman has written several entertaining films, including *Bolt, Cars 2* and *Tangled*; but this is his most inspired yet.

As for directors Glenn Ficarra and John Requa, this is more humane than their scriptwriting efforts on *Bad Santa*, and infinitely superior to their previous attempt to direct a Hollywood movie, *I Love You Phillip Morris*. There's an especially eye-catching tracking shot, establishing Carell's newly found prowess as a womaniser.

The picture raises plenty of laughs but also has heart – plus a couple of crafty plot twists. It's commercially shrewd, too, delivering a multi-generational love story that gives all age-groups within the audience characters to whom it's easy to relate.

Most romantic comedies are aimed at women, but there's enough here for men to like. Gosling, in a rare comic role, is a revelation in a part that a lesser actor might easily have made crude and unsympathetic. I shudder to think how Vince Vaughn or Ashton Kutcher would have interpreted it. Gosling finds the vulnerability behind Jacob's bluster, just as Carell discovers the iron in the soul of his apparently staid family man.

The film is distinguished from almost every other recent Hollywood comedy not just by its intelligence, but also by generosity of spirit. Romcoms don't come much better than this, and in the context of recent gross-out comedies from Tinseltown it's little short of a miracle.

CYRANO DE BERGERAC *(1990)*

A man with a big nose (Gérard Depardieu) is too shy to tell a pretty girl he loves her but finally summons up courage to do so, with unfortunate consequences.

In his finest performance, Depardieu definitively captures Cyrano's self-loathing, his pathos and, above all, his panache. Depardieu's masculinity is reminiscent of Olivier in his prime; his swashbuckling is on a par with Errol Flynn's; and he miraculously combines all this with the more modern, anti-heroic, screen subtlety of a de Niro. On a screen filled with distractions – beautiful scenery, wonderfully detailed costumes, thousands of extras – it is hard to take your eyes off him. Depardieu alone would make the film worth seeing twice.

But as Roxane, the cousin who doesn't quite requite, Anne Brochet is a match for him. Even though the character might cruelly be summarised as an insensitive pseud infatuated with her illusions, she is still delightful: you can understand why Cyrano has fallen head-over-nose in love.

The usually tedious role of Christian, Roxane's stupid paramour, is played with nobility by Vincent Perez. The villains have complexity and humanity. Even in the crowd scenes, everyone seems to know what he's doing.

The screenplay is (bravely) in verse, and a reminder of how elegant French can sound. Anthony Burgess's rhyming subtitles capture the meaning and spirit perfectly. Even the spelling mistakes in the subtitles (inexcusable in a film with such meticulous attention to detail in every other respect) are not too distracting.

This is a splendid, moving, lyrical romance, brilliantly filmed by director Jean-Paul Rappeneau, who also wrote the screenplay with Jean-Claude Carriere. It is not static, like so many adaptations of classic stage plays; the beauty of the lighting, the fluidity of the camerawork and the energy of the staging make it better than the best of Zeffirelli. It's a masterpiece, and on a scale which means that it should be enjoyed first on the big screen.

DANCES WITH WOLVES *(1991)*

A white soldier (Kevin Costner) stationed on the frontier of the Old West learns to love the Indians.

This is, above all, a good yarn. The epic set-pieces – such as the buffalo-hunt, the battles and the cross-country journeys – are magnificent. And, whenever the story seems to be lapsing into cliché, it always manages some clever inversion of our expectations.

Most praise was rightly showered on Costner, who co-produced, starred and made an outstanding directorial debut. But Australian cinematographer Dean Semler, who displayed his eye for lighting and landscape in *Mad Max Beyond Thunderdome* and *Young Guns*, surpassed himself with shots worthy of a David Lean epic. The film's loving attention to detail also reflected credit on production designer Jeffrey Beechcroft, costume designer Elsa Zamperelli, and Michael Blake for his well-researched screenplay.

To the great credit of Costner's team, they don't allow period authenticity to overwhelm the story. Nor do they allow their modern concerns – for the environment, and about the need to respect other cultures – to become preachy or anachronistic. They have been content to tell a simple tale which illuminates great truths, with a sincerity and humour which speedily involves the emotions of an audience.

The three hour print feels longer than the four-hour version, the "director's cut", which avoids the pro-Sioux sentimentality of the original, fills in holes in the plot, and makes more sense of the romantic interludes. Most crucially, the full version is sceptical about whether Costner can ever become, or truly wants to become, an Indian – he never understands their marriage traditions, and even at the end we see him stopping a Sioux warrior from scalping a white officer. This makes much better sense of the ending, when Costner decides that his future lies in returning to white society.

Even in its shorter, commercially viable form, the film was a handsome piece of story-telling, and one of the more impressive Oscar-winners of recent years – though some critics have never forgiven it for beating another worthy candidate, *GoodFellas*. Revealed on the scale intended by its director, *Dances With Wolves* is much richer, complex and sophisticated. It deserves to take its place among the classic westerns.

THE DESCENDANTS (2011)

This is a grown-up, perceptive, funny film about family and responsibility, subjects rarely covered in movies except in clichéd, romantic terms.

Rich, complacent lawyer Matt King (George Clooney) has been able to behave selfishly until well into middle age, but suddenly has to come to terms with responsibilities to wife, daughters, family, ancestors and community.

He tries to cope with several crises in his life, simultaneously. First, as the senior member of a huge Hawaiian family that can trace its roots back to King Kamehameha, who united the islands of Hawaii in 1810, Matt is the major shareholder in his family trust. Cousins are pressing him to let them cash in on 25,000 acres of prime, unspoiled land on a beautiful island.

Secondly, Matt's wife Elizabeth (Patti Hastie) is in a coma after a boating accident, and so he has to behave as stoically as possible in front of friends and relatives, and become more than a "back-up parent" to his daughters, a vulnerable 10 year-old (Amara Miller) and a rebellious 17 year-old (Shailene Woodley). It doesn't help that she's going out with a dopey surfer dude (Nick Krause) whom Matt instinctively despises.

Matt can't understand why his daughters don't obey him: "It's like you don't respect anything!" he cries, unaware that it's mostly him they disrespect.

Thirdly, Matt discovers that his wife was having an affair with a local real-estate agent (Matthew Lillard). This makes him even more angry. "Nothing is ever a woman's fault!" he snarls, defiantly.

At the heart of the movie is Matt's damaged relationship with his daughters, especially the elder one, beautifully played by Woodley. Her character development is superbly written and acted, and it's movingly obvious that she is in some ways more emotionally mature than her father, and he desperately needs her help.

Robert Forster is exceptional as Elizabeth's father, a bad-tempered man who never much liked Matt. Judy Greer also turns in in a career-best performance that I can't describe without giving away the plot.

Clooney is rarely better than as a smart-alec learning not to be an idiot, and this performance is on a par with his Oscar-nominated turn in *Up In The Air*. Some of his early acting smacked of vanity. Now, he's unafraid to be seen in unflattering costumes, doing undignified things.

I can't recall any actor who has had the suave charisma of Cary Grant, coupled with the comic timing of Jack Lemmon. Clooney nails that combination here; in his early films, he was content to be a matinee idol, keeping most of himself well hidden. He's grown into the real deal, an authentically great screen actor.

He has many fabulous scenes, especially one where he confronts the man who nearly wrecked his family. In this sequence and many others, writer-director Alexander Payne shows the same skill as the great Billy Wilder, in being able to combine tragedy and comedy in the same scene and move between the two without any tonal dissonance.

Payne specialises in wise and witty tragi-comedies. This

is in the tradition of his previous best films, *Election, About Schmidt* and *Sideways*, and it's his warmest, kindliest yet. It confirms him as one of the most thought-provoking film-makers in the world today – and one of the most entertaining.

This is a film of rare maturity, and as such it may leave younger audiences cold. I can quite see how they might find it rambling and uneventful. Much of the "action" is taking place below the surface and behind people's eyes.

It's also the least satirical of Payne's films, the one in which he seems the most disposed to forgive his characters their sins; and that may not please those who are looking for something "edgier".

But I make no apology for liking it. In a world full of cinematic junk food, this is *haute cuisine*.

THE DISH *(2000)*

The Dish enables us to recall – and a younger generation to see for the first time – the men who walked on the Moon, back in 1969. But the adventure is seen from an entertainingly skewed angle – that of the men whose satellite dish beamed the TV satellite pictures to the world from the middle of a sheep paddock.

Based on a true story, this tonic from down under is from the team of writers who gave us *The Castle*. That was the funniest comedy of 1997, even if it hardly got a release elsewhere, driven out of the multiplexes by more heavily publicised American product. Both films have many of the most treasurable qualities of our own Ealing comedy – especially affection for the underdog.

The Dish opens with an elderly man (Sam Neill plus latex make-up) hobbling up to see a gigantic dish in a field. A security guard intercepts him. He's come in via the old entrance. There's a new one now, and if he would like to enter the proper way he can be taken on a guided tour. Neill shakes his head. The security man doesn't know he used to be in command there. But there's no "Do you know who I am?" springing to Neill's lips. He accepts that he's forgotten. He's more concerned that the things he did are remembered.

It's a moment that's typical of the comedy. It's touching,

self-deprecating, and it celebrates teamwork over the individual.

In its way, this is a patriotic movie, celebrating a real Australian achievement, but it avoids jingoism. It makes clear the fallibility of all concerned, and the somewhat ludicrous pretensions of the politicians, both local and national, who tried to make capital out of the event. Edmund Choi's deliberately histrionic score and well-chosen pop hits from the period add to the fun.

The heroes are the small-town Australians manning the dish – all the way down the intellectual ladder from shy mathematician Glenn (Tom Long) to Rudy (Tayler Kane), the lone security man. Rudy is handsome, good-natured but amazingly dim, and his beautiful sister (Eliza Szonert) is shocked to see he's been given a gun ("Does mum know?"). One of the film's running gags is Rudy's lumbering attempts to appear efficient, which are treated with good-humoured contempt by the workmates he is annoying.

This is a more innocent world where terrorism and sabotage aren't really on the cards. You can assume that any call by Rudy of "Halt! Who goes there?" will be followed by the sound of a bewildered sheep clearing its throat.

The parochialism of the people involved is comically at odds with the grandeur of the enterprise. "I can't believe I'm part of it!" says engineer Mitch (Kevin Harrington), before adding in a worried tone "I certainly can't believe Rudy is part of it".

Mayor Bob (Roy Billing) is thrilled to hear that the solitary American stationed at the dish (Al Burnett) has inquired in the town if there are any pretzels. "Pretzels!" gurgles the local dignitary, barely able to contain his joy and excitement. "It's a world event!"

Mayor Bob's teenage daughter Marie (Lenka Kripac) thinks of herself as counter-cultural and is visibly unimpressed. "If you ask me," she grumbles, "it's the biggest chauvinistic exercise in the history of the world." "That," replies her mother (Genevieve Mooy), who has a hideous selection of cocktail dresses and a practical answer for everything, "is why nobody asks you, darling!"

Naturally, things go wrong. Mistakes have to be covered up. A last-minute hitch means the guys at the Dish have to risk their lives to make the whole thing happen. But happen, it does. (This is not me spoiling the plot – you've already seen the TV pictures.)

The US Ambassador (John McMartin) doesn't mind that the local rock group thinks his national anthem is the theme from *Hawaii 5-O*. The Prime Minister of Australia (Bille Brown) is too drunk or stupid to notice that the banner welcoming him to the town is spelt "Prime Minaster". As long as he's getting whisky poured surreptitiously into his teacup, he's happy.

This is an unusually charming movie – funny, in a gentle, kindly way that is far too rare. It shows respect for the people behind the scenes, affection for dogged amateurs, for scientists, even for the boffins at NASA (whom it suggests are merely the Australian telescope people writ large). And though the film is on a small scale, it says important things about the human spirit.

In particular, it celebrates the importance of taking risks. The people at the Dish risk their lives to transmit the pictures. The shy mathematician has to risk rejection if he is to take out the most gorgeous girl in town. And the over-keen young Australian army recruit (Matthew Moore) who unaccountably fancies the mayor's daughter turns out to be the hero of his own particular sub-plot, with his inability to take no for an answer.

"Marie," he says, "I was wondering if you'd like to dance?"

"Are you stupid?" she replies, scathingly.

"No," says Keith, who takes everything at face value and adds doggedly "Do you want to?"

In the end he gets the girl. And even Mayor Bob, who fought in World War II, has to admire Keith's courage under fire.

Whenever I'm able to prise myself away from cinemas and screening rooms and meet real people, I'm struck by how unlike they are from everyone I've been watching all week on screen. Hardly any of them are violent. Virtually all are well-meaning. If they have faults – a certain pretentiousness, say, or a tendency to be materialistic – these tend to be counterbalanced by other strengths, such as a love of children or animals, a concern for those less fortunate in the community, a desire to make something better of themselves, or a sense of humour. They are, in short, precisely the kind of people you'll see in *The Dish*.

DISTRICT 9 *(2009)*

Highly original action movies don't come along every week – or every year, come to think of it. *District 9* is the understated name for a science fiction horror movie that might, in bygone decades, have been made on a shoestring, released to a few American drive-ins and called something a lot more exciting, like *Killer Prawns from Outer Space.*

Helped along by the production expertise of Peter "*Lord of the Rings*" Jackson, along with his 30-million dollar investment, this is a modern classic, easily the most imaginative of 2009's summer spectaculars. Though the first ever mega co-production between South Africa and New Zealand, it puts to shame all those big, brainless Hollywood product this year – and yes, I do mean you, *Transformers 2, GI Joe* and *X-Men Origins: Wolverine.* It's going to be a huge, world-wide hit.

We've become used to movie aliens who are either superior beings paying us a patronising visit – *Close Encounters, The Day The Earth Stood Still* – or aggressive creatures bent on world domination – *Independence Day, Mars Attacks!*

This time round, they're confused, helpless creatures who look as if they smell bad and wouldn't make ideal neighbours. Emotionally, they resemble ET in that they would like to go home. But they're not cute. They're ugly. They breed. They scavenge around garbage. Essentially, they're ten-foot cockroaches.

They refuse to assimilate or learn English. Their mother-ship remains immobilised over Johannesburg, but they have no way of getting it moving again. So they are confined to District 9, a shanty town rife with crime.

The human authorities, white and black, treat the extra-terrestrials as illegal aliens, while Nigerian gangs run a black market exploiting the newcomers' nauseating addiction to cat food. The poor "prawns" live in corrugated iron shacks and squalid poverty, slinking around and grumbling crabbily, like an entire race of exoskeletal Gollums.

The film's human anti-hero starts out as the principal villain, a brave move by screenwriters Terri Tatchell and Neil Blomkamp, possibly influenced by the great German film *The Lives of Others*. He's nerdy, unconsciously racist middle-manager Wikus Van De Merwe, brilliantly played by Sharlto Copley, a non-professional actor who is South Africa's answer to Steve Carell.

He has the job of evicting the prawns and transporting them to District 10, a concentration camp far away from the city. He approaches this task with groundless self-confidence, a dangerously patronising manner and a cheerful disregard for inter-galactic civil rights.

Little does Wikus know that his boss (Louis Minaar), who happens also to be his father-in-law, is interested in making a killing from understanding the aliens' weaponry, which will only fire if you have prawn DNA. Unfortunately for Wikus, he suffers an accident which results in him absorbing some crustacean goo, and one of his arms starts turning into a pincer.

The good news is that suddenly he can shoot alien weapons. The bad news is that Wikus' blonde, beautiful wife (Vanessa Haywood) thinks he's been sleeping with prawn prostitutes and caught some terrible disease. Even worse news is that he's turning into one of the inferior life-forms he's previously despised.

As if that wasn't enough, he's being chased by his homicidal father-in-law who's interested in his weapons potential and a Nigerian gang-leader who wants to amputate and eat his new limb, which he believes will give him superhuman powers. I suppose you could call this an arms race, kill-or-be-krill, or even torture prawn.

Running alongside this story is a tender tale of a father prawn who's been working on a plan to save his race, and his shrimp of a son, who has a talent for technology. They need the help of our mutating hero, or they'll end up as an exploding seafood cocktail.

Obviously there's an element of political satire. Through implicit references to Zimbabwean immigrants, apartheid and Jewish concentration camps, the film suggests that it's part of the human condition to find outsiders to victimise.

Hard-line vegans might also argue that it takes a beady-eyed view of man's inhumanity to crustacean, but first-time director Neil Blomkamp (a Canada-based, South Africa-born director who's expanded *District 9* from a 7-minute short called *Alive in Joburg*) doesn't labour this. He's primarily interested in making a fast and furious action movie, with black comedy elements reminiscent of *RoboCop*, *The Fly* and *Starship Troopers*.

Thanks, I suspect, to the valuable assistance of producers Peter Jackson and Philippa Boyens (who also collaborated on *Lord of the Rings* and *King Kong*) and first-rate special effects by New Zealand's Weta workshop, he carries off his objective with great flair.

Stylistically, the start and finish of the film are shot as mockumentary, with implied satirical jabs at gabbling 24-hour newsgatherers and pundits who dispense prejudice rather than information.

But elsewhere Blomkamp makes us care, despite our initial misgivings, about poor, mutating Wikus (whose love for his wife becomes all the more pathetic as he increasingly resembles a giant cockroach) and the prawns, who aren't as dumb as they appear, and may in fact be more instinctively humane than the humans.

The result is a thinking person's *Transformers*, with plenty of shoot-outs and explosions to please undemanding fanboys, but enough of everything else to persuade mature audiences to keep watching.

For my money, the apocalyptic finale goes on too long, and lacks the innovative spirit that has gone before – some of it, unluckily, has been foreshadowed by the recent movie of *Iron Man*. The overuse of the F-word becomes oppressive, as does the gory violence.

But it would be churlish to deny that this film's a lot of fun, highly original and the most entertaining action sci-fi to hit our screens for many years. Whereas the recently revived *Star Trek* was cheerfully old-fashioned, grandiose space opera, *District 9* feels very modern, cynical and hard-edged. I liked – and admired – it enormously.

DODGEBALL: A TRUE UNDERDOG
(2004)

Ben Stiller owes us a decent comedy, and here he revels in the role of a tiny, muscle-bound gym owner who thinks he's God's gift to wimps and women. Stiller proved in *Zoolander* that he is most inventive when he's not trying to be ingratiating, and *Dodgeball* shows him at his funniest (stay to the end of the credits, by the way).

Vince Vaughn is also at his deadpan best, laugh-out-loud funny for the first time since *Swingers*, as a nice-guy gym owner whose place is about to be taken over and turned into a car park by Stiller's fitness company unless Vaughn can raise $50,000.

How will he raise the money? By assembling his motley crew of weeds and misfits (and a friendly banker, played by Christine Fisher, the real-life Mrs Ben Stiller) to win the Las Vegas world final of Dodgeball – a genuine, though none too subtle game which basically involves bombarding your opponents with large rubber balls.

This is no small challenge, however, especially as first Vaughn and his team have to win a qualifying round against a mean-looking bunch of girl guides.

No one is likely to confuse *Dodgeball* with art, but it's one of the few gross-out comedies America has produced that is actually funny.

Writer-director Rawson Marshall Thurber has his mean-spirited moments – there's a horrible gag involving an overweight cheerleader that totally undermines his message that it's all right to be different. The sexual references are far too crude and copious for a 12A movie. And an enormous amount of the comedy is sadistic.

However, a lot of the slapstick is so well-timed (and aimed) that it's genuinely amusing. The movie has an underlying satirical thrust against the world's increasingly frenzied pursuit of the body beautiful and the mind vacant. And there's a refreshing amount of verbal wit in the script.

Dodgeball is on one level a conventional sports movie in which the underdogs overcome ridiculous odds – but it's also clever in the way it lampoons the whole genre of sports movies, and the increasingly idiotic, self-important way that sport is portrayed on TV. Neatly timed for the end of the Olympics, it's a refreshing breath of foul air.

EAST IS EAST *(1999)*

This account of the trials and tribulations of an Anglo-Pakistani family in the north of England is up there with the very best comedies. It's extremely funny, with more laugh-out-loud moments than you can count, and a climax that made me weep with laughter. It also has depth, with a sensitive approach to such heavyweight topics as racism and domestic violence.

The masterly screenplay and lively direction are by exciting new talents. Its warmth and generosity of spirit deserve to make it a smash-hit around the world. The best British comedy since *The Full Monty*? No. It's far better.

Om Puri, who has impressed before in less distinguished British films, gives the performance of his life as George Khan, a proud Muslim, Pakistani and Salford chip-shop owner. He has Ella (Linda Bassett), a no-nonsense, hard-working Lancashire lass as his wife, plus six sons and a daughter, who respect and fear him, calling him "Genghis" behind his back. Like an Islamic Tevye the Milkman, he is bent on marrying off his oldest offspring through arranged marriages.

When his oldest son (Ian Aspinall) humiliates his father with a bolt from imminent wedlock, George removes his photograph from the wall and declares him dead. "No, he's not," his wife points out placidly. "He's living in Eccles". The rest of the story revolves around Dad's iron determination to marry off his next two sons to two of the ugliest girls in Bradford.

The film is set in 1971, but it could almost be today. The period just offers scope for lovely little nostalgic touches – such as the ubiquitous space hopper – and a wealth of character detail: the cocktail barman who's too smooth for the safety of his own drinks, the youngest boy's constant use of his parka as a comforter…

Linda Bassett gives a blissful performance, which brings together the best qualities of Brenda Blethyn's befuddled mum in *Secrets and Lies,* and Kathy Burke as the battered wife in *Nil By Mouth.* It is partly because of her obvious affection for George, despite everything, that he doesn't become a monster, and the whole film doesn't descend into laughter-freezing melodrama. Yet the scene where she is beaten up is as terrible in its way as the equivalent moment in that great drama from New Zealand about domestic violence, *Once Were Warriors.*

As in *The Full Monty,* you have the feeling that there is real pain here and real joy. The moment when Ella finally speaks her mind constitutes one of the triumphant moments in cinema. I can imagine people – especially women – cheering her, in cinemas around the world.

The mostly inexperienced actors produce faultless performances, winning big laughs without straining for them, creating a rich tapestry of character with minimal dialogue. This is a huge tribute to director Damien O'Donnell. His work here is better than promising. It's terrific, with a vigour and relaxed invention reminiscent of Alan Parker in *The Commitments.*

Credit, too, should go to producer Leslee Udwin (who's also a fine actress), for spotting the universality of the film's theme. Everyone will respond to the children's problems here, which exist regardless of race, colour or creed. It's one of the few films that advocates freedom for children without downgrading the responsibilities of adulthood.

But the star here is the script, clearly written from the heart by first-timer Ayub Khan Din, and brilliantly adapted from his own play. Can he write another screenplay this good ? It is a hard act to follow, since it has the robust good humour of Bill Forsyth's *Gregory's Girl,* the quirky one-liners of *The Commitments* and the social observation of Mike Leigh's *Secrets and Lies.* But my guess is that we'll be hearing a lot more from him.

Despite the film's Anglo-Pakistani setting, the film is very British. It's firmly in the tradition of other great tragi-comedies about British patriarchs, such as Harold Brighouse's *Hobson's Choice* and Bill Naughton's *Spring and Port Wine.*

It also has that treasurable Ealing-comedy quality of helping to redefine Britishness. It shows a marvellously common-sense approach to race relations, appreciating and embracing the differences between cultures, not pretending that they don't exist.

It understands that racism is not a purely white-against-black phenomenon, but often a product of sincere commitment to a set of values, mingled with fear of the unknown. Like *Beautiful People* earlier this year, it celebrates tolerance as one of the great British virtues, and one from which all cultures can learn.

There is coarse language and behaviour, but all of it is true to the film's setting, and I don't think many will find *East Is East* any more offensive than a Donald McGill postcard. I can't find anything in this movie about which I would be seriously critical.

The only failure surrounds its commissioning. Astonishingly, the BBC (which developed the film) couldn't or wouldn't find the money to shoot it, whereupon the project passed to Channel 4. Who passed on this, yet gave the go-ahead to such horrors as *Bring Me the Head of Mavis Davis*? I trust the people who made that decision will regret it for the rest of their lives.

EASY A *(2010)*

I loved this movie – and its heroine. *Easy A* is easily the most entertaining high school comedy since *Ten Things I Hate About You* (1999), and the first great teen movie of the 21st century. It bears the same relationship to Nathaniel Hawthorne's classic novel about nonconformity, *The Scarlet Letter*, that *Clueless* did to *Emma*, and *Ten Things* did to *The Taming of the Shrew*.

From its ear-catching first line, spoken by a 17 year-old virgin – "The rumours of my promiscuity have been greatly exaggerated" – Bert V. Royal's literate screenplay is the sharpest piece of screenwriting since Diablo Cody's Oscar-winning script for *Juno*; and, in many ways, this is superior, because all its snappy one-liners feel based in character, and don't rely on one performer to generate the laughs.

Easy A introduces one of the most likeable heroines in screen history. Just as Elle Woods in *Legally Blonde* was the breakthrough for Reese Witherspoon, the uniquely adorable role of Olive Penderghast is sure to make a star out of Emma Stone. She impressed as a supporting actress in *Superbad* and *Zombieland*, but looked too like Lindsay Lohan for comfort. Here, she finds her own voice, and is intelligent, sexy and charming. She can sing, too.

Olive is the sort of teenager to whom no one at school pays much attention. This struck me as hard to accept, since she is gorgeous, quick-witted and funny enough to be worthy of worship, but I could certainly believe that boys her own age might be scared of someone this obviously bright, especially when she makes double-edged comments like "Don't worry, I'm not nearly as smart as I think I am".

The catalyst comes when she tells her more worldly best friend (Aly Michalka) a seemingly harmless lie – that she has lost her virginity – which is overheard by the school's most self-righteous Christian (Amanda Bynes), who spreads the story around the school.

Suddenly, Olive acquires a measure of celebrity, which becomes even greater when she pretends that she has had sex with a friend (Dan Byrd) who's being bullied for his homosexuality.

From here on, her reputation as a slut grows until in a spirit of resentful irony Olive starts wearing tarty clothes and the scarlet A (for adultery) that Hester Prynne wears in Hawthorne's novel, which her class is reading in English.

Olive's revolt brings her into conflict with the school principal, played by Malcolm McDowell, in a role that's the polar opposite of the rebel he played in *If...*, (this is only one of many knowing – and amusing – cinematic references). The poor man doesn't regard her as the worst problem he has to face. "This is public school," he sighs, "If I can keep the girls off the pole and the boys off the pipe, I get a bonus."

From there, events spiral entertainingly out of control. Stanley Tucci and Patricia Clarkson give exquisite performances as Olive's loving, liberal and embarrassingly over-frank parents, as even they become concerned at their daughter's behaviour.

"No judgment," says mom, "but you kind of look like a stripper," "A high-end stripper," adds her ever-supportive dad, in an endearingly hopeless attempt to reinforce his daughter's self-confidence. "For governors. Or athletes."

Despite the film's overall generosity of spirit, there's an edge to it that's very uncommon in modern Tinseltown comedies, and is evocative of Hollywood's greatest Austrian import, Billy Wilder. By no means all these characters are lovable or redeemable.

Up-and-coming director Will Gluck's film is far from a simplistic piece of Christian-bashing, but it does make timely fun at the expense of intolerant members of America's religious Right. Amanda Bynes has often played the cutesy role in high school movies, but she's hilariously nasty to Olive. "We need to pray for her," she simpers to her entourage of fellow-Christians, "but we also need her to get the hell out of here".

There are no pat happy endings. Thomas Haden Church, as Olive's sympathetic but also slightly pathetic English teacher, reminds us again of the multi-faceted actor he was in *Sideways*, and Lisa Kudrow is outstanding in a remarkably unsentimental role as his wife, the school's guidance counsellor, who's more of a mess than the students.

This is the best film about the viral nature of gossip and bullying peer pressure in the era of texting and the internet, and its heart is very much in the right place.

The sex element is portrayed in a refreshingly non-voyeuristic way, and the underlying morality (ironically, for a movie which has already incurred the wrath of some on the religious Right) strikes me as thoroughly compatible with modern Christianity. In a way, Olive is herself a martyr and a Jesus figure, exposing how hypocritical society can be towards its chosen pariahs.

The film celebrates family life in a delightfully humorous, unsentimental way – Clarkson and Tucci must be the most charming, understanding and exhilaratingly supportive big-screen parents since the ones in *Juno*.

Funny, feelgood movies that are this intelligent are extremely rare. Do see this, even if you would normally run a mile from an American high school movie. This is the jolliest, and in some ways the wisest, film of the year.

ED WOOD *(1994)*

Citizen Kane showed the downside of the American Dream by taking a success story, peeling away the layers and revealing the man beneath to be a loser. Ed Wood does precisely the opposite, taking the ultimate loser – Edward D. Wood Jr, an eccentric, unemployable transvestite generally acknowledged as the Worst Director of All Time – and revealing him to be a winner, a supreme individualist, an inspiring embodiment of the human spirit.

Underrated by critics and a disaster at the box office, *Ed Wood* did at least win an Oscar for Martin Landau, plus another for the wonderful make-up by Rick Baker, Ve Neill and Yolanda Toussieng.

Some of the great movies of all time were flops on first release – *The Wizard of Oz, It's A Wonderful Life*, even *Citizen Kane*. To that illustrious number we can now add *Ed Wood*. Hollywood's most visually talented director, Tim Burton reunited himself with actor Johnny Depp for the first time since *Edward Scissorhands*, and the result is a masterpiece.

It would have been the easiest thing in the world to poke fun at director Edward D. Wood. After all, if you sit through any of his most notorious films of the Fifties – *Glen or Glenda, Bride of the Monster* or *Plan 9 From Outer Space* – it is impossible to imagine how he got funding for them, persuaded actors to speak his dialogue, or directed with such breathtaking ineptitude. Burton's film succeeds in showing not only how he managed it – but why.

There is a fictitious but magical scene towards the end when Wood meets his hero and fellow auteur Orson Welles, magnificently impersonated by Vincent d'Onofrio. Wood, clad in his favourite ensemble of angora sweater, skirt and blonde wig, commiserates presumptuously with Welles on being unable to finish his movie of *Don Quixote*. The point is well made. Welles and Wood are reverse sides of the same artistic personality, both daring to tilt at windmills, though with very different levels of talent.

If *Ed Wood* is a touching film about artistic self-expression, it is also a celebration of go-getting entrepreneurialism. Wood's films were so appalling that he must have been a better salesman than Welles ever was. The scenes where Wood wheedles money out of the unlikeliest sources are worthy of Arthur Daley in the heyday of *Minder*.

This is also a moving study of friendship. Wood was a bad film-maker, but a good friend – not least to the bitter, burned-out star of Dracula, Bela Lugosi (Martin Landau). Landau thoroughly deserved his Academy Award for both an uncanny impersonation and a towering, tragic portrayal of human disintegration.

But it is Depp who carries the picture, at the head of a flawless supporting cast which includes Bill Murray as Wood's greatest fan and Patricia Arquette as the woman Wood woos and weds. Depp has played weird misfits before, but never so brilliantly. Unrecognisable from the handsome romantic lead of *Don Juan de Marco*, he is frantic, funny and sincere. He makes the warm, well-meaning, woolly-minded Wood seem a genuine hero in a world which has lost its values and settled for a dull, mercenary conformity.

The lesson may well be lost on our own, censorious and selfish times. Some – and perhaps a majority of film-goers – will find themselves on the outside looking in, like Wood's increasingly unimpressed fiancée, Dolores Fuller (Sarah Jessica Parker). "I see the usual gang of misfits and dope addicts are here," she remarks witheringly, of Ed's friends.

The rest of us will come to care about Wood's odd entourage of deadbeats and dead wood (it comes as no great surprise to learn that his cinematographer is colour-blind). It is impossible not to admire his determination to live on his own terms, however cockeyed they may be.

Scott Alexander and Larry Karaszewski's screenplay is touching, funny and economical, so much so that I wished they could have presented even more examples of Wood's peerless incompetence – his ill-judged adventures into visual surrealism, his wildly inappropriate use of language ("He's as gentle as a kitchen," says Lugosi of his huge sidekick in *Bride of the Monster*), his imperishably awful dialogue (Man in *Plan Nine From Outer Space*: "I saw a flying saucer." Woman: "Saucer? You mean the kind from up there?" Man: "Yeah. Or its counterpart."). But there are still enough examples to leave any audience weeping with laughter.

Howard Shore's witty score, Tom Duffield's tongue-in-cheek design and Stefan Czapsky's lustrous black-and-white cinematography all enhance a movie which is very much in the tradition of Tim Burton's other movies about outsiders, from *Pee Wee's Big Adventure* through *Batman* to *The Nightmare Before Christmas*.

This is easily his best picture, and perhaps his most personal one. Wood's friendship with Lugosi reflects Burton's own relationship with veteran horror actors Vincent Price and Christopher Lee. But it also has a universality.

There is no picture which captures better the importance of art, friendship, resilience, optimism, respect for others and for history. Try to see it. *Ed Wood* is a triumph, a twentieth century *Don Quixote*.

EDEN LAKE *(2008)*

At last! Here's a really first-rate British horror film, that taps into our deepest fears and offers a thought-provoking insight into such topical subjects as knife crime and gang culture.

Though nightmarish and visceral, it's easily the most intelligent horror film to have been made by a British director since Jack Clayton's *The Innocents*, way back in 1960. And it fulfils the two basic purposes of horror films: it involves you emotionally, and it's frightening.

One of our finest young actresses, Kelly Reilly, plays Jenny, a primary school teacher first seen playing peek-a-boo with her small, charmingly innocent pupils. She's as pretty, defiantly English and as child-friendly as Julie Andrews in *The Sound of Music*. She goes off camping for the weekend with boyfriend Steve (Michael Fassbender), little knowing that he is about to propose marriage and get seriously in tents.

Ominous portents abound: a woman slaps her child in a supermarket, rude cyclists casually ride through a red light, causing Steve's Jeep to brake, and an advertising hoarding announces that Steve's favourite lake is to be redeveloped into a "gated community".

"Who are they so afraid of?" asks Jenny, with the blitheness of someone probably recruited for her job through the pages of the Guardian. She's about to find out, and a strong hint is afforded by the obscene, unpunctuated graffiti on the back of the billboard.

Jenny and Steve laugh as they leave the road and receive an menacing message from the bossy girl's voice on their sat nav: "At your first opportunity, turn around."

They swim, sunbathe and enjoy the peace of the lake, which is really a man-made quarry. But their idyll is spoiled by teenagers aged between 12 and 16. They are playing their music loud and failing to control their Rottweiler. Jenny wants to move on. "Boys will be boys" she says, not noticing that one of the gang is a girl.

Steve is all for approaching the group and believes they'll see reason. When Jenny says "No, Steve, it's not worth it", he replies "If everyone said that, where would we be?"

It's a thoroughly credible set-up, and the process of escalation whereby Jenny and Steve alienate, then anger these feral youths until they're ready to stab, torture and even burn them to death is worryingly authentic too.

Unlike most horror films, in which the heroes steer themselves into danger by their own stupidity, *Eden Lake* has Jenny and Steve behave with complete plausibility and a tragically unrequited sense of kindness and social responsibility.

Be warned that events turn extremely gruesome. Some of it even I, desensitised as I have been by many hours of watching big-screen violence, found hard to watch. But for once the violence has a point, and it's treated responsibly.

Never has knife crime been less glamorised. We watch someone bleeding to death from stab wounds, and it's a shocking sight. And there's darkly comic horror to be experienced as we watch the ringleader's girlfriend impassively recording acts of extreme violence on her cellphone.

We even see the horrifying effects on Jenny, as she's transformed from a nice young teacher into... well, I'll leave you to find out. Unlike the torture porn it superficially resembles, it makes sure our sympathies are always with the victims.

The film delivers plenty of tension and vicarious excitement. But it's also willing to say what other films have been too scared or politically correct to mention: that the true horrors we fear from day to day are not supernatural bogeymen, or monsters created by scientists. They're our own youth.

Eden Lake will doubtless be accused of class hatred, and demonising chavs, especially by those who accuse newspapers of "whipping up" public concern over innocent victims of street-gangs.

The obvious point never seems to occur to these people, that we are right to feel concerned about, say, the stabbing of headmaster Philip Lawrence outside his own school gates in 1995, or the way the murderers of Stephen Lawrence are still walking free. We wouldn't be fully human if we weren't.

And it's made abundantly clear within the film that the guilty youths are often the offspring of parents who have jobs and might reasonably be called middle class, but who have lost their moral compass and any feelings of responsibility towards their kids.

Far from demonising the gang-members, there's an underlying compassion towards them, along with a sad realism about mankind's potential for barbarism. It's the same feeling that made a classic of William Golding's *Lord of the Flies*.

The film is remarkably strong on the dynamics of the gang, with its psychotic leader (played by Jack O'Connell as a variation on Malcolm McDowell in *A Clockwork Orange*) bullying, manipulating and incriminating his less daring colleagues until they become as vicious as he is. You can see from his attachment to his dog Bonnie that hers is the only love he has in his life – and wait until you meet his parents.

Uncaring or absentee parents are the true villains of the picture, mostly unseen until a truly unpleasant end, but an implied presence throughout.

There's a world of pathos in the reply of a young boy whom Jenny meets in the woods and asks "Where's your mother?" (obviously considering it's safest to assume he has no father), whereupon he answers sadly "She's working".

Time will tell whether first-time writer-director James Watkins is a major new talent or just a flash in the pan. Either way, he has made a terrific directorial debut. Even though the picture was shot in only six weeks on an obviously limited budget, I was much taken with cinematographer Chris Ross's use of backlighting at the start, when our couple seems to be embarking on an idyllic holiday, and his shift to harsher, less flattering light and hand-held camerawork as things go wrong.

Eden Lake may sound like yet another story about nice people straying into hostile territory – like *Straw Dogs, Deliverance* or the recent *Timber Falls* – but it has five virtues you don't often see in horror films: believability, leading characters you care about, a responsible attitude towards violence, a willingness to get inside the heads of the "bad guys", and a recognition that aggression may brutalise even the victim.

A sixth virtue is that it doesn't fight shy of a truly frightening final twist, which makes *Eden Lake* not only bleaker but also more truthful than virtually every other movie in this genre, which all too often is over-populated and under-humanised.

AN EDUCATION *(2009)*

Here's a hit movie that's small in scale, but big in heart. It has a female protagonist who's flawed, pretentious and frequently misguided, but grows into a character as memorable as Holly Golightly in *Breakfast at Tiffany's*.

Best of all, it introduces a sensational British actress who combines the gamine innocence of Audrey Hepburn with the warmth, intelligence and mischief of the young Judi Dench. The chances are that you haven't heard of Carey Mulligan, even though she had a small role in the Keira Knightley *Pride and Prejudice*, and a bigger one in the BBC's serialisation of *Bleak House*, but she's going to be gracing the big screen for decades to come. The camera loves her, and her face has a miraculous transparency of emotion. A star is born – and, more importantly, a wonderful actress.

Based on a memoir by journalist Lynn Barber, this is the potentially sleazy but ultimately uplifting story of a 16 year-old schoolgirl who – bored with her staid, suburban parents' ambitions for her to study hard and get into Oxford – allows herself to be seduced by a man more than double her age.

As played by Peter Sarsgaard, David is a sophisticated smoothie with just a hint of Jewish exoticism, who offers an alluring world of classical concerts, art auctions and cabarets. He's glib enough to persuade her domineering but socially insecure father (Alfred Molina) and easily flattered mother (Cara Seymour) that he wants the best for their daughter. He offers to introduce her to his old tutor, C.S. Lewis, who might be able to help her get into Oxford.

Even early on, we suspect that David is too good to be true. But he's good-looking, generous and offers Jenny more fun and excitement than her hesitant teenage boyfriend Graham (Matthew Beard, the promising young actor from *And When Did You Last See Your Father?*). David and his chums (Dominic Cooper, amusingly shifty, and Rosamund Pike, hilariously vacuous, like a less fearsomely intellectual Holly Willoughby) show her an entertaining mixture of high life and low pleasures, such as a visit to the dog track and an introduction to property racketeer Peter Rachman.

Though Carey Mulligan is bound to attract most of the critical plaudits, Sarsgaard is terrific in the role of tempter. His smile is engaging but reserved. His eyes are friendly but watchful. His easy self-assurance is just a little bit too manufactured, but what is it concealing: shyness? weakness? a guilty secret? Still, he knows how to give a girl a good time – drive her around in his maroon sports car, buy her presents, take her to Oxford and Paris… Who could resist?

Certainly not Jenny, who disappoints her English teacher (Olivia Williams, delightfully prim and buttoned up) and enrages her headmistress (Emma Thompson, who makes a splendidly blue-stocking, anti-semitic gorgon). David seems like a short-cut to a life that previously Jenny had thought she could only achieve through higher education and a successful career.

Nick Hornby's screenplay contains a handful of speech anachronisms and a couple of moments when the dialogue teeters on the edge of soap opera and caricature, but is a likely Oscar nominee for its quiet wit, and the way it offers every member of a superb cast their moment.

Sally Hawkins, so delightful in Mike Leigh's *Happy Go Lucky*, has a late, moving cameo that confirms her as an actress of rare versatility; and Rosamund Pike shows talents as a comic actress that have never been obvious before. It's a tribute to the writing that virtually every subsidiary character has so much vibrancy and texture that it's easy to imagine an entire film being constructed around each of their lives.

Hornby's books have all had humour and humanity, and he fleshes out Lynn Barber's short memoir with a real feeling for Sixties glamour, adolescent longings and adult insecurities. From *High Fidelity* onwards, he's always been skilled at noting how people let their cultural tastes define them, both as they are and as they would like to be. Jenny sees herself as a French, bohemian sophisticate in the Juliette Greco mould, which makes her all the more delightful as she fails to be as worldly as she thinks she is.

The title *An Education* is deliberately ambiguous, referring both to academic training and the process by which life leads us towards maturity.

Although Carey Mulligan was 22 when she played the role, she doesn't condescend to her 16 year-old. It's easy to empathise as she makes choices that don't exactly go the way she planned. Female director Lone Scherfig (who made the promising *Italian for Beginners*) handles the sexual side of the relationship with delicacy, never allowing it to become exploitative.

The story could easily have been treated more sensationalistically, over-seriously or melodramatically, but even as comedy it remains a moral, cautionary tale. Hornby has softened Barber's memoir to make us see David through

Jenny's eyes and understand how she made some foolish choices. But he remains true to its bitter-sweet essence.

It depicts life as a cruel kind of farce, in which everyone makes mistakes but most people somehow pick themselves up and make the best of a bad job. Its stiff-upper-lip bravery, and refusal to wallow in self-pity or see its leading character as a victim, is peculiarly British – and refreshingly rare in modern cinema.

Some will dismiss this as a film about not very much. The only thing at stake is a silly, middle-class girl's place at university, so why should we care? The extraordinary thing is that we do. And though the film may appear small and slight, it takes on a deeper resonance because of its impeccably observed sense of period.

Jenny is not just a silly girl. She represents Britain emerging from the austerity of the post-war era and experiencing the dangerous allure of entrepreneurial capitalism and the Swinging Sixties. Her story is the story of a generation.

EDWARD SCISSORHANDS *(1990)*

An old inventor (Vincent Price) dies as he is about to fit hands to his finest creation: a real, live boy called Edward (Johnny Depp). A kindly Avon Lady (Dianne Wiest) takes Edward down to her neighbourhood, where he wins popularity through his talent for topiary, hair-cutting and dog-grooming. The tone darkens as he allows himself to become exploited by Mrs Bogg's teenage daughter Kim (Winona Ryder) and her yobbish boy-friend (Anthony Michael Hall). Edward's nonconformity becomes a threat, and his scissors are no longer creative tools, but weapons.

This is several dozen cuts above the Hollywood average: the story is a weird but wonderful mix of American suburban comedy and Gothic romance – a bit like *Happy Days*, re-written by Roald Dahl. There are delightful performances from Johnny Depp and Dianne Weist. Anyone who enjoys character acting will enjoy Alan Arkin as the well-meaning, blue-collar Mr Boggs, and Kathy Baker as the neighbourhod man-eater in man-made fibres. There's a deliberate lack of depth to these characters: they have the kind of simplicity you find in fairy tales. Yet they're convincing: Winona Ryder's teenager is oddly lovable in her adolescent weakness, and touching when she realizes the extent of her awfulness. The scene where she dances in the snow is one of the most magical moments in cinema.

The film is plainly an allegory; and like all the richest allegories, you will find your own meaning. On one level, it's about handicap: Edward is both handicapped and "special", like an autistic child with miraculous drawing ability. Edward also represents the artist, tolerated and celebrated by "normal" people – but only as long as he is not unduly threatening. Others may spot the affinity that Edward has with Christ – there are hints at the end that he has the power to control the weather and that he's immortal. All in all, it's a highly original, modern fairy-tale about the eternal gulf between conformism and creativity.

Pedants should give the film a wide berth. Its tone is deliberately unrealistic in the juxtaposition of suburban normality next to Gothic horror, and in the conscious use of anachronism (colour television, aerobics and videotape are all around, even though the setting seems to be the late 50s). Cinéastes, however, should enjoy the film's wealth of cinematic allusions (which range from *The 5000 Fingers of Dr T* to *Nightmare On Elm Street*, the slasher movie in which Johnny Depp had his first role). And lovers of legend will have a fine time spotting influences which range from *Beauty and the Beast* to *Struwwelpeter*.

There was evidence of director Tim Burton's visual flair in his three previous films, *Pee Wee's Big Adventure*, *Beetlejuice* and *Batman*. Here, he had reason to thank his co-screenwriter, Caroline Thompson (who wrote a deceptively simple script which would be enjoyable without subtitles in any country), and a superb design team. *Edward Scissorhands* attracted mixed reviews and didn't set the box office on fire, but posterity may recognize it for what it was: a fantastic achievement.

ELECTION
(1999)

An obnoxiously ambitious girl (Reese Witherspoon) strives to be elected High School President. One of her teachers (Matthew Broderick) resents her ability to trample over anyone who stands in her way, and persuades a popular but inarticulate sports jock (Chris Klein) to stand against her. Whereupon a third candidate emerges, in the form of the nice lad's 14 year-old, adopted sister (Jessica Campbell). She is a spiky lesbian jealous of her brother's latest girl-friend, but she makes the most rousing speech of the campaign, inviting her schoolfellows to vote for her because she is the only candidate who can see that the election is a pointless charade.

Tom Perotta's novel, on which this is based, is an allegory. The lesbian nihilist is Ross Perot. The nice guy probably destined to finish last is George Bush. The unscrupulous, ideology-free student who must be stopped at all cost is a composite of Bill and Hillary Clinton. The film stands up very well as satire, and is a lot more perceptive about politics than either *Wag The Dog* or *Primary Colors*.

Where the film scores is in its ruthless analysis of the kind of person who stands for office. One of the chief arguments against big government is: look at the people it attracts. Power not only corrupts; it attracts those who are already corrupted.

The film's most controversial aspect is the way it probes into the relationships between the sexes. The men on display are flawed, easy-going and resigned to shouldering any blame that's going. But they also know about duty, personal responsibility, teamwork and a lot of things that don't seem fashionable right now, least of all among women.

Is the movie misogynistic? I don't think so, for writer/director Alexander Payne takes the trouble to create sympathetic female characters alongside the harridans.

The film won't be a big hit, because it deals in irony and satire rather than smart one-liners, and Matthew Broderick and Reese Witherspoon are not big stars. However, both offer flawless, richly humorous performances, supported by a perfect cast, many of them real teachers and high-school students.

Another artistic strength which may be a weakness at the box office is that the screenplay sees events from everyone's point of view. It deliberately makes its discussion of morality and ethics far more sophisticated than the usual Hollywood good guy/ bad guy dichotomy.

The most sympathetic figure is the teacher played by Broderick; yet he cheats on his wife, watches porno, attempts to pervert the course of democracy and ends up a pitiful study in masculine alienation.

Anyone interested in the malaise of late twentieth century politics, the cult of the personality or the current balance of power between the sexes will find much food for thought here.

Reese Witherspoon's character is a splendidly awful creation, as monstrous yet immediately recognisable as Nicole Kidman's homicidal weathergirl in *To Die For*. This is far more than just another teen comedy – it's a great little movie.

ENCHANTED *(2007)*

Enchanted is fantastic fun for all the family. Though it may seem at first to be designed for little girls, it's really aimed at anyone with a sense of humour and a willingness to be entertained. This touching romantic comedy is also the most tuneful musical since *Beauty and the Beast*, and the most inventive combination of animation and live action ever (yes – even better than *Mary Poppins* and *Who Framed Roger Rabbit?*). It deserves to make a household name of its leading actress, the gorgeous, witty and sublimely talented Amy Adams.

The film starts out as a deliciously camp, over-the-top parody of Disney cartoon at its most sickeningly sweet, though children may take it at face value.

Giselle (voiced by Adams) is a fairytale princess who sings to woodland creatures with the sweet soprano soppiness of Disney's Snow White. She is about to marry the ridiculously handsome but extremely thick Prince Edward (James Marsden), only a day after literally falling into his arms, when his stepmother, a wicked Queen (a splendidly vicious Susan Sarandon), pushes her down a magic well and into a terrible land where there is no such thing as "Happily ever after". That's present-day New York City.

Within minutes, the live-action princess (now played by

Amy Adams in the flesh) has been robbed of her tiara by an elderly vagrant. "You are not a very nice old man!" she scolds him. She is rescued by a six year-old girl (Rachel Covey) who believes she is a real princess. The child's lawyer father Robert (Patrick Dempsey), considers more realistically that Giselle is probably a mental case. She offers to move in with any local dwarves she can find ("I hear they're very hospitable!") but none seems to be available.

Hardly has she woken up the next morning and impulsively turned Robert's curtains into a new dress (the first of several affectionate nods to Julie Andrews in *The Sound of Music*) than she is clearing up his bachelor-style mess with the help of the local Manhattan fauna – not the usual Disney bunnies, deer and lovebirds but a grisly collection of rats, pigeons and cockroaches performing Busby Berkeley routines – to *The Happy Working Song*, an inspired mix of lilting melody and witty lyrics that actually made me weep with laughter.

Against his will, Robert – a jaded realist about love, who is contemplating getting engaged to his girlfriend of five years – becomes weirdly enchanted by Giselle's innocence, ultra-femininity and all-round adorability. She has pretty much the same effect on everyone in Central Park, whom she incorporates into the biggest and best production number since *Oliver!*, entitled *That's How You Know*.

More and more fairytale characters cascade into New York, either to save or murder the princess: the impulsive Prince Edward, who finds Manhattan more than a little confusing and needs time to work out how to use a revolving door; a helpful animated chipmunk appalled to find himself in a world where chipmunks can't talk; the Queen's obedient sidekick Nathaniel (played by the great Timothy Spall); and finally the wicked Queen herself.

I won't tell you more, except that the story takes many delightfully unexpected directions, and artfully incorporates computer-generated effects into its storyline – not to mention a glass slipper, poisoned apples, a fancy dress ball and a dragon. It's never less than marvellously magical.

It doesn't end up as a savage satire on the tweeness of Disney – a wise decision, but one that is bound to disappoint some critics. Instead, it's a heartfelt celebration of innocence, kindness and the kind of love that lives happily ever after, as long as you work at it.

The brilliance of *Enchanted* is that it's a generous homage to the traditional Disney virtues, but with a new, knowing twist. It's bound to be compared with *Shrek*, but it has more charm and sincerity, a praiseworthy determination to be wholesome and family-friendly, and much catchier songs.

If I were to nitpick, it could have done with one or two more production numbers and a few better jokes for Timothy Spall, but *Enchanted* achieves a joyous near-perfection. It's the kind of movie, like *It's A Wonderful Life*, that audiences instinctively applaud at the end, then find themselves wanting to see again and again.

The music is by one of the few melodic geniuses working in musicals today, Alan Mencken, and every number from the hilariously cheesy opening love duet *True Love's Kiss* onwards is a knockout, in the finest tradition of his work on *The Little Mermaid* and *Beauty and the Beast*.

The clever lyrics are by Stephen Schwartz, who also worked with Ashman on the excellent score for *The Hunchback of Notre Dame*. The director is Kevin Lima, who made the superior cartoon version of *Tarzan*. The inspired script is by Bill Kelly, who penned that underrated charmer starring Brendan Fraser, *Blast From The Past*, another comedy about an innocent fish-out-of-water trying to survive and find love in a big, cynical city.

Even the costume designs are funny and romantic enough to warrant the price of admission. They're by Mona May, whose previous credits include the similarly witty *Clueless* and *The Wedding Singer*.

But the star of the show is Amy Adams. I first noticed her talent as the touchingly shy young wife of the con-man anti-hero (Leonardo DiCaprio) in Spielberg's *Catch Me If You Can*. She was funny as the heroine's self-absorbed sister in *The Wedding Date*, and brilliant as the naïve, not-very-bright sister-in-law in *Junebug*, for which she rightly won an Oscar nomination. She even managed to shine in a minor comic role in the blokish Will Ferrell vehicle, *Talladega Nights: The Ballad of Ricky Bobby*. But *Enchanted* is the movie which will catapult her to the top of every Hollywood casting director's A-list.

It's easy to see that Princess Giselle could have been camped up and made thoroughly annoying, if played by the wrong actress. Adams is emphatically the right one, taking her as seriously as if she had been created by Chekhov, but never forgetting to make her adorable and fun. Not since Julie Andrews burst upon the Hollywood scene with *Mary Poppins* and *The Sound of Music* has a musical comedy marvel of this magnitude appeared.

THE ENGLISH PATIENT *(1996)*

In the Second World War, a French-Canadian Nurse (Juliette Binoche) finds that everyone she loves gets killed. Emotionally numbed by the end of the war, she stays in a ruined Tuscan monastery to tend a hideously scarred man (Ralph Fiennes), the nameless survivor of a plane shot down in the Sahara. Unable to heal him physically, she lessens his pain through morphine, tends to his emotional wounds and heals her own with the help of a Sikh lieutenant (Naveen Andrews) who's disposing of bombs in the area.

The second, central story unfolds as the dying man unburdens himself of his history, encouraged by the nurse's tenderness and spurred on by the hostility of a Canadian thief-turned-spy (Willem Dafoe) who turns up at the monastery, recognises him and blames him for the loss of his thumbs. The so-called English Patient turns out to be neither English, nor patient. He is – or was – an impetuous, Hungarian Count, a mapmaker before the war for Britain's National Geographical Society, tempted into adultery by passion for the wife (Kristin Scott Thomas) of an English colleague (Colin Firth). His act of personal treachery has far-reaching, fatal consequences.

Here is the highest of high romance, an epic love story which swept the Oscars and created two new superstars.

Kristin Scott Thomas has never been more gorgeous – which, as her admirers will know, is saying something. In this film she casts the kind of spell which transported her into the first rank of screen goddesses, up there alongside Garbo and Ingrid Bergman.

Ralph Fiennes left no one in any doubt as to his acting ability in the role which should have won him an Oscar, the German Commandant in *Schindler's List*. This film, in which he is ridiculously handsome, established him as the world's number one matinee idol.

Though he couldn't hope to compete with their cheek-bones, a third Briton was always a more probable Oscar-winner than either of his stars. Writer-director Anthony Minghella did an astoundingly skilful job of organising Michael Ondaatje's complex, Booker Prize-winning novel into two, parallel stories. Somewhat perversely, the Academy rewarded his direction but not his writing.

This is a sublime piece of film-making, from start to finish. The opening sequence is among the most playfully cinematic ever committed to celluloid. The first shot resembles a vast, flat desert, until a paintbrush enters frame to reveal that it is in fact an intimate close-up of paper.

The second shot seems to be a sensuous study of the curves and hollows of a woman's body, but turns out to be an aerial shot of a desert's undulating hills and valleys.

The third presents a scene from some idyllic, costume drama – a pilot steering a biplane, with a beautiful woman asleep in the passenger seat – but then their plane is shot at by artillery, and the woman remains asleep (or dead?).

Within seconds, and without a word of dialogue, the film has set up an intriguing mystery, a sense of danger and the central conflicts of the film: between the intimate and the epic, between human sensuality and the wider world, between love and war.

The film is not quite perfect. The love story told in flashback is so powerful and sensuous that every return to the monastery is a minor irritation, even though relieved by superb cinematography and the luminous beauty of Juliette Binoche (who won an Oscar as Best Supporting Actress).

The racial taboos which would have affected any affair between a white nurse and a Sikh are scarcely acknowledged; the relationship between the Indian lieutenant and his trusty British subordinate (Kevin Whately) is underwritten; and the extent to which most of the characters are grappling with the aftermath of British colonialism is less clear than in the novel.

It's hard to understand why the hero has the real name of Count Almasy, since he is so heavily fictionalised. The real count appears to have been a homosexual Nazi spy, who lived on until 1951.

The film also lacks a certain nobility which one tends to find in the best loved films. There's none of the soul-searching about adultery which made the lovers so sympathetic in *Brief Encounter*, and there isn't the moral perspective of *Casablanca*, where personal feelings are renounced for the greater good.

The hero's biggest moral choice – between personal loyalty and public treachery – is glossed over in a curiously cursory manner. It's a strange war film which evades wider questions of right and wrong, of why a war is being fought in the first place – although I suppose one might raise the same objection to *Gone With The Wind*.

The production values are first-rate, if unrealistically glossy (these map-makers evidently carry round their own hair stylists and dry-cleaners). The success of the film lies in the intensity of its lyricism, its ability to reveal character through action and landscape, and the extraordinary charisma of its three leading actors. Some simplification of Michael Ondaatje's long, literary novel was inevitable, and Minghella chose intelligently to dwell on the central love story, which is as moving as it is romantic.

It is not often I say this, but I would like it to have been longer, and would love to see a director's cut which would tell us more about the subsidiary characters. Still, few who see it will fail to recognise that this is film-making of the very highest quality.

FARGO *(1996)*

A financially embarrassed car salesman Jerry Lundegaard (William H. Macy) arrives an hour late for an appointment – not with a potential customer, but with two sleazy hoodlums-for-hire (Steve Buscemi and Peter Stormare). Jerry commissions them to kidnap his wife (Kristin Rudrud). His plan is to get a million dollars ransom money from his rich, ruthless father-in-law (Harve Presnell), give the gangsters $40,000 and keep the other $960,000 for himself.

The trouble is that Jerry is a poor liar, much too easily dominated, and so incompetent that, when the kidnapping is no longer a financial necessity, he can't call off the crooks because he doesn't know their phone number. One of the gangsters he's hired (Buscemi) is panicky. The other (Stormare) is a psychopath. Virtually everything that might go wrong duly does; and a crime which starts out as mean and pathetic becomes brutal and bloody, as potent a warning not to get mixed up in criminality as any Home Secretary might wish.

Fargo is a cool, black comedy set in the very white wastes of northern Minnesota. It's about a crime gone so hideously wrong that it might have sprung from the brain of Quentin Tarantino. The message is a variation on the old homily which used to be instilled in children by their parents – that small lies have a nasty habit of having to be disguised by bigger ones, until you become enmeshed in a web of your own duplicity. William H. Macy gives a sensational performance, funny but also sad, as a weak but not intrinsically evil man entangled in just such a waking nightmare.

Equally impressive, in the role of crime-fighter, is Frances McDormand, who probably won the part through being married to director Joel Coen, but also happens to be one of America's finest screen actresses. Here she plays a decent, hard-working cop who – despite being heavily pregnant, eating for two and stopping off to buy worms for fisherman-artist husband Norm – solves the case through old-fashioned detection and persistence.

Not even Columbo treated witnesses with this much respect. You get the sense of a woman whose perspective on criminal behaviour is limited and uncomprehending, yet she is so fundamentally decent and grounded in common sense that she's immediately sympathetic. The performance is a delight, and so is the character.

Another pleasure is the Coen brothers' detailed observation of their own roots in Minnesota, which has the same quirky affection as Bill Forsyth's early films about Scotland. It's the kind of place, full of first-generation Americans, where English is spoken with the lilting accents of the Muppets' Swedish chef. The first impulse is to laugh at these people's banality. Then you warm to their normality, their competence, their innate kindliness.

The Coens' films tend to be underplotted and anti-climactic. This time, real events from 1987 have presented them with an extraordinary yarn, full of narrative twists to the end. Even more surprising is the fact that this moral tale comes from filmmakers as cool as the Coen Brothers, who previously brought us such hip, affectionate homages to criminality as *Miller's Crossing, Blood Simple* and *Raising Arizona*.

The bad language and gruesomeness are justified within the context, and this is the Coens' most generous-spirited film.

FIELD OF DREAMS *(1989)*

A 36 year-old farmer in Iowa (Kevin Costner) appears a contented family man but has nagging regrets. He never got on with his dead father; he has not achieved his ambitions; and 60s idealism has given way to narrower concerns. Suddenly, he hears a mysterious voice, telling him to plough up a cornfield and turn it into a baseball park. Sceptical at first, he becomes obsessed with following his dream – or delusion.

Ignore anyone who tells you that *Field of Dreams* is about baseball: it is no more about baseball than *Harvey* was about rabbits. Baseball is a metaphor for personal achievement, reconciliation, and a less mean-spirited society. The story is about exorcising the ghosts, or regrets, from one's past.

Most of the major studios turned down the screenplay; and it certainly strays close to being fey, whimsical and pseudo-religious. Perhaps the film's greatest achievement is that the acting – and not just Costner's – is so realistic that the audience becomes as caught up as the characters in solving the mystery.

If Gabriel Garcia Marques had written *Field of Dreams*, intellectuals might have hailed it as magic realism. Just because it is a Hollywood project which moves at a decent pace, is humorous and entertaining, and made many million dollars at the box office does not make it any less successful as a modern ghost story. This is an offbeat, lyrical, moving film, pretty much in the same class as Frank Capra's *It's A Wonderful Life*.

FIGHT CLUB *(1999)*

This violent but intelligent movie falls into three sections, with an ever-darkening tone. The first act is a lively social comedy, in which the narrator (Edward Norton) becomes ill-at-ease with his existence as a corporate employee. He has misgivings about the work he is doing: helping a big car company get away with making vehicles that don't comply with safety standards. He is increasingly unable to sleep and can't feel any emotion other than generalised discontent. Most of all, he feels emasculated.

His doctor, though, can't find anything wrong with him ("you can't die from insomnia") and unsympathetically recommends that, if he wants to know what real male suffering is about, he attend a local men's support-group for sufferers from testicular cancer. So he does. At first, he is a callous observer of such support groups, but he gets a taste for them and becomes a fascinated tourist through their weirder excesses. This culminates in a showdown between himself and a fellow-tourist, a bored girl in black (Helena Bonham Carter) with a bad attitude. Rather than keep ruining each other's fun, they share out the best-value support groups between them.

The second, less comedic section begins when the narrator encounters a stranger called Tyler Durden (Brad

Pitt). Tyler seems to possess an uncanny insight into his brain. The narrator's bachelor pad explodes in a gas explosion that looks at first like an accident, so he moves in with Tyler and falls under his influence.

Tyler introduces him to the dubious pleasures of getting beaten up and feeling pain. Gradually their bare-knuckle fights become underground institutions, as men line up to get in touch with their brutal sides, as opposed to the lovey-dovey stuff they are allowed to express in conventional support groups.

The tone darkens as Bonham Carter's character moves in and annoys the narrator by having noisy sex with Tyler. Tyler takes the credit for inventing fight clubs and uses his motivational skills to organise his ever-increasing band of followers into eco-warriors, using their ill-defined grievances to support a fascist-style terrorist movement from which the narrator finds himself increasingly alienated.

The third section begins with a twist that I really didn't expect – even more audacious and disturbing than the one in *The Usual Suspects* – and turns into a psychological thriller, as the narrator does battle with Tyler's evil empire and engineers a final cathartic show-down.

Fight Club arrived with a worse reputation for on-screen violence than the Arsenal midfield. It has been savaged by some American reviewers as brutalising, infantile and fascistic. One of Britain's most respected critics, Alexander Walker, has denounced it as "not only anti-capitalism but anti-society, and, indeed, anti-God." Even the normally pusillanimous British censors have made cuts, complaining of the film's sadism.

Well, it certainly proves the adage that no two people have the same experience while watching a film. For *Fight*

Club strikes me as witty, grown-up and extremely unlikely to brutalise anyone. It has an original, funny, literate screenplay, contains three of the year's best performances, and is the most brilliantly directed picture since *Saving Private Ryan*. And, like Spielberg's film, it skilfully uses the shock of extreme violence to make points that are profound and revelatory about the human condition.

If director David Fincher gave you any time to think about the plot, it might strike you as wildly implausible. No one who behaved like the narrator would last long in a corporation. The violence undergone by the central characters is so excessive (and, for once, the horrible effects on them are clearly visible) that only a fool would wish to suffer it in real life, so it's hard to imagine fight clubs really springing up. And the characters lack parents, children and friends to a preposterous extent.

But *Fight Club* is about as naturalistic as a painting by Hieronymus Bosch. That's because it is a vision of Hell, and a dystopic satire on modern society. Like *The Full Monty*, it shows a deliberately exaggerated world where men feel they no longer fit in, where their old aggressive instincts, once valued, are now condemned as anti-social.

It's also a perceptive analysis of cults and Fascism. Both, the film argues, arise from the psychological need some people have for authoritarian leaders, the comfort which the weak can derive from unthinking conformism. Brad Pitt is wonderfully charismatic as Tyler, a daredevil with no self-doubt, the sort of person who rises to the top everywhere. There's a distinct hint of Tony Blair about the eyes.

Though the film has been likened to *A Clockwork Orange*, it is far from sympathetic to the kind of gang mentality and violence which Stanley Kubrick unintentionally glorified.

Tyler's followers are anything but an advertisement for fascism. On the contrary, they're humorously portrayed as utter dolts, absurdly gullible and without an original thought in their heads.

Accusations of the film being fascist are wildly off-beam. Norton's and Bonham Carter's characters eventually find a moral perspective on Tyler which the audience is meant to share and, audibly, does. Although *Fight Club* captures the allure of fascism to an extent that many may find alarming, it must be the most anti-fascist film of the year.

The violence in the film is graphic, and the reason why some people will find it hard to watch. However, the emphasis is on the pleasures of being hurt, not – as in so many of Michael Winner's films – on the joys of hurting and killing others.

Fight Club digs deeper than any other film I have seen into the causes of violence, about why people go on killing sprees in Bosnia or pupils turn guns upon their schoolmates in America. Violent, anti-social role-models in screen entertainment and inadequate gun control undoubtedly play a part in encouraging such horrors, but the roots go much deeper, into the emptiness of materialism, the breakdown of family ties and the way human (especially male) drives can become perverted if society provides no useful outlet for them.

There is always something verging on hypocrisy in films that claim to be anti-materialistic while allowing product placement and accepting finance from big corporations such as Twentieth Century Fox, but *Fight Club* carries apocalyptic warnings that we ignore at our peril.

Even those who don't understand the film's social message will emerge disturbed by its power to suck us into the nightmarish world of a deranged personality. It's a powerful experience, even more thrilling and visceral than previous tours of disturbed minds in Hitchcock's *Psycho* and David Lynch's *Blue Velvet*.

Like *Blade Runner*, another film that was misunderstood on release, *Fight Club* depicts the world as seen by a single character, the narrator. It is, therefore, shot like an expressionist nightmare.

Unlike the German expressionists of the 1920s, however, director David Fincher (whose previous masterpiece was the equally apocalyptic but less challenging thriller, *Se7en*) and screenwriter Jim Uhls have a sense of humour. The bravura camerawork and lighting lend it the nightmarish intensity of Charles Laughton's *Night of The Hunter*; but the crackling one-liners, many from Chuck Palahniuk's original novel, mean that the film also has the cool irony of a Raymond Chandler thriller.

In lesser hands, the story might have ended up looking silly; but thanks to Fincher's mastery of grungy style and unsettling imagery it's a triumph. Pitt and Bonham Carter are terrific in the chief supporting roles, but it's Edward Norton – who hasn't given a bad performance since his memorable debut in *Primal Fear* – who delivers a *tour de force*.

FINDING NEMO *(2003)*

Finding Nemo is that delightful rarity – a family film that genuinely appeals to all the family, and not only children. It will enchant the most fidgety four year-old, but most grown-ups will also fall for it, hook, line and sinker. It's one of the best yet from Pixar, the animators who made the *Toy Story* movies, *A Bug's Life* and *Monsters Inc.* And it's a magnificent piece of story-telling.

Marlin (voiced by Albert Brooks) is a perennially anxious clownfish who can't tell jokes and doesn't have much to laugh about, especially when – and this is only the pre-titles sequence – a barracuda destroys his home and eats his wife and 399 eggs. The 400th survives and becomes Nemo (Alexander Gould).

On his first day at school, Nemo doesn't heed the advice of his understandably over-protective dad and swims out to inspect a boat – whereupon he's scooped up by a diver and taken off to a tropical fish tank in a Sydney dentist's surgery.

From then on, the story divides in two, as Nemo tries to escape the tank with the help of his fellow internees, led by a scarred old-timer called Gill (Willem Dafoe). Marlin attempts to find Nemo with the help of an eternally optimistic blue fish called Dory (Ellen de Generes).

Along the way, they encounter such characters as Bruce

the shark (Barry Humphries) who's formed a self-help group with a couple of like-minded predators in order to turn themselves into nice guys, not mindless eating machines; Nigel, an accident-prone pelican (Geoffrey Rush) and Crush (played by the film's director and co-writer, Andrew Stanton), a 150 year-old turtle who believes like any surfer dude that, hey, you just go with the flow.

The clownfishes' adventures are suspenseful, unpredictable and ceaselessly inventive. The visuals are gorgeous, and make marvellous use of reflection, refraction and the brilliant colours of aquatic life. The gags are often very funny, and – wonder of wonders – the film espouses "family" values without ever becoming earnest or preachy.

It's arguably the best film ever made about parental anxiety. Marlin learns not to become quite so over-protective. But Nemo discovers the importance of caution and that his father's twitchiness is born out of love, not just a determination to be a spoilsport.

The film even tackles the potentially schmaltzy, politically correct subject of disability and does so in a positive, thoughtful way. Nemo is born with one fin smaller than the other and is no great swimmer – but he largely overcomes his disability through courage.

Marlin's friend Dory has a mental defect – short-term memory loss – but conquers that too, thanks to her friendliness and optimistic outlook. The script carries off the difficult task of making her disability funny, yet at the same time sad and sympathetic. Ellen de Generes, not the warmest of performers in the flesh, comes across in fish form as a terrific comedienne. The scene where she attempts to talk fluent whale is a classic.

Finding Nemo is charmingly acted, beautifully scripted,

and pacily directed, with a wit – verbal, visual and even musical – that raise it to the highest level of film-making. Its success in America has already made it the most successful animated picture of all time. Artistically, it's up there with the all-time animated greats.

FINDING NEVERLAND *(2004)*

Finding Neverland is literally a wonderful film. It's full of wonders we too often take for granted. It celebrates imagination, creativity, family life in general and fatherhood in particular. Without pompous moralising or cheap mawkishness, it reminds us of how life inspires art, and art gives meaning to life.

It's the deceptively simple story of how the successful but childless playwright Sir James Barrie (Johnny Depp) was rescued from a low ebb in both his career and his marriage to a beautiful would-be socialite – exquisitely played by Radha Mitchell with an elegance that explains why Barrie married her, and an icy self-righteousness that shows why he must have wished he hadn't.

Barrie found a kind of deliverance from his lonely marriage in four boys (there were five in real life) and their recently widowed mother, Sylvia Llewelyn Davies (Kate Winslet), whom he met by chance in Kensington Gardens. They transformed both his private life and his career, for Barrie's games with them provided the inspiration for his greatest artistic triumph, *Peter Pan*.

Screenwriter David Magee can be faulted for the odd verbal anachronism (no Edwardian would ever have called a theatre interval "the intermission"), but his screenplay –

based on Alan Knee's play *The Man Who Was Peter Pan* – is in all other respects remarkable, teasing out the themes from Barrie's life that influenced the creation of *Peter Pan*, without this ever seeming an academic exercise. Every scene is sensitively crafted, and the film never feels wordy or constricted, unlike so many adaptations of stage plays.

Director Marc Forster (who previously gave us *Monster's Ball*, the film that earned Halle Berry an Oscar) does a superb job of visualising Barrie's fantasies. One of the most touching moments comes when Barrie and his wife retire to their separate bedrooms, and we see through Barrie's half-open door a glimpse of an imaginary landscape beyond, where his wife has only wallpaper.

The backstage sequences have the same love of theatre and its eccentricities that made *Shakespeare in Love* so magical. Angus Barnett is splendidly lugubrious as an actor lumbered with the task of playing Nana the dog, and Paul Whitehouse shines in his brief cameo as a harassed stage manager trying to master the rudiments of stage flying.

Finding Neverland is marvellously acted throughout. Dustin Hoffman offers first-rate support as Barrie's long-suffering producer, driven to distraction by the obviously suicidal notion of putting a children's fantasy in front of curmudgeonly theatre critics. Julie Christie also contributes her best work in decades as the boys' severe matriarch of a grandmother, suspicious of Barrie's motives in attempting to become one of her family.

Kate Winslet is excellent as Sylvia Llewelyn Davies, attempting to shield her children from the pain of losing their father, and then trying not to acknowledge that she herself is seriously ill. This is a role that could easily have been over-played; but Winslet approaches it without histrionics and with a matter-of-factness that makes it all the more affecting.

Freddie Highmore is sensational as Peter Llewelyn Davies, who was not only the inspiration for Peter Pan, the boy who wouldn't grow up, but also that character's antithesis (because of his father's death, he had grown up more than a child of his age should have had to). Many of the laughs in the film emanate from his also being Barrie's harshest critic. This is, in its way, as amazing a child-acting performance as the one that earned Haley Joel Osment an Oscar nomination for *The Sixth Sense*.

As for Johnny Depp, *Neverland* makes great use of his innocent, childlike quality, previously seen to miraculous effect in Tim Burton's *Edward Scissorhands* and *Ed Wood*. Depp's Scottish accent never slips, and he uses it brilliantly to establish his curious status in London society – as an established theatrical figure, but also an outsider, and a man who had never lost the accent or enthusiasms of his youth.

Depp's ability to be both subtle and flamboyant is as evident here as in his Oscar-nominated turn in *Pirates of the Caribbean*, which he shot after *Finding Neverland*, the release of which was delayed in order not to clash with last Christmas's release of *Peter Pan*. It also neatly avoided the near-certain fate of losing out at last year's Academy Awards to *The Return of the King*.

The story has been written and filmed before, in Andrew Birkin's memorable 3-part TV series *The Lost Boys*, in which Ian Holm played Barrie as a closet paedophile. That interpretation, because it was darker, will be held in some quarters to be more "realistic" than the new one. But, in fact, there is no evidence to suggest that Barrie had sexual yearnings for the Llewelyn Davies boys.

The new film makes tasteful reference to those rumours,

both through Julie Christie's suspicious grandma and through an exchange between Barrie and his friend Sir Arthur Conan Doyle (Ian Hart), in which Barrie is warned of what others are saying about him, but the film takes Barrie's interest in the boys as essentially paternal – rightly, in my view. Anyone who has done as I have and read all of Barrie's plays is bound to be struck by their extraordinary innocence, rather than anything remotely sinister.

Of the two versions, *The Lost Boys* – fine achievement though it was – is the more guilty of seeing the past through the distorting lens of the present. None of the boys themselves ever suggested any element of impropriety, and the new film argues persuasively that Barrie saw in the boys the children that he had never had, and in Sylvia Llewelyn Davies the good mother that he had failed to marry.

Finding Neverland is a film that explores some harsh realities of disease and death (the Neverland of the title is both the realm of the imagination and the very different "awfully big adventure" of death) but it does so in a way that entrances and uplifts.

There aren't many films nowadays that you could enjoy with a fidgety five year-old or your 90 year-old maiden aunt; this is one of them. Under no circumstances should you miss *Finding Neverland* for it's one of the great emotional experiences of our time. But be warned: take handkerchiefs.

FLIRTING WITH DISASTER *(1996)*

My favourite of all David O. Russell's films – and his Oscar nominees include *The Fighter, Silver Linings Playbook* and *American Hustle* are all of high quality – this is his early, dark comedy about the quest of an adopted man, Mel (Ben Stiller), for his real parents.

Mel feels in psychological limbo and unable to name his five month-old son until he finds out the truth. Besides, his adoptive mum and dad leave much to be desired as grandparents. She (Mary Tyler Moore) is shrill and insensitive; he (George Segal) is pessimistic and paranoid. Mel's wife Nancy (Patricia Arquette) understands his need to discover his roots, and would like to reinvigorate their sex life, which has ground to a halt. She also considers it advisable that the baby should have a name before he starts shaving. And when she sees the gorgeous, leggy, trainee psychologist from the adoption agency (Tea Leoni) who is so keen to video Mel 's encounter with his biological mother, she is even more determined to tag along.

From then on, it's a comedy of errors, as Mel is introduced to more and more people who may or may not be his parents (including Lily Tomlin and Alan Alda, hilariously flaky as the hippies from hell) and finds himself attracted to the dangerously unbalanced shrink.

Flirting With Disaster is funny, fresh and an inspired mixture of road movie, screwball comedy and slapstick farce. It offers its four comic veterans – Segal, Moore, Alda and Tomlin – the sparkiest roles they've had in years, but the younger cast-members acquit themselves just as well. Patricia Arquette is delightful as the moral centre of the movie, making sweetly earnest attempts to be supportive to Mel, even as each new disaster makes him ever more hopelessly neurotic.

The other characters teeter on the brink of caricature, but they are far from clichéd. These are the kind of exuberant eccentrics that a modern Dickens might create: people starved of self-knowledge and following their enthusiasms to the point of lunacy.

Writer-director David O. Russell pokes fun at blinkered conservatism, but is equally perceptive about knee-jerk liberalism, which he diagnoses as being a by-product of stultifying middle-class politeness.

Mel's desperate attempts to conform non-judgmentally to whatever type of family he currently thinks he's part of – from southern Reaganites to hippie radicals, from Californian blondes to redneck truckers, are both pathetic and endearing. There hasn't been a more penetrative satire on the desire to play safe by following fashion and blending into the crowd.

Russell likes flirting with dangerous subjects. This is funnier and much more mainstream than his debut, *Spanking the Monkey*, but his irreverence about family values may strike some people as tasteless, as may his frankness on matters sexual. Even so, *Flirting With Disaster* has an energy lacking in the cinema since the Forties heyday of Preston Sturges – and it's very, very funny.

FOUR WEDDINGS AND A FUNERAL
(1994)

A tongue-tied, disorganized Englishman falls for an American beauty and spends the whole movie trying to get together with her on a permanent basis. Subsidiary characters either marry or die.

That crude summary of the story may sound predictable, and ultimately it is. But it's brilliantly structured as a series of surprises, and incorporates more sub-plots even than two of the other great comedy scripts of recent years: *Parenthood* and *Singles*. It's written with both verbal and visual wit by the creator of Mr Bean, Richard Curtis.

It is superbly acted by a virtually all-British cast (the casting director, Michelle Guish, deserved her own Oscar). I particularly liked James Fleet's engagingly cloddish Tom, the seventh-richest man in England – but in this film, even Simon Callow gives a good performance. It's directed by Mike Newell with the pace and eye for comic detail which he first showed on Jack Rosenthal's TV film, *Ready When You Are Mr McGill*.

Grant extracts every ounce of laughter and pathos from his role as a young man who's always late or making gaffes, and has a phobia about matrimony, concealed under an attractive veneer of self-mockery. American critics have likened him to Cary Grant, David Niven, even (a bit more disturbingly) a grown up Macaulay Culkin. His timing is a joy to behold; and perhaps the best thing about him is that he manages to be cute without appearing narcissistic.

The film has also made a transatlantic star out of Rowan Atkinson, who does a short revue sketch early on, as a nervous priest conducting his first marriage ceremony. Strictly speaking, it's irrelevant to the plot: it's the equivalent of those speciality acts which used to bring pre-war musical comedies to a halt, while someone juggled or did farmyard impressions. Its justification is that it's very, very funny, and adds to the gentle bonhomie of a film which all through takes a generous-spirited view of human failings.

Four Weddings has an underlying liberalism which stops it from being the conservative, middle-class escapism which some critics accused it of being. It recognizes – and condones – the fact that some people decide to have children together but not marry; it makes abundant use of four-letter expletives (to thankfully comic effect); and it suggests that a longstanding "gay" couple may have just as rewarding and profound an emotional relationship as a heterosexual one. All these attitudes may be a far cry from Ealing days, but they do reflect the central Ealing ideal: that we should celebrate our differences, and then appreciate our underlying similarities.

In the same way, the inclusion of a deaf character – the hero's brother (David Bower) – is not just a "politically correct" sop to a minority group, or a plea for easy sympathy. Sign-language leads to some of the film's funniest moments, and is brilliantly used to trigger the denouement.

Even the pathetic scenes are carried off with panache. So often in comedies these seem sentimental and included to give a spurious depth, or an opportunity for an actor to show off. But John Hannah's funeral oration is wonderfully written and performed, as is the scene where the delectable Kristin Scott Thomas reveals her unrequited passion for another character. The ease with which Curtis moves from comedy to pathos reminded me, I kid you not, of Chekhov.

The film is very commercial – there's a scene with the obligatory American guest-star Andie MacDowell (who is the one weak acting link) trying on wedding dresses which has a clear affinity with Julia Roberts's equivalent scene in *Pretty Woman* – and it has obviously been made with an eye to a transatlantic audience. Why else would the very first wedding invitation carry the gratuitous information that Somerset is in England? But frankly, who cares?

Four Weddings And A Funeral is one of the great romantic comedies of all time, cleverer even than *When Harry Met Sally* or *Annie Hall*. Curtis's script is perfection, and will be studied for years to come by film students. Impeccably produced by our most talented young producer, Duncan Kenworthy, this is the funniest British comedy since *The Lavender Hill Mob*.

FRAILTY *(2001)*

A charmingly folksy Texan father (Bill Paxton) has an angelic vision one night... and brings his two sons up to become serial axe-murderers, assuring them that they are killing demons and doing the Lord's work.

Bill Paxton's first feature as a director was dismissed unfairly by some critics as B-movie horror, rather as another actor-turned-director Charles Laughton's not dissimilar *Night of the Hunter* was in its day.

I agree with Stephen King, Sam Raimi and James Cameron, who see it as a highly accomplished piece of American Gothic. This is an outstanding thriller, ingenious and atmospheric, with a twist that's as outrageous as the ones in *The Usual Suspects* and *The Sixth Sense*. Like all the best twists, it makes you re-examine the whole movie again, from a wholly new perspective

The subject-matter may sound off-puttingly like a slasher film. Though most of the violence is wisely left to the imagination, *Frailty* is hard to watch, because it shows boyish innocence and trust in their father corrupted, religious fanaticism turning two ordinary children's lives into horrific nightmares.

The elder boy's anguish as he stands up to his father is brilliantly played by young Matthew O'Leary, and just as splendidly narrated by a blank-eyed Matthew McConaughey, as one of the boys, now grown up.

Frailty could easily have descended into Grand Guignol and many moments deliberately teeter on the edge of black comedy, but the film is so wonderfully acted, and directed with such restraint by Paxton, that it always retains a sense of authenticity. It's very creepy, and packed with tension and suspense.

Just as you think this may turn into yet another smug liberal movie bashing ignorant Southerners, inveighing against religious fundamentalism and the perils of patriarchy, Brent Hanley's screenplay takes the first of a series of unexpected turns, until it ends up in an entirely different genre from the one it seemed to be inhabiting.

FROST/ NIXON *(2008)*

Making easily the finest film of a career that has included *Apollo 13*, *Cinderella Man* and *A Beautiful Mind*, along with such misfires as *The Da Vinci Code*, Ron Howard has done a clever job, along with screenwriter Peter Morgan, of opening out Morgan's acclaimed stage play. It never looks like filmed theatre.

They have retained two strengths of Michael Grandage's stage production – the magnificent performances of Michael Sheen as David Frost, and Frank Langella as Richard Nixon – and added the structure of a first-class fly-on-the-wall documentary. You could say it's a mockumentary, except that it's in deadly earnest, with a great deal riding on the central personality clash.

Langella gives the performance of his life as Nixon, making him a bruised, brooding intellectual, comically inept at basic social intercourse but still canny enough to knock even a practised schmoozer like Frost off-balance. It's hard to watch him without a twinge of nostalgia for a man who is obviously at least twenty IQ points above the last Republican incumbent.

Nixon may be the villain of the piece; but Langella makes us aware that in Nixon's mind he was the misunderstood hero. There's a lesson here for all film-makers:

always give the devil his due, for acknowledging there are more sides than one to every question will make your drama all the richer.

Another reason the movie works brilliantly lies with the supporting cast. Toby Jones is hilariously ferocious as Irving "Swifty" Lazar, Nixon's Hollywood agent.

The reliably marvellous Kevin Bacon makes a convincing character out of Jack Brennan, the ex-President's steely-eyed but affectionate aide, proud of his employer's intellectual capacity but secretly worried that the old man's human frailties will find him out. The real Brennan is affable and funny, but never mind.

Platt and Sam Rockwell are excellent as Frost's principal researchers, the urbanely witty Bob Zelnick and the wiry attack-dog James Reston. They capture beautifully the tension I have noticed in most first-rate researchers, between mistrusting their famous front man (Will he do his homework? Will he let the interviewee off too lightly? Why won't he do as I say?) and being helplessly dependent on him for any chance of reaching a mass audience.

One weakness of the film lies in two underwritten parts, but even here fine actors do their best with the material. Morgan wittily uses Frost's producer, John Birt (Matthew MacFadyen, accomplishing the tricky task of humanising the future BBC boss), and Frost's lover, Caroline Cushing (Rebecca Hall), as sounding boards for the chat-show host.

MacFadyen is entertainingly nervous as things start turning from bad to worse. Ms Hall is so gorgeous and supportive that it's hard to know why her relationship with Frost didn't work out.

Morgan's screenplay takes liberties with the truth. As in *The Queen*, he invents events which he believes will illuminate character – including, here, a late night telephone call to Frost by Nixon, in which the ex-President rails against snobbery, while the interviewer wonders if Nixon is mad or drunk.

The fact that Nixon never made such a call is, within the context of a drama, irrelevant. Morgan is right to believe that Nixon resented the easy graces and, as he saw it, snobbery of those who would never accept him socially. It's an important component of Nixon's character and it fed his paranoia, which in turn led to Watergate. So dramatically the scene is justified. It enables us to see the Shakespearean scale of Nixon's tragedy.

Morgan also takes liberties with Frost, to give him a more dramatic character arc. I've met David Frost socially and when I was a producer-director in TV, and I've been interviewed by him. He certainly didn't learn to be sharper, tougher and more conscientious through his dealings with Nixon; he was all those things already.

Were I Frost, I wouldn't be too pleased to be portrayed as a lightweight. I'd be pointing to my track record of previous interviews with world leaders, and my on-air skewering of such rascals as Emil Savundra. But Morgan accurately conveys a sense of how Frost was underestimated by his enemies. If Nixon's advisors hadn't regarded Frost as a pushover, Nixon would never have agreed to be interviewed by him.

Morgan also expertly conveys the feeling of how far, especially in the cut-throat world of US television, you're only as good as your last hit. Frost had everything to lose, personally and financially, if his Nixon interviews had turned out to be a succession of boring, long-winded Presidential anecdotes.

Morgan's most dubious departure from the truth is when he makes Nixon confess to the cover-up. Frost asks "Are you really saying the President can do something illegal?" and

Nixon replies I'm saying that when the President does it, that means it's not illegal!"

Nixon did speak those words, and they do give an insight into his mind, but he didn't state them in the context of Watergate. Indeed, he explicitly denied his guilt with the words "You're wanting me to say that I participated in an illegal cover-up. No!"

Nixon's departure from office was humiliating, but it wasn't Frost who humiliated him. Still, *Frost/Nixon* is drama, not history. And the film persuades us that "trial by television", a term used pejoratively at the time, was in fact the public's only option, when the establishment was determined to close ranks protectively around its ex-President.

Why, despite its distortions, is *Frost/Nixon* entertaining? Because it manages to turn the process behind a talk show into a riveting thriller, even though most of us already think we know the outcome.

Why is it important? I reckon, and here I realise I'm bringing my own baggage to the party, it's because it reminds us, at a time when parts of the media and certain well-known practitioners have rock-bottom standards, of what good journalism should be: it's holding people to account, whether they be film-makers or US presidents.

True, the people don't elect film critics, any more than they voted for David Frost; but they are at liberty to stop reading or watching.

For the journalists' part, it is their responsibility to do their research, accrue relevant knowledge and think deeply, so that they can act as informed commentators and ask probing questions. *Frost/Nixon* knows this – which is why it's the finest celebration of journalism since *All The President's Men*.

FUNNY GAMES *(1998)*

A pleasant, civilised, friendly, middle-class family on holiday in the European equivalent of the Norfolk Broads is terrorised, tortured (mentally and physically) and killed by two apparently polite but cold and remorseless young men (Frank Goering and Arno Frisch). Why? Simply for kicks, and to give the young men a feeling of their own power.

Funny Games is the most suspenseful, wickedly intelligent thriller since *The Vanishing*. It is not for the faint-hearted. Austrian writer-director Michael Haneke's film is horribly authentic in its portrayal of late twentieth-century psychosis.

The reason the film is important and profound, however, is that it examines a much more widespread psychosis in society's and cinema's attitudes towards violence. There's more than a hint that the young men are doing it for the audience's entertainment; and this is the factor which gives the piece added creepiness.

The film is an unpalatable but necessary antidote to the daily diet of movies which trivialise violence and are drugging, if not poisoning, an entire generation.

The violence in *Funny Games* – which occurs offscreen and is none the less upsetting for that – has all the painful impact of true crime, and it comes as a shock to be reminded in the cinema of this reality.

The cumulative tension of the plotting and horribly real performances – especially by Susanne Lothar as the wife – make no concessions to movie cliche or audience wish-fulfilment, and create a terror that is almost unbearable. Seldom has a great film been so difficult to watch.

GLADIATOR *(2000)*

Maximus (Russell Crowe), a brave Spanish general, is favoured by the Emperor Marcus Aurelius (Richard Harris) to take over the empire and ensure that it is governed by the Senate under the kindly guidance of Gracchus, played by Derek Jacobi. However, the Emperor's son Commodus (Joaquin Phoenix) has other ideas and murders his father before he can make the plan public. Not only this: he orders Maximus to be executed, and his wife and son to be burned and crucified alive.

Though Maximus escapes, he is captured, enslaved and then turned into a gladiator by the owner of a touring gladiator company (Oliver Reed in his last film, brought back to life by computer magic for his final scenes). Whereupon Maximus is brought to Rome, wows the audience and his fellow-slaves, is elevated to superstardom and finally gets the chance to gain his revenge on Commodus.

Gladiator is the kind of sword-and-sandals spectacular that seemed to have died out 40 years previously, with *Spartacus*. However, it's back – and great fun. Director Ridley Scott is just the man to re-imagine Ancient Rome in all its glory and brutality.

The Roman Coliseum – partly built, partly computer-generated – is marvellously realised. The action sequences, whether they be men fighting tigers or a high-speed chariot battle, are tremendous.

The opening spectacle of a Roman army overcoming the Germanic tribes amidst oceans of mud (actually shot near Farnham, in Surrey) is a scene to rival anything in *Braveheart*. Indeed, Ridley Scott's coverage is plainly influenced by Spielberg's brilliant portrayal of the Normandy landings in *Saving Private Ryan*.

Scott is an expert at using landscape to denote characters' emotions – this was one of the undervalued strengths in the way he directed *Thelma and Louise* – and he uses this talent to great effect throughout. The work by British cinematographer John Matheson is as lyrical as it is thrilling.

Storywise, the formula is pretty much as it was when Charlton Heston and Kirk Douglas used to do this kind of thing. A handsome, hunky if not particularly humorous hero is reduced to slavery but wins through against his eminently hissable enemies.

One of the film's biggest assets is Russell Crowe who is, as he showed in *L.A. Confidential* and *The Insider*, a very fine actor. Here, he is a long way from the paunchy, middle-aged scientist he played in *The Insider*. The script is nothing if not ponderous and po-faced, but Crowe invests it with quiet heroism, brooding menace and gravitas. His accent has a tendency to turn Antipodean in moments of stress, but he has that Charlton Heston quality of not making you laugh, however pompous the dialogue. He makes it seem the most natural thing in the world to conduct a man-to-man swordfight in a skirt, while a live tiger is mauling his shoulders.

Phoenix is convincingly nasty, and finds the pathos within Commodus: here is a weak man who knows he is weak, and resorts to brutality to hide it. The most intriguing character, because we rarely know which way she is going to jump, is Commodus' beautiful sister Lucilla (Connie Nielsen), an old flame of Maximus but ambitious for her small son Lucius (Spencer Treat Clark) and unsure how to treat her brother's incestuous cravings for her.

Few viewers are likely to take the film very seriously as history. A few issues are raised – about democracy and the distracting power of violent entertainment – but they aren't allowed to get in the way of the action.

At two and a half hours, the film does drag a bit between bloodbaths, and the Gladiator-versus-Emperor climax is too obviously contrived. The film has nothing new to say and no higher purpose than to make money; and Derek Jacobi's presence is a reminder that the TV series *I Claudius* had more depth and intellectual daring.

But, as long as you can put up with the gore and extreme violence, you'll come out of *Gladiator* feeling you've had your money's worth. This is escapist entertainment rather than art; but it delivers the same kind of thrills and high romance that *The Mask of Zorro* did. It's good to see new life being breathed into old genres.

GONE BABY GONE (2007)

For years it's been obvious that Ben Affleck doesn't have his heart in acting, and here at last is the explanation. His first cinema release as writer-director is a masterly adaptation of the novel he proclaims as his favourite, a labour of love that reflects his Boston roots. It's great at communicating the atmosphere of blue-collar neighbourhoods, the sleaziest regions of the criminal underworld, and the mindset of police who have been paddling through moral sewage for too long.

It's a tough thriller touching on sordid behaviour, but don't let that put you off. For once, the foul language and violence are authentic, not gratuitous.

The set-up is intriguing, and horribly topical in view of recent child disappearances. Private eyes Patrick Kenzie (Casey Affleck, Ben's younger brother) and his girl-friend Angie Gennaro (Michelle Monaghan) specialise in tracking down missing persons, and are hired by a stern, working-class matriarch (Amy Madigan, who you may remember as Kevin Costner's longsuffering wife in *Field of Dreams*) and her reformed alcoholic husband Lionel (Titus Welliver from *Deadwood*) to track down their missing, four year-old niece.

She's pretty, blonde and looks like Madeleine McCann, which is the reason this picture has taken so long to reach these shores. But fear not: this is no exploitation movie – the book on which it's based was published in 1994 – and that is where the similarities end.

The more obviously caring of the two gumshoes, played by Monaghan, voices the resistance many of us feel towards films which involve child abduction: "I don't want to find a child in a dumpster. I don't want to find a kid after she's been abused for three days."

Casey Affleck, though no tough guy, is more hard-boiled, even cracking a joke when he sees the abducted child's pathetically empty bedroom: "Did they kidnap the furniture too?"

The girl's single mother Helene (Amy Ryan) personifies the undeserving underclass. She's a mess, a negligent mother who's drunk when she isn't sniffing cocaine. Our hero and heroine use their underworld contacts to discover that Helene has stolen money from a drugs supplier nicknamed Cheese, who may have kidnapped the girl as a bargaining counter.

The investigating cops (who include Morgan Freeman and Ed Harris) are on the trail of a local paedophile, and resent the private eyes' interference, viewing them as too young and inexperienced to be helpful. "Go back to your Harry Potter book," rasps Harris.

But the cops become aware that Helene isn't telling them the whole truth. When Harris follows up the private eyes' theory and asks the child's befuddled mother if she knows an underworld figure called Cheese Jean Baptiste, she mumbles "Who?" then mutters "Sounds familiar". Whereupon Harris loses his temper: "No, it don't sound familiar, Helene. He's a violent, sociopathic, Haitian criminal named Cheese – either you know him or you don't!"

Together, the hardened cops and noticeably softer private eyes follow the clues deep into the Bostonian underworld.

Ben Affleck won an Academy Award for his screenplay (with Matt Damon) for *Good Will Hunting*. Even though his script here, co-written with childhood friend Aaron Stockard, failed to be nominated for an Oscar, it is vastly superior, with cracking dialogue and the deftest plotting since *LA Confidential*.

Twists in Hollywood thrillers are far too often designed merely to trick the audience, and cheat by introducing new evidence that we can't possibly know about. There's a double twist here which – though admittedly far-fetched – is highly ingenious, and Affleck cleverly parades the clues before us in advance without cheating.

The film also raises important moral issues which are anything but clear-cut. Indeed, our hero and heroine can't even agree about them. See this movie with someone else, and I guarantee it will have you arguing afterwards about who did the right thing, and who didn't.

Emotionally, this is powerful stuff, partly because it is so brilliantly acted. The ensemble cast is superior even to the one in that other Bostonian thriller based on a Dennis Lehane novel, Mystic River, where director Clint Eastwood allowed one of his actors, Sean Penn, to go over-the-top. Penn won an Oscar for his histrionics but, to my mind at least, he detracted from the movie's plausibility.

Ben Affleck keeps his actors under control, and they respond with some of the most truthful performances they have ever given. Casey Affleck and Michelle Monaghan are competent, rather than revelatory. But they're always realistic, and they unselfishly allow Ed Harris, Morgan Freeman, Amy Ryan and Amy Madigan to give Oscar-worthy supporting performances – though only Ryan won a nomination.

Gone Baby Gone is a thriller of rare intelligence and maturity.

GOODFELLAS *(1990)*

GoodFellas recounts 30 years in the career of real-life gangster Henry Hill (Ray Liotta), who descends into a self-made hell and the FBI's witness protection programme, accompanied by his wife (Lorraine Bracco), a nice Jewish girl seduced by wealth and the glamour of gangsterism.

The trouble with most gangster movies, from *Public Enemy* to *The Godfather*, is that, even though the film-makers dutifully ensure that their anti-heroes meet a nasty end, they usually glamorize the lifestyle, loyalty and competence of the criminal fraternity so much that any final come-uppance fails to outweigh the gangsters' overall attractiveness.

Scorsese avoids this trap by constantly revealing the skull behind the smile. Seldom has violence has been portrayed less glamorously, or with more moral effectiveness. Whether it's the slaying of a dying, defenceless rival in a car boot, or the shooting of a harmless waiter, there's never any doubt that violence is repellent: the work of inadequate, scared men.

And yet, Scorsese's anti-heroes make us care. Dangerous psychopath though Joe Pesci's character is, we are still shocked when he himself is gunned down. We sense Lorraine Bracco's fear of De Niro. We feel Liotta's panic when the FBI is on to him. We even share De Niro's sense of betrayal when Liotta testifies against him. All this is a tribute to some magnificent acting, but also to Scorsese's direction, which constantly changes our viewpoint with consummate ease.

Technically, too, Scorsese manages some startling effects: there is one masterly steadicam shot, as Liotta leads the woman he is trying to impress (Bracco) into a nightclub by a side entrance. Another tour de force is the scene in a diner where Liotta realizes that De Niro is out to kill him, and the back-projection enlarges subliminally, to give the effect of Liotta's world closing in. Every shot shows a director at the height of his powers, with the entire vocabulary of film at his fingertips.

But the main reason why this is more than just another study of the Mafia is that Scorsese depicts criminality as being a temptation for all of us. His portrayal of Ms Bracco's seduction, in particular, is a memorable study of how anyone might be enticed into criminality.

Some critics objected that there was little depth or complexity in Scorsese's characterisation; but in doing so they missed the point. In other movies, such as *Raging Bull* and *Taxi Driver*, Scorsese chose to investigate an individual's psychology. In this film, he is doing something different: portraying a whole society of people who lack depth, who simply don't see any problem with what they're doing.

Good Fellas is full of detailed observation, humour and realism; but it's also a parable, a reminder that Scorsese once intended to become a priest. It's a sustained attack not only on gangsterism, but also on the three big, post-Marxist "isms": opportunism, conformism and materialism. It's timely, horrible and devastating, the greatest of all gangster movies. Thelma Schoonmaker's editing was nominated for an Oscar; it remains a mystery as to why Michael Ballhaus's cinematography was ignored, and it's even more unfathomable why Scorsese wasn't even nominated for Best Director.

GRAN TORINO *(2008)*

Clint Eastwood used to play The Man With No Name. Now, he is The Man With No Shame. In what he threatens will be his final performance, the 78 year-old actor-director stars as arguably his nastiest character ever. Walt Kowalski is a cantankerous, beer-swilling veteran of the Korean war, and a former Ford worker who's living in a Detroit neighbourhood taken over by immigrants. Recently widowed, Walt reacts to anything modern that he doesn't like – which is just about everything – with a low growl and a snarled "Get off my lawn!"

So politically incorrect that he makes Carol Thatcher look like Sir Ian Blair, he doesn't like "chinks", "zipper-heads" or "gooks", especially when one tries to steal his lovingly tended car, the 1972 Gran Torino of the title.

But the oriental boy and girl next door make him see the good in gooks, especially contrasted with Walt's selfish relatives, and he becomes their unlikely father-figure.

This could have become a tediously pious fable about a racist learning the error of his ways, or – in its final act – an audience-pleasing revenge fantasy in the tradition of *Death Wish*; but Eastwood bravely avoids both extremes.

Walt may mellow too quickly to be entirely credible, and I can sympathise with those who feel that the movie condescends to Asian–Americans by making them dependent on a white authority figure.

Yet how many other mainstream films can you name which have this much empathy with Asian-Americans? In any case, the whole film is about the central character's change from bigotry to redemption, isolation to neighbourliness, villain to role-model.

The denouement is essentially an urban remake of Don Siegel's John Wayne western, *The Shootist* (1976). Both films commemorate the end of the old, non-multicultural West, for which Eastwood has replaced Wayne as a potent icon.

Eastwood is great fun and rivetingly watchable, as a character who is in many ways a comedic variation on his own Dirty Harry. There is an especially funny scene where the Polish-American Walt and an Italian-American barber reveal the mutual affection underlying their apparently racist banter.

The film might have been a little more realistic about the difficulty of dispelling bigotry, and better-acted by Clint's inexperienced Asian co-stars. All the same, this wise, likeable and extremely entertaining picture is very much a must-see. It is already the highest-grossing movie in Eastwood's illustrious career.

GROUNDHOG DAY (1992)

A TV weatherman (Bill Murray) has to relive the same day over and over again, in his least favourite small town in America, on the occasion of the festival he most hates – one on which he has to hand over weather-forecasting duties, because of a local superstition, to an overgrown, underground squirrel. He is cursed – or blessed – with reliving this most demeaning day of his year until he gets it right.

Groundhog Day poses a question we all ask ourselves. What would I do if I had my life to live over again? I know I'd do things differently, but would I do them any better?

The anti-hero of this movie reverts initially to the traditional pursuits of younger men. Since he doesn't have to care about consequences, he drinks heavily, drives like a maniac, pursues meaningless sex. Growing up a little, he tries to impress the woman he fancies (Andie MacDowell) by pretending they have a lot in common. Maturing still further, he realizes that to win her he must actually improve himself – in his case, by finding new skills (he turns into a demon piano-player) and developing something he has previously found anathema: community spirit.

The resulting film of self-redemption owes something to Dickens's novel *A Christmas Carol*, but more to Frank Capra's masterpiece, *It's A Wonderful Life*. In both films, the hero begins with so self-centred and restricted a view of his universe that he contemplates suicide. In both, he learns through supernatural intervention that he is part of a wider community, and he comes to appreciate small-town American values.

There are, however, dissimilarities. The outcome of *It's A Wonderful Life* is, in a way, pessimistic: its hero, played by James Stewart, has to learn that his own thwarted personal ambitions are relatively unimportant, and he needs to sacrifice them for the good of his family and community. In *Groundhog Day*, the message is more upbeat: by improving yourself, you may learn that family and community are more important than career, but there's no reason why you shouldn't have your career as well.

All this may sound over-optimistic, and perhaps it is. Americans like to see life as a series of opportunities; Europeans tend to be more cynical and fatalistic. Murray's character is so entertaining when sneering at small-town Americana, popular taste and pushy life-insurance salesman that it's almost a disappointment when he turns into a nice guy who might have voted for A Better Tomorrow With President Clinton. Murray's at his funniest, like his spiritual ancestor W.C.Fields, when being a curmudgeon.

But at least Murray has learned to mellow convincingly. At the end of a not dissimilar process in a Hollywood update of *A Christmas Carol*, *Scrooged* (1988), he seemed to be sneering at the sentimentality of the script. Maturity has turned Murray into a much more sympathetic comedian. So why was *Groundhog Day* such a success? Not even excellent performances by Murray could make hits out of his previous two movies, *Quick Change* and *What About Bob?* The answer, as so often, lies in the script. Given the highly restrictive premise, the film might have turned out over-repetitive and mechanical but it didn't: a tribute to writer Danny Rubin and his co-writer and director, Harold Ramis.

The film is, like a previous "surprise" hit, *Ghost*, a very clever mixture of genres. Some American critics dismissed *Groundhog Day* as just another time travel picture, like *Back To The Future* or *The Terminator*. But the film is completely uninterested in the logic or mechanism of time travel. *Groundhog Day* is more like those rather dated J.B.Priestley plays (*Dangerous Corner, I Have Been Here Before*) when time repeats itself without explanation.

It is also a middle-aged romantic comedy, like the underrated *Frankie and Johnny*, where both members of the duo bring their own hopes and insecurities to the party – and a middle-age crisis movie. The Bill Murray we see in the opening scenes is old before his time. He has forgotten how to enjoy himself: he even turns down a date with Andie MacDowell to read a book. As in Spielberg's *Hook*, he has to find the child – or at least the optimistic young man – within himself.

But the aspect which makes *Groundhog Day* so original and such a huge success is that this is a computer-age comedy. The American critics failed to notice something that will be obvious to most young moviegoers: Murray's character lives his new life just like the hero of an interactive adventure in a computer game. If he dies, he can always go back and make another choice; and he can use knowledge gained beforehand to make more informed choices next time. This was certainly the most ingenious comedy of 1993, and among the funniest and most heart-warming.

THE HANGOVER (*2009*)

The Hangover is 100 minutes of men behaving incredibly badly, shameless ethnic stereotyping, gratuitous violence and unattractive nudity. It's also extremely inventive and entertaining, providing the most consistent source of laughter since *Dodgeball*.

Rude, crude and defiantly male, it's the ultimate phallocentric antidote to *Sex and the City*, and easily the funniest American comedy of the year.

The movie begins in a deliberately misleading, fragrantly feminine way with preparations for an elegant Californian wedding. But bride-to-be Tracy (Sasha Barrese) has a problem. She keeps asking variations on the question "Where is Doug?" Then she gets the answer. Well, kind of. His best friend Phil (Bradley Cooper) phones her from the Mojave Desert. He has a bleeding lip and three male companions, none of whom is Doug. He tells her they've lost her groom, and there's no way the wedding is going to happen.

We flash back two days, to the start of a uniquely disastrous bachelor party. Doug (Justin Bartha) seems to be the most responsible member of the group, and promises his father-in-law that he won't let anyone else drive the classic Mercedes convertible he's borrowing for his bachelor trip to Las Vegas. Huh.

Then there's Stu (Ed Hels), a quiet, brow-beaten dentist who has assured his hectoring girlfriend (Rachael Harris, as a sort of transatlantic Polly Toynbee) that he's off on a genteel, wine-tasting tour of the Napa valley. Cocky lounge-lizard of the trio is Phil, a married but discontented schoolteacher, who thinks nothing of stealing from his students to pay for the trip, and clearly doesn't like children.

The fourth member of the quartet seems to like children a little too much. "I'm not supposed to be within 200 feet of a school," he mumbles, "or a Chuckee Cheeze." He's the bride's chubby, bearded brother Alan (Zach Galifianakis) who is understandably friendless and dismayingly unpredictable. Doug has been told not to let him near alcohol or a gambling table, or presumably children. "You mean like a gremlin?" asks Phil. "He comes with instructions?"

This ill-assorted quartet checks in to an expensive suite at Caesar's Palace, where Alan gives further hints that he may be dangerously stupid. "Is this the real Caesar's Palace?" he asks the receptionist. "Did Caesar live here?"

Convening on the roof of the hotel, they toast "an evening we'll never forget" with drinks poured by Alan. Uh-oh. Cut to the following morning, after a night none of them can remember. The hotel suite is trashed. Stu is minus a front tooth. Phil has a wrist tag, which suggests he's been in hospital. There's a chicken wandering through the debris, a crying baby in the wardrobe, and a tiger in the bathroom. Doug has disappeared, and when his father-in-law's cherished Mercedes is brought for them it's changed, ominously, into a police car.

Thus begins a comedic form of *Saving Private Ryan*, as the three of them try to track down poor, doomed Doug, and remember what happened when, and how on earth that tiger got into the bathroom. The answer to this conundrum turns out to involve Mike Tyson, who plays a slightly more articulate version of himself and reveals a memorably atrocious singing voice.

Nothing in the dismal previous output of these writers, Jon Lucas and Scott Moore (*Four Christmases, Ghosts of Girlfriends Past*), or director Todd Phillips (*Road Trip, Old School*) would suggest they were capable of anything as entertaining as this. The delight of the script lies in its continual inventiveness and its frenetic pace. Just as you think things can't get any worse, they do... and how. It's as hilariously catastrophic as Gordon Brown attempting to reshuffle a cabinet.

But, despite the male characters' glaring faults, they become likeable in their befuddlement, as they sink below a rising tide of anxiety, humiliation and panic. It's all cleverly structured and there's never a dull moment, even if they never do get round to explaining the chicken.

I could, I suppose, reprimand the movie for misogyny. The only appealing female character is that most tired of clichés, a tart with a heart, engagingly played by Heather Graham. And yes, ladies, she could be described as window-dressing.

But men don't come out of the movie well, either, and the entire movie could be seen as a descent into the heart of masculine darkness. It's like *Apocalypse Now*, but with Mike Tyson instead of Marlon Brando as a symbol of corrupted masculinity. Ultimately, men are portrayed as dangerously out of control if they don't come to terms with their responsibilities to females and family. The happy ending comes only when they grow up.

The last ten years have thrown up – and I use the term advisedly – numerous movies that have explored the notion of masculinity in crisis. The most serious of these was *Fight Club*. The funniest by far is *The Hangover*.

HAPPINESS *(1998)*

Various Americans try to connect emotionally and sexually in this story of various individuals who are all, in different ways, losers. Seven of them belong to the same family, though the only family gathering is a cheerless one, towards the end. It is the characters' sense of isolation and their fear of being alone that resonate throughout the film. The only scenes where members of the family reveal their true emotions to each other are a sequence in which a psychiatrist (Dylan Baker) attempts to help his 11 year-old son (Rufus Read) through the onset of puberty.

These scenes are enough to make anyone uneasy, since we know that the father is sexually attracted to boys of his son's age and is wrestling with his own warring instincts towards the child: paternal and predatory. The scenes are hard to watch, but brilliantly written, acted and directed – and they serve a moral purpose.

They remind us that even paedophiles have normal feelings too. Without condoning anything the offender does to children, without titillating us with his acts, and without saying that he does not deserve severe punishment, Solondz shows us why we should not demonize such people – because in doing so, we behave as they do towards their victims: we treat them as objects, and deny them their humanity.

Dylan Baker courageously produces the most authentic portrait of a paedophile since Peter Lorre's in Fritz Lang's *M*.

Solondz will be criticised for rubbing people's noses in the sordid sex lives of inadequate people; but there must be room in the cinema for analysing the dark sides of humanity, as long as this is done with taste and wisdom. There will be those who find the subject-matter – sexual deviancy, child abuse, self-abuse, self-destructive behaviour of various kinds – too disgusting to cope with, and they should avoid this movie.

But *Happiness* is a fine film that hardly ever stoops to the cheap gag, and constantly confounds our expectations.

The character who comes across immediately as a sicko – a stalker who likes to terrorise women with obscene phone calls (Philip Seymour Hoffman) – turns out to be no more sad and twisted than the glamorous writer he's pursuing (Lara Flynn Boyle, hilariously pretentious) and less of a menace to society than the amorous fat lady who lives down the corridor (Camryn Manheim).

The loveless marriage between two elderly people who can't stand each other (Ben Gazzara and Louise Lasser) survives – but only because the alternative loneliness is too ghastly to contemplate. Many will find this cold-eyed observation of Darby and Joanhood horribly authentic.

Even the most attractive character, a droopy 30 year-old bachelor girl called Joy (Jane Adams), suffers a series of personal and professional embarrassments as she causes the suicide of one boyfriend (Jon Lovitz, terrific in the film's opening scene), and is ripped off by a seemingly romantic Russian (Jared Harris). The crowning irony is that she is patronised even by her sister (Cyntha Stevenson, in a Penelope Keith-style role), who thinks she has it all but is in fact married to the man who's a serial child-rapist.

All this may sound tacky, tasteless and cruel, but curiously it isn't. Solondz's sympathy for the underdog was visible in his previous film, *Welcome to the Dollhouse*, and saves him from patronizing even his creepiest and most complacent characters.

The result is social observation which compares favourably with the very best films of Robert Altman and Mike Leigh. The actors play every part with intelligence, sympathy and integrity. Solondz doesn't claim that his characters are likeable, and he certainly finds them funny; but he also illuminates their pathos and humanity. His argument is that people are not either good or evil, but on a continuum of dysfunctionality.

The dialogue is sharp, authentic and fresh (there are obscenities, but for once they are used to dramatic and comic effect). A word of praise, too, for Robbie Kondor's witty, cod middle-of-the-road score.

Happiness is not for everyone, but it's the most innovative, challenging film to have come out of America since *Pulp Fiction*.

HEARTS OF DARKNESS: A FILMMAKER'S APOCALYPSE
(1991)

Warren Beatty has described film-making as "like trying to keep a 95,000-ton souffle from falling". Francis Ford Coppola says it's like attempting to walk on a floor covered with vaseline. *Hearts of Darkness: A Film-Maker's Apocalypse* shows why it's more dangerous than that. This documentary tells such an amazing story that it should appeal to many more people than just film-buffs.

Coppola's production was dogged by disasters, some of them self-made. Coppola had to reshoot after he fired the leading man (Harvey Keitel). On location in the Philippines, the crew found themselves in a civil war between President Marcos and guerillas. A typhoon wrecked most of the film's sets. The new leading man (Martin Sheen) almost died of a heart attack. The guest star, Marlon Brando, threatened to pull out and then arrived overweight, underprepared, and unwilling to perform the part as written, so that scenes involving him had to be improvised (one reason why the feature film itself becomes grossly distended in the final half hour). Other actors performed scenes drunk or on drugs.

It's hardly surprising that Coppola, who was risking his

personal fortune on the project, ended up having a nervous breakdown and a near-fatal seizure. The film ultimately took three and a half years to complete, by which time it was horribly over-budget and known throughout Hollywood as *Apocalypse When?*

Such a story would be interesting in itself, but it's all the more resonant since it reflects not only the theme of *Apocalypse Now* – one man's descent into a self-created hell – but also the entire history of the Americans in Vietnam. Even Coppola sees the ironic comparison: "My film is not *about* Vietnam," he says, "it *is* Vietnam... We were in the jungle; there were too many of us; we had access to too much money, too much equipment; and little by little we went insane".

Co-directors Fax Bahr and George Hickenlooper organize the original material (shot, while the feature was made, by Coppola's wife Eleanor) with great intelligence, and have succeeded in gaining access 14 years later to almost all the principals, who look back on the experience with humorous detachment.

The hero of the documentary emerges as Coppola's wife, apparently willing – even enthusiastic – to lose everything in order to support her husband's artistic quest. Coppola himself is a surprisingly sympathetic, though chaotic, anti-hero: no one can doubt his courage or commitment, and there's considerable pathos in the fact that he has never risen to such heights again. Always intriguing and often hilarious, this is the best film about a film ever made.

HEAT *(1995)*

It's the oldest cliché in gangster movies – when the killer comes face to face with the cop who's hunting him, and they realise that they are two sides of the same, bent coin. They exchange glances of grudging respect, and you know that one is going to wind up killing the other.

It's a measure of this film's excellence that the scene is played here with such freshness and wry self-knowledge that it seems to be telling us something new about human nature. Mind you, it helps that the cop is Al Pacino and the criminal, Robert De Niro.

Three hours long and never dull for a second, *Heat* is one of the all-time-great thrillers.

What's so great about it? Writer-director Michael Mann has taken a commonplace story and shot it with a flair that borders on the poetic (the miraculous cinematography is by Dante Spinotti). He has staged exciting, inventive set-pieces and terrifying shoot-outs, then deepened the picture with superb dialogue, actors and sub-plots which cleverly illuminate the central theme.

Some women will be irritated by that theme – which is essentially an update of the old John Wayne maxim, "A man's gotta do what a man's gotta do".

Stern moralists may deplore the film-maker's obvious

respect for professionalism, however criminal. The not altogether benign influence of Quentin Tarantino on both style and substance is never far below the surface.

Michael Mann directed the best episodes of *Miami Vice*, went on to make the stylish *Manhunter* and the scenic if violent *Last of the Mohicans*. This is by far his finest movie – not only a masterly thriller, but a penetrating analysis of what it means to be a modern, workaholic male. It's an action movie about men who prefer action to thought.

Those who dislike *Heat* might argue that it is also *for* men who prefer action to thought.

Pacino's performance has its irritations – especially when he is indulging his favourite mannerism of speaking very softly and then suddenly exploding at top VOLUME! Some of his policing decisions are reprehensible, and much of his behaviour is bizarre bordering on psychotic. But he is never less than riveting. Whether barking orders at subordinates or suffering while his third wife (Diane Venora) pronounces on his shortcomings, he has a power which few screen actors could hope to match.

Except De Niro. His performances recently have been uneven, which may be why he has to take second billing to Pacino; but this is one of his best efforts. He is cool, where Pacino is hot; careful, where Pacino is impetuous; as the criminal mastermind, he leads and makes Pacino follow. All the more touching, then, when this lonely man with an inhospitable life loses his heart to an attractive graphic artist (Amy Brenneman) with whom he plans to move to New Zealand... except, of course, that there is always one more heist to pull, one last enemy to eliminate.

The structure of Mann's screenplay is as fiendishly complicated as any episode of *Hill Street Blues*, and he even allows himself a third storyline about De Niro's fellow-thief (Val Kilmer) whose marriage (to Ashley Judd) is in trouble because of his gambling. You can gauge how good the script is by the fact that Jon Voight, Wes Studi, Tom Sizemore and Natalie Portman take minor parts.

The final shoot-out has two of Hollywood's greatest actors, De Niro and Pacino, disorientated on an airfield, dwarfed by jets coming in to land, marionettes of their own gigantic machismo. They come across as both mythic and pathetic, which I'm sure is precisely what Mann had in mind.

HEAVENLY CREATURES *(1994)*

In 1954, respectable, buttoned-down New Zealand was shocked by a horrible murder – one of those landmark events, like the trial of O.J. Simpson in America or the James Bulger case in Britain, which makes an entire nation take stock of itself. Two outwardly ordinary 15 year-old schoolgirls – one English, one a New Zealander – were put on trial for battering the Kiwi girl's mother to death. Their crime was all the more senseless, since the victim was a mild, caring woman who had never done her daughter any harm.

The press searched for some glib, copycat explanation for their crime. But the diaries of the New Zealand girl revealed no media influences more sinister than crushes on Mario Lanza, Orson Welles and James Mason. Nor did the girls appear to be mad. The diaries revealed a strong physical relationship between the girls, and a shared fantasy world inhabited by princesses, unicorns and chivalrous (if murderous) princes.

In most other ways, the girls appeared normal, except in the area of art and creative writing, where they were exceptionally talented and imaginative. Most damningly for their lawyers' plea of insanity, the diaries revealed the murder to have been premeditated. "Our main idea for the day," ran one matter-of-fact entry, "was to murder mother. We decided to use a rock in a stocking."

The girls were duly imprisoned; but youth and good behaviour ensured that they were released within five years, on condition they never saw one another again. Neither girl re-offended. One has gone on – under the name of Anne Perry – to become a respected crime novelist, and now lives in Scotland.

It's a fascinating story, but the stuff of which lurid exploitation movies are often made. And writer-director Peter Jackson has previously been responsible for *Bad Taste*, *Meet the Feebles* and *Braindead*, three of the most puerile and revolting films of all time.

Astonishingly, under the influence perhaps of his co-writer Frances Walsh, Jackson has turned out a film unrecognizable from the rest of his oeuvre – mature, sensitive and profound.

The film establishes a realistic picture of a society not dissimilar from Britain in the same period. Virtually every scene has been shot where it actually took place; and, since the script quotes verbatim from the diaries, it has the power and authenticity of documentary.

It is magnificently acted by the entire cast, including such familiar British actors as Clive Merrison; and the two leading performances are stunning.

17 year-old Kate Winslet, fresh from playing Pandora in the TV series *Adrian Mole*, is wonderfully touching as the bright, attractive English girl, afflicted by TB, and uncertain if her professional-class parents care either for her or each other.

Just as much of a revelation is 15 year-old New Zealander Melanie Lynskey, a first-time actress, as a dumpy working-class girl first in awe of her more sophisticated friend, then in love with her. Increasingly isolated by feelings of being misunderstood, she retreats ever further into fantasy, ultimately transferring all her guilt and shame on to her hapless, harmless mother.

Heaven knows whether this film really tells the truth, but it is remarkably persuasive at making sense of a seemingly senseless crime. It neither glamorizes nor whitewashes the girls. The murder is portrayed (with commendable restraint and brevity) as a horrific, irrational, yet understandable act.

The film is often funny about the stiff, ultra-conventional nature of New Zealand at the time, but it does not take the easy, over-familiar route of blaming Society, or Emotional Repression, or Bad Parents. Instead, it explores the dark side of the girls' imagination with a nightmarish intensity unseen in the cinema since David Lynch's *Blue Velvet*.

This is a splendidly unconventional "coming of age" story – depicting adolescence in immediately recognizable terms, as a hormonal and psychological battleground. And it succeeds in showing how two apparently "normal" individuals can merge to become an abnormal entity, collectively insane and capable of terrible savagery. Canine psychologists might call this the "pack" mentality; but no one looking at the history of the twentieth century can doubt that humans suffer from it too.

Amusingly and intelligently scripted, this is a powerful film on a serious topic – and brilliantly crafted. Perhaps Alun Bollinger's camerawork is over-obtrusive at times, but much of it has a strange, dreamlike clarity. The special effects - especially the evocation of the girls' cod-mediaeval fantasy world – are amazingly impressive for a low-budget production.

This is not a movie for those who watch films only for entertainment or stories with a clear and conventional morality. But if you're interested in seeing one of the most unusual and gripping films of the 90s, I would advise you to put this at the top of your list of films to see.

HIDDEN/ CACHE *(2005)*

Hidden is about an upmarket, arty, liberal French couple (superbly acted by Daniel Auteuil and Juliette Binoche) who are quietly terrorised by someone sending them videos – first of the outside of their home, then of the house where Auteuil's character was born, and then... well, I won't spoil it for you.

The build-up of tension, suspense and menace is worthy of Hitchcock at his best, and director Michael Haneke reveals the same quality he exhibited in the extremely frightening *Funny Games* of making us empathise with his flawed leading characters as they find themselves under attack.

Some critics have called the film "cold", because of its clinical detachment and air of creepiness, but that's misleading. I defy anyone to watch *Hidden* and not become involved with the husband and wife at its centre.

The less you know about *Hidden*, the more you'll enjoy it. It works as a conventional thriller, with one or two extremely nasty shocks, but it's also adventurous in the way Haneke plays with form – often, we're unsure if we're watching something happen, or watching a tape of something happen, which helps us to identify with the leading characters' uneasiness at being under surveillance.

Hidden also raises important issues. It is one of the best movies I've seen about the casual cruelty of children – and teenagers, come to that. It shatters the smugness of liberals who favour liberalism as long as it doesn't impinge on their own interests. And it raises awkward questions about post-colonialism and immigration that not only the French have been slow to confront.

I would urge you to catch *Hidden* on the big screen if you can. Haneke reveals – or rather, strongly hints at – who sent the threatening tapes in his very last shot of steps outside a building, but if you are not looking at the appropriate area of the screen (over to the left) you might easily miss it.

Haneke clearly doesn't care much if you notice it or not, and is never one for cosy endings that restore a sense of balance and normalcy. His point is not so much that a particular person sent the tapes – it is that we all have secrets to hide, we could get found out at any time, and every one of us is, to a greater or lesser extent, a victim of our own secrets and hypocrisies.

HOOP DREAMS *(1995)*

The bad news is that this is yet another documentary about the plight of black youth in American inner cities. The really bad news is that it is a three-hour movie about basketball. The good news is that this is one of the great documentaries of all time. I defy anyone to sit through it and not feel enriched and altered by the experience.

Hoop Dreams shows us the American Dream in all its nightmarishness and splendour. It offers insights into sport, race, family and human aspiration. It is inspiring and unforgettable. Though it was not even nominated at the Oscars for Best Documentary, it deserved to be a shoo-in for Best Film. It is the antidote to the complacency of *Forrest Gump*.

The unique project began in 1986, when three white basketball-fans from Chicago – Steve James, Frederick Marx and Peter Gilbert – started on what was intended to be a half-hour documentary for public service television. They began with only $2,500 in their pockets, and selected – with the aid of a school talent-scout – two black, 14 year-old basketball players from the ghetto.

One was Arthur Agee – skinny, talented, but undisciplined. The other was William Gates – a muscular, more mature boy, tipped for the top by professional coaches.

Over the next five years and 250 hours of footage, an extraordinary story of the two youths and their families built up, spanning comedy and tragedy, disaster and triumph. Fate and family continually sprang surprises. Stereotypical situations had unexpected consequences. On the evidence of this film, God is one hell of a screenwriter.

The film-makers must not have been able to believe their luck, and have rightly asked critics not to say what happens. Suffice it to say that losers become winners, and vice versa. The film's one tragic figure turns out to be William's older brother, Curtis, a former high school basketball star, growing ever more defeated, drab and dejected as his own dreams recede inexorably into the past.

The film's most unfamiliar insight is into how early the recruiting of athletes begins in America. This has one welcome effect – white suburban schools help to give black children chances they might otherwise not have, of receiving a proper education. It is equally clear, however, that the schools drop them speedily and brutally, if they are no longer considered to be fulfilling their athletic potential. The children's educational needs and personal efforts – and their family's financial sacrifices – count for nothing.

The players, coaches and fans are all part of a highly competitive system which works in the best interests of a tiny minority, but cruelly ignores the needs of the vast majority.

It would be impossible to devise a more telling indictment of how white society uses and discards young black men. The film-makers have no need to preach; they simply show the difference between one boy – humiliated and dubbed a failure at 15, and having to study remedial English in a dark, crowded room – and the other, still with star potential and receiving treatment for a cartilage problem, free of charge, in a luxurious treatment centre. A fine documentary might have finished at the end of the first hour, with this downbeat but devastating conclusion.

The achievement of the film-makers – not to mention the young men and their families – is that they keep going. The story which unfolds over the final two hours contains as many emotional highs and lows as a novel by Charles Dickens. We witness games and other crucial events with hope, anxiety and even dread, for we know this is real life, which guarantees no happy endings, and we increasingly understand how far these children have to fall.

Hoop Dreams demonstrates the importance of family, the courage of mothers compelled to bring up children single-handed, and – on a much bleaker note – the defects of the grown men on display.

Most of all, it enables us to see how heavily the odds are stacked against these youths. One of the most moving moments comes at a simple birthday party, as one of the boys' mothers weeps tears of pride and joy that he has managed to survive, unlike so many of his contemporaries, to the grand old age of 18.

By the end, we know what we didn't understand before – that the boys' dreams of becoming professional basketball-players may always have been delusions. Of the half a million children who play high-school ball, only 14,000 make a college team, and of those only 25 turn professional. But having a dream, however unachievable, has given these young men hope, and the spirit to improve themselves beyond any realistic expectation.

The growing involvement of the film-makers with their subjects gives the movie much of its strength; ironically, it may also have undermined its realism. One fact unrecorded in the film is that when Arthur's family went through especially hard times and their electricity was cut off, the film-makers arranged for the bill to be paid and power restored. And the experience of being filmed may have given these two young men a greater determination not to fail publicly.

Still, I would not wish to detract from what is truly one of the great, inspirational movies of all time. Seeing it is an emotional experience which you should put yourself through. Set aside three hours of your life, and I promise it will leave you humbler and wiser.

THE HURT LOCKER (2009)

Kathryn Bigelow's thriller about bomb disposal is not only the best movie about the war in Iraq; it's one of the most revealing films ever about war in general.

Like all Ms Bigelow's movies, it's obsessed with manliness and machismo – but in a much more serious, searching way than anything she's done before. Her anti-hero is a gung-ho sergeant (Jeremy Renner) who feels alive only when defusing bombs.

The trouble is that he's so reckless, he endangers the lives of the two other members of his team (Anthony Mackie and Brian Geraghty).

Ms Bigelow has always been clever at creating suspense, and several sequences – especially a scene of sniper attack – rank among the most gruelling ever committed to celluloid.

Journalist and screenwriter Mark Boai spent weeks embedded with a US army bomb squad, and everything about the movie feels real. It's the nearest thing to serving in Iraq, and a heck of a lot safer.

The movie wowed American critics but failed to attract much of an audience at the box office. This could be because the film has no stars. The only well-known actors – Guy Pearce, Ralph Fiennes and David Morse, all excellent in brief appearances – are swiftly blown up, shot or moved on.

But that's deliberate, and adds greatly to audience involvement.

Because there's no Tom Cruise, Bruce Willis or Brad Pitt involved, we can't be certain which, if any, of the three leading characters will survive. There's a real feeling of life and death at stake.

Some of the story-telling feels confused – especially in two night sequences late on, where the leading character is bent on vengeance and explores a nightmarish world where he is more dangerously exposed than ever. At first I thought these descents into chaos were a mistake, until I realised that emotionally and intellectually both scenes fulfil a purpose.

They make us experience the sergeant's emotional turmoil by proxy, as the lighting and camerawork, previously neat and documentary-style, turn jagged and expressionistic. We discover for ourselves just how narrow the line is between heroism and foolishness, courage and madness. It has the same feeling of nervous breakdown as the most memorable parts of *Apocalypse Now*.

The Hurt Locker is not a political movie. It's uninterested in why US forces are in Iraq, or in pointing a finger of blame. It's primarily interested in making us understand why men volunteer to do something this dangerous. The truths it reveals are equally applicable to Afghanistan in the 21st century, or the Thirty Years War in the 17th.

The most quietly insightful scenes come when we see the leading character clearing leaves out of a gutter at home, and standing in a supermarket, bemused by the number of choices in front of him. Here, he feels weak and unimportant – something he never experienced in action.

He simply feels more of a man when he's doing something useful.

THE ICE STORM *(1997)*

The Ice Storm is an in-depth study of two middle-class families interconnecting in the Seventies. They are linked at first by lust, and finally by a freak event which makes them re-evaluate the way they have been conducting their lives.

Ben (Kevin Kline) and Elena (Joan Allen) have grown apart as husband and wife. Their sexual interest in each other is about as warm as the ice in their drinks, and Ben is having a clumsily concealed affair with a neighbour's wife Janey (Sigourney Weaver). It's not much of an affair, since Janey is exasperated by him in every way but sexually. "You're boring me," she tells him, interrupting as he drones on about golf. "I have a husband. I don't feel the need for another."

Elena has started getting her kicks from shoplifting, and is being chatted up by the local clergyman (Michael Cumpsty), a long-haired hippie with a keen interest in wifeswapping, even though he has no wife of his own to swap. "Sometimes the shepherd needs the comfort of the sheep," he tells Elena, by way of self-justification. "I'm going to try hard," she replies, " not to understand the implications of that."

Ben and Elena love their teenage children, but are spectacularly useless at giving sound advice to them about growing up – hardly surprising, since they are hardly in a position to preach.

For her part, Janey knows something is wrong when she finds Ben's daughter (Christina Ricci) exposing herself to her small son (Adam Hann-Byrd), but can't come up with any moral reasons for her misgivings, so she launches into a confused, quasi-feminist account of sexual practices in Samoa, half-remembered from anthropologist Margaret Mead.

A freak storm during a wife-swapping party brings about the nemesis that has been looming throughout the picture, and brings home the overriding power and importance of a parent-child relationship.

Here is a rarity indeed – a Hollywood drama, set in the past but without a hint of nostalgia, able to grip an audience without a single car-chase or act of violence. It has intelligence and passion, superb acting and flawless production, delightful comic touches but real seriousness of purpose.

Director Ang Lee has never made a bad film, and *The Ice Storm* is as impressive as Lee's previous success, *Sense and Sensibility*. (An alternative title for *The Ice Storm* might have been *Sense and Sensuality*.) Even at first sight, it has the kind of maturity and depth which leave you confident that further viewings will bring even greater rewards.

No film has so wittily shown the disparity that can exist between intellectual and emotional intelligence. It also explores – with rigour, yet a certain charity – the limitations of permissiveness, the way people are trapped by the promise of sexual liberation into ways of life that they eventually find joyless, demeaning and unsatisfying.

The film has enormous sympathy for its liberal characters, yet it isn't afraid to come down squarely – and persuasively – in favour of traditional family values.

The social and period observation of James Schamus's script, skilfully crafted from Rick Moody's novel, is wonderfully astute, helped by Lee's mastery of mood, unrivalled sensitivity towards actors, and underrated, unflashy pictorial sense (the ice storm itself is ferocious yet beautiful).

The story is serious but never gloomy. The climactic wife-swapping party, worthy of Alan Ayckbourn at his best, is a perfect illustration of how profound personal tragedy can exist side-by-side with comic social embarrassment. Throughout the film, I laughed more than I do at most comedies.

Sigourney Weaver is hard and abrasively defensive, in the way she has made her own in the *Alien* movies, yet she also manages to suggest an aching vulnerability beneath, an intelligence that has deteriorated through lack of use into self-destructive cynicism. This is her best screen performance, but she is only one actor in a brilliant ensemble.

Joan Allen makes desperation seem sexy, in a quiet yet intense performance no less superb than her Oscar-worthy performances in *Nixon* and *The Crucible*.

Kevin Kline has never been better, effortlessly shifting between comedy and tragedy, giving a marvellously rounded portrait of a man grappling with his own weakness, pomposity and sexual urges, troubled that he can no longer play the role he wants most – that of father – with any degree of authority.

The younger members of the cast – especially Christina Ricci, Elijah Wood, Tobey Maguire and Adam Hann-Byrd – are equally astonishing; and the film would be a masterpiece were it only a rites-of-passage movie about sexual awakening.

But the picture is more than that. It finds telling contrasts and parallels, funny and sad, between the ways the two generations behave, and is mercilessly truthful about the impact of parents' poor judgment upon their children.

The most refreshing aspect of *The Ice Storm* is that it

seems to be about real people, not types. It presents characters so truthfully that it never has to analyse them, subject us to long passages of exposition, or preach about what is wrong with them. We know these people, because we have met children and adults just like them. In fact, if we didn't know how to behave ourselves, we might even be them.

THE IDES OF MARCH *(2011)*

Beware missing it. For my money, this thriller – with its dark view of human nature and satisfyingly twisty plot – is one of the most entertaining films ever made about the political process.

George Clooney has directed four films so far, and *The Ides of March* is by far his best. That's not to say it will be his most critically acclaimed or commercially successful. Most reviewers admired his *Good Night, And Good Luck* more than I did, and took at face value his reverential, not entirely accurate portrait of liberal broadcaster Edward D. Murrow. *The Ides of March* is a more world-weary and fearlessly realistic film, and the most persuasive account yet of working inside politics.

The anti-hero is Stephen Meyers (Ryan Gosling), idealistic thirty year-old press secretary to an attractive, left-wing Democrat Presidential hopeful, Pennsylvania governor Mike Morris (Clooney). Stephen is second-in-command in the whole campaign to likeable, paunchy, chain-smoking veteran Paul Zara (Philip Seymour Hoffman).

Stephen's on the way up, and that attracts a beautiful young intern (Evan Rachel Wood), for whom power is evidently an aphrodisiac.

A different kind of temptation arrives in the seedy form of rival campaign manager Tom Duffy (Paul Giamatti), who offers Stephen a job in the team of the other Democrat candidate, Senator Pullman (Michael Mantell).

Pullman's more conservative politics don't appeal to Stephen, and he tells his boss, Paul, about the approach. Somehow news of the offer reaches a New York Times journalist (Marisa Tomei).

Suddenly, Stephen's future doesn't look so bright. Paul lectures him on disloyalty and fires him. The job offer that seemed so certain fails to materialise. Has this naïve young man been outwitted?

It would be unfair to reveal the bargaining card that could save Stephen's career, though anyone familiar with the history of Democrat candidates Bill Clinton and John Edwards may be able to hazard an educated guess.

The film is based on a stage play, *Farragut North* by Beau Willimon, but you'd never know it. Clooney and his co-writers Grant Heslov and Willimon (who spent part of his twenties working for Hillary Clinton), have cleverly opened it up and made flesh a character who was offstage in the play but here plays a pivotal role: that's the candidate played by Clooney himself.

Clooney, like Gosling, is terrific at keeping his real emotions hidden behind a friendly façade. Their big confrontation at the end is all the more effective for being understated. Both are splendid here. The showiest performance is Hoffman's, though Giamatti's memorable demonstration of ratlike cunning steals every scene he's in.

The film has plenty to say about the dirty compromises of politics, and it's applicable to either American party, and indeed all major parties on this side of the Atlantic. Every aspiring politician should see it, if only as a warning.

The title may suggest the assassination of Julius Caesar,

but this film is more about the death of integrity, or at any rate the extent to which perfect integrity is unsustainable in an imperfect world.

At first sight, the suave sophistication of this film could easily be mistaken for facile cynicism. Okay, it's sceptical, but through that scepticism it discovers some uncomfortable truths, among them the familiar but accurate axiom that politics is, first and foremost, about acquiring power. Although the dialogue is so sparky it might easily have been written by Aaron Sorkin (responsible for *The Social Network* and TV's *The West Wing*), it's the noir atmosphere and moral choices facing the anti-hero that really grip.

The darkening mood is brilliantly captured by Phedon Papamichael's widescreen cinematography, with nods to *All The President's Men* and *In Cold Blood*. In its maturity and refusal to bend to sentimentality, it is closest in feel to Alexander Mackendrick's great *film noir* about the misuse of media power, *The Sweet Smell of Success* – now universally considered a classic but, on release, a commercial flop.

IL POSTINO *(1995)*

A simple postman (Massimo Troisi) feels out of place on his dead-end Italian island full of uncommunicative illiterates. He becomes doggedly devoted to the exiled Chilean poet Pablo Neruda (Philippe Noiret), mainly in the hope that by cultivating a more "poetic" temperament he may be able to win the affections of the proud, sulky beauty in the local bar (Maria Grazia Cucinotta).

This marvellous film is a reminder of how good European movies can be, and is for anyone who prizes honest sentiment above phoney sentimentality. The events may owe something to *Educating Rita* and *Cyrano de Bergerac*, but have a magic all of their own. Excellent writing and wonderful performances neatly avoid the danger of patronising the central character, or his community of fisherfolk.

The film is about the postman rather than Neruda, but the great French actor Philippe Noiret gives a memorable impression of a a Socialist who doesn't care much for human society – a civilised man coping uneasily with celebrity, wishing for privacy, but responding to friendship. The rest of the supporting cast is no less superb.

But the central performance is the one to relish and remember, a miraculous combination of comic technique with emotional honesty. The film was a labour of love for its

Italian star, who refused a heart transplant so that the film could go ahead, and died of heart failure the day after filming finished. Ten thousand people attended his funeral in Naples, and *Il Postino* offers conclusive evidence that 41 year-old Massimo Troisi was a great actor.

This touching testament to the power of art, words and friendship has been beautifully directed by a Briton, Michael Radford. It is in a different class from anything he has directed before – *Another Time Another Place, 1984* and *White Mischief.* It is as though the Italian sun has burned away all his miserablist, Anglo-Saxon tendencies.

Because of Noiret's presence and its power to jerk the audience's tears, it will inevitably be compared to *Cinema Paradiso*, but I would argue that this film is superior, for it never runs out of steam and has an underlying toughness.

Il Postino is among the most beautiful, life-affirming romantic comedy-dramas of recent years in any language, and it would be difficult for anyone to see it and not emerge with a rosy glow of affection for humanity. Treat yourself to this, and you'll feel as if you've been on a gorgeous Summer holiday.

THE INCREDIBLES *(2004)*

Pixar's previous animated hits include such gems as *Toy Story* and *Finding Nemo*. *The Incredibles* is not as good. It's even better, and in years to come I suspect it will be regarded as Pixar's masterpiece. For grown-ups, it's a highly intelligent, wonderfully witty satire on modern society. But for almost every age, it's a very funny comedy and thrillingly entertaining adventure (though it may be too loud and frightening for the very young). It raises animated film to a whole new level.

A bald recounting of the plot might suggest that this is just another Superhero saga torn from a Marvel comic. Its premise echoes films such as *X-Men* and *Spider-Man*, and indeed the *Watchmen* series of graphic novels. But it's funnier and more ingenious than any of them.

Bob Parr (voiced by Craig T. Nelson) is an old-fashioned, square-jawed, all-American super-hero who enjoys nothing more than to put on his Mr. Incredible tights and mask, and perform daring deeds to save the world. But a series of expensive lawsuits brought by disgruntled citizens and frustrated suicides who abhor his can-do, pro-life behaviour, turns the public against him and his kind.

So he and his super-hero wife Elastigirl (Holly Hunter) are reassimilated into society via a Superhero Relocation Program. For 15 years they try to pass as a normal couple with their three children. Bob squeezes himself into a small cubicle at the office where he works unhappily for a mean-minded insurance company. Then he crams himself into an even smaller car to drive home, where he plays the role of any suburban dad, patching up rows between his children, humouring his wife and going for Wednesday nights out with his best friend Frozone (Samuel L. Jackson), doing good in surreptitious ways that their respective wives know nothing about.

But one day Bob loses his desk job, and a glamorous young lady (Elizabeth Pena) offers him the chance to return to Superhero duties; but he's walking into a trap. A new super-villain Syndrome (voiced by Jason Lee) has secretly killed off many of the surviving superheroes around the world, and now he is targeting Bob and his family.

The second half of the movie changes tone. As the hilarious Bond-pastiche score by Michael Giacchino emphasises, it becomes more of an action movie, while retaining a sense of humour and making use of effects that only animated characters could possibly achieve.

A few American critics have lambasted the second half for being violent, and it's true that when the Incredible family fights back in self-defence, it does indeed fight.

When the bad guy sends a deadly plane flying into Manhattan (the 9/11 symbolism could hardly be more explicit), the message is clear: you can't negotiate with such people, you have to defeat them. The heroes of this movie are not called The Empathisers or The Peacemakers, and the film will undoubtedly be seen as a Bush-era movie par excellence.

But commentators who castigate the movie as pro-Bush are missing a number of points. For a start, the film's writer-director, Brad Bird, is politically left of centre. His work on

The Simpsons betrays an irreverent approach to the US Establishment, and his last cartoon, *The Iron Giant* (1999) wore its left-wing prejudices on its sleeve.

The argument of *The Iron Giant*, which was popular with critics but failed to endear it to a mass audience, followed the Michael Moore-Oliver Stone line that the military-industrial complex is bad, and environmentalists, peace campaigners and anti-hunt lobbyists are good.

The Incredibles suggests that Bird has either changed his mind, or reassessed the political and social climate, and come up with a film that far more accurately reflects the conservative spirit of our age.

Key to his new film's success is the way it taps deep into our notions of what life, especially family life, should be about. In the old days, family films celebrated the all-powerful rule of Dad – but that's not the case here. Mr Incredible may be the breadwinner; but Mrs I is the one who has to stretch herself in all directions to meet her family's needs, like a domesticated version of the super-flexible Elastigirl she once was. And she's the one who works hardest to keep her family safe, by ensuring that their superheroic attributes remain under wraps.

Brad Bird's most brilliant idea is to make the Incredible family both super-heroic and archetypal. Violet Incredible is a typical teenage girl, hiding from the world behind her hair and, although she isn't allowed to use her superhero power of invisibility, like many teenage girls she feels so under-appreciated as to be invisible.

Her younger brother, Dash, is a mass of suppressed energy but isn't allowed to show off his superheroic power of speed, because that would make him "different". So he's barred from the very thing he's best at: athletics.

As for the seemingly angelic baby Jack-Jack, his superhero powers remain a mystery until the end of the film, when he too joins in to save the day.

So the movie celebrates the traditional family unit, but recognises the mother as equal partner, and points out that even the children in a family have responsibilities.

It departs from the Hollywood norm by laying unfashionable emphasis on the sanctity of marriage. Mr and Mrs Incredible live by their vow in church to be together until death do them part. And for their children, the strength of their parent's marriage is central. At one point, young Violet inspires her younger brother with the words "Mom and dad's lives could be in danger – or, worse, their marriage!"

The film also embraces the truth, unpalatable to so many on the Left, that intelligent conservatism can be more progressive than left-wing dogma. The Incredible family suffers from an unthinking egalitarianism in society that results in blandness, mediocrity and a system that rewards failure, undervalues success and won't allow people to be the best they can be. It's rather a good metaphor for Tony Blair's Britain.

When Mrs Incredible pays dutiful lip service to prevailing notions of equality by saying "The world just wants us to fit in", young Dash grumbles "Dad says our powers make us special."

"Everyone is special, Dash." Mom chides him.

"Which is another way of saying nobody is!" replies Dash. He has a point.

So no wonder that this extremely entertaining movie is going to drive some po-faced, liberal commentators into paroxysms of rage. Actually, they're wrong to label it as reactionary – it celebrates racial tolerance, compassion and social activism, among other values too frequently commandeered by the Left.

Where the movie is daringly conservative is that it isn't afraid to champion the importance of competitive sports and the right to self-defence, and it acknowledges the idiocy of pretending that everyone is equal. It espouses Christian values, whether or not you happen to believe in God, and it sensitively updates the idea of family to the 21st century. Not bad going for a kids' movie.

INDEPENDENCE DAY *(1996)*

Aliens invade Earth. Humans – under American leadership, naturally – band together to defeat them.

Director Roland Emmerich applies Nineties technology – super 35mm film, computer graphics and state-of-the-art model work – to a classic, mythic storyline (people meet aliens, aliens destroy people, people destroy aliens). The result is spectacle, sensation and entertainment on an epic scale – the greatest of great fun. No wonder it broke American box office records: it is one of the best action-adventures of all time.

The screenplay, by Emmerich and Dean Devlin, is as funny as it exciting, and expertly interweaves a multitude of characters. It proves – even more than Emmerich's two previous successes, *Stargate* and *Universal Soldier* – that if you're going to steal from other film-makers, you may as well do so on a massive scale.

The movie will appeal to every age group because it plunders films from so many eras: Forties war movies where everyone learns to pull together for the common good, those Fifties B-movies which encoded fear of foreigners and their sinister beliefs into a terror of monsters from outer space, and Seventies disaster movies which first created a gallery of stereotypical characters and then gleefully set about slaughtering them. Most of all, though, it's an affectionate hommage and cynical counterblast to the childlike optimism of Spielberg's *Close Encounters* and *E.T.*

All this shameless pilfering is done with such wit and panache (there's even a tongue-in-cheek parody of Henry V's speech to his troops before Agincourt) that you can only admire the film-makers' cheek. The plot may beg any number of logical questions, but it moves so fast that it becomes a duty and a pleasure to suspend your disbelief.

The special effects are astonishing, and include the wholesale destruction of Los Angeles, Washington and New York. *Independence Day* must have the highest bodycount of any film in the history of cinema, so it's a tribute to its makers that the film doesn't trivialise death and suffering. Every so often, we are brought up short by the real terror and pain which such events would create.

That we become involved emotionally – and, even in the sedate circumstances of a press screening, whoop as characters and even dogs are delivered from Armageddon – is a tribute to the actors who, as is inevitable in the action-adventure genre, have to construct living characters out of skeletal dialogue.

There's somebody for everyone to identify with. I empathised most with the peace-loving family-man who also happens to be the US President (Bill Pullman), but others will go for the cocky but charming black fighter-pilot (Will Smith), the apparently clapped-out Vietnam veteran (Randy Quaid), the Jewish computer genius (Jeff Goldblum) or their various womenfolk.

Even though the characters are unashamedly flippant variations on familiar stereotypes, *Independence Day* does touch emotions deep within our psyche. It taps, very entertainingly, into our suspicion of government secrecy and into the fear (or hope) that there is something "out there", which are bound to be encouraged by those recent discoveries about Mars. In some ways, it resembles a wildly ambitious episode of *The X-Files*.

Like *Apollo 13* and *Forrest Gump*, it appeals to Americans to unite in spite of their differences. The device of an alien aggressor is, of course, a transparent ploy to avoid antagonizing interest groups, but it works.

It won't win friends on the Left. The view of international politics is as "gung ho" as in any classic British war movie, and the film invents an uncomplicated world where other countries are eager for America to give a moral and military lead against terrorism (no bickering here over investment in Cuba, Libya or Iran).

Nostalgic references are made to the Gulf War, and there's a determination that this time round, the aggressor won't live to fight another day.

The film puts forward highly conservative images of masculinity and femininity which may not appeal to the chattering classes, but will to the vast majority of moviegoers. The young black man (Will Smith) has to learn the value of commitment and marry his girl-friend (Vivica Fox) before he can fly off to confront the enemy.

The Jewish "save the world" eco-freak (Jeff Goldblum) who was not ambitious enough for his career-woman ex-wife (Margaret Colin) learns to become supremely ambitious – convinced that only his brainwave can save the world.

The President (Bill Pullman) who, like so many western leaders, has acquired a reputation as a wimp, steels himself to order a nuclear attack on the aliens, then goes up there himself – he's a retired fighter-pilot – to finish the job.

The apparently worthless drunk (Randy Quaid) redeems himself by wreaking explosive revenge on aliens who, he claims (though no one believed him until they started blowing up the White House), sexually abused him when they kidnapped him ten years earlier.

In short, all four leading men in the movie learn the value of commitment, ambition, aggressive leadership and hatred of deviants.

Symptomatic of the film's politics are the facts that the one homosexual in the film (Harvey Fierstein) is used for light relief and dispatched early; that the one woman who disobeys her man (a Hillary Clintonesque First Lady, played by Mary McDonnell) pays dearly; and the dippy hippies who welcome the aliens by dancing with welcome signs on a skyscraper are among the first to be torched.

Independence Day is a film you must see in the cinema. It's easily the most enjoyable piece of sci-fi escapism since *Star Wars*, but also fascinating on a deeper level, as one of the most outrageously and entertainingly conservative works of modern cinema – Leftist wishful thinking is blown to smithereens in a series of apocalyptic explosions. The anti-terrorism message is clear: give war a chance.

ISN'T SHE GREAT? *(1999)*

This hugely underrated film is a humorous biography of Jacqueline Susann. She achieved notoriety and enormous wealth as the author of *Valley of the Dolls*, a soft-porn blockbuster of the Sixties about pill-popping actresses in Hollywood.

Isn't She Great celebrates Susann as a trashy optimist, and Bette Midler plays her with the same bravura dynamism she brought to the musical film of *Gypsy*. It's a marvellously vituperative satire on Hollywood's own prevailing values and bad taste. Depressingly, few of the American critics or members of the public seemed to get the joke.

The ironic aspect of Susann's ambition is that she desires not to write a work of literature, but to be famous. "I need mass love," she announces. But for much of the film she has to make do with the doglike devotion of her husband/agent, Irving Mansfield, superbly played by Nathan Lane without a hint of condescension to the fact that he is playing one of the scummier examples of pondlife.

When Irving ploughs through to the end of her first, near-illiterate manuscript, the failed actress Susann is a twittering mass of insecurities, not so much an authoress as an actress playing an authoress: "You think it's like... a book that could win an Oscar?" she asks. And he, like a true agent, beams at her and nods: "It's like *Gone With The Wind*. Only filthy!"

There is a wonderfully funny supporting performance from Stockard Channing as the egotistical, hard-drinking actress who is Susann's best friend and encourages her to write. "Fame can happen to you!" she assures her, based on her own knowledge of Hollywood. "Talent isn't everything!"

And she has a great line when helping Susann's husband select a necklace for his wife: "If a man bought me those pearls, not only would I have sex with him – I'd enjoy it!"

David Hyde Pierce, best known as Frasier's brother, is enjoyably starchy and disapproving as Susann's reluctant editor. "It's salacious, perverted, soft-core porn!" he splutters at his publisher boss (John Cleese). "Can we put that on the cover?" comes the reply.

The film works best as a sequence of uproarious comedy sketches, shot in the Sixties style by Andrew Bergman (who made *Honeymoon in Vegas* and co-wrote *Blazing Saddles*). But Paul Rudnick's sharp, cynical script – he wrote the enjoyable comedy *In and Out*, starring Kevin Kline – also hints at why Susann and her husband pursued fame and wealth so relentlessly.

There is something pathetic, bordering on the tragic, when you see the same incorrigible optimism they brought to marketing her books applied to their depressingly autistic son and the breast cancer which eventually killed her in her fifties.

Rather like another brilliant flop, *Ed Wood*, the film celebrates the "can do" mentality against all the odds, and portrays the crass, sleazy side of American entertainment with real affection.

This is an unashamed yet tongue-in-cheek glorification

of lewdness, self-publicity, materialism, marketing and lots of other things that it is politically incorrect to like. It is not fashionable to admire people like Susann and her husband, least of all in critical circles.

Jacqueline Susann's writing may have been trashy and her influence on popular culture far from beneficial; but she was refreshingly truthful about many things that hitherto couldn't be said in books. *Valley of the Dolls* was the *Bridget Jones' Diary* of its day, capturing a mood about women of its decade, and this film shows her bravery in forging ahead when everything was against her.

Isn't She Great is boldly determined to look on the bright side of her life. As her husband says at the end. "She never got the breaks, so she made her own. You gotta love that". Well, I did. This is a funny and perversely inspiring movie, insufficiently appreciated.

JERRY MAGUIRE
(1996)

Jerry Maguire (Tom Cruise) is a master of his own particular universe. He's a top sports agent, a ruthless hustler with a seductive smile and no time for intimacy or family. He has a gorgeous, sexy fiancee (Kelly Preston) who is even harder than he is. Jerry subscribes to the tough-guy philosophy expounded by Gordon Gekko in Wall Street, that "greed is good". He adds to this a scary degree of personal commitment. "I will kill for you, I will maim for you!" he roars down the phone at clients. "I will rape and pillage for you!" Jerry is, in short, a nasty, glib, superficial jerk.

Then, in a lonely hotel room, he has a long, darkish night of the soul and pens a memo to his colleagues at Sports Management International, about the need to be kinder, more caring, less obsessed with making money. It's such a grand, moralising document that Jerry doesn't even call it a memo: it's a "mission statement".

The next day, his colleagues applaud the height and breadth of his vision, smile encouragingly, and predict behind his back that he'll be fired within a week. Sure enough, he's axed by a young turk (Jay Mohr) who's learnt his callous methods from the old Jerry – including the idea of firing him in a crowded restaurant, where he won't make too much of a scene.

Jerry's insincere loyalty to his clients is duly repaid, when all but one leave him. The one who doesn't is his most hopeless, least idealistic client: a black American football-player called Rod Tidwell (Cuba Gooding, Jr). Rod is nearing the end of his career, and has "attitude problems" which make him unpopular with fellow-players and spectators alike. Rod's wife (Regina King) is even greedier for instant cash. "Show me the money!" is their catch-phrase.

The one bright spot on Jerry's horizon, and the only employee of the sports agency who's loyal to him, is Dorothy (Renee Zellweger) an accountant who's a single mother of a cute five year-old (Jonathan Lipnicki). She admires Jerry's memo and the way he's trying to turn his life around: "I love him for the man he almost is," she confides to her co-habiting sister (Bonnie Hunt), who's divorced, cynical and runs a self-help group for women who have been through lots of relationships with creeps like Jerry.

Cameron Crowe's Oscar-nominated comedy is a strange film, and some people won't like it at all. It's over two hours – long for a romantic comedy – and Crowe crams in so much incidental detail that the shape of the central love story sometimes gets lost. The characters lack the instant likeability of those in Crowe's underrated *Singles*.

A lot of people will sit through the satirical, early scenes and expect Crowe to make an overt, anti-Capitalist statement. But although the film captures more cleverly than any recent film the ruthlessness of corporate America, he doesn't condemn it out of hand. Crowe doesn't like the hypocrisy of the people who stab Jerry in the back, but he accepts it as a fact of life. How could he not? Hollywood is full of it.

Many British people may find it hard to believe that people as awful as Jerry and his colleagues exist; but they do, and Crowe knows that they are part of the reason why America has a successful economy. Jerry doesn't whinge when he's branded a loser, nor does he start campaigning for higher welfare benefits. He fights back – and makes himself a better person, in doing so.

This is all very American, very "can-do", and it will put many non-American people's teeth on edge. But Crowe slips in a subtle point: that business success and failure owe as much to luck, as they do to skill and determination. The plot turns upon an accident to Jerry's one and only client, and for several moments the fate of everybody we care about in the movie is beyond anyone's control, including Jerry's. It's a reminder of how cruel and arbitrary jungle capitalism can be.

Tom Cruise moves through the film at hurricane force. Watching him here in his finest performance, you can realise why the word "star" is appropriate about some actors: he radiates a superhuman energy.

Most good screen actors thrive by having faces which show every emotion. Cruise is more physical, using his whole body like the old silent comedians, and his face here is a series of dazzling masks. It's fascinating to watch them gradually being peeled away, to reveal first a wistful vulnerability, then a fearful reserve, and finally a dawning emotional maturity.

It's a sensational piece of acting, and Crowe surrounds Cruise with enjoyable and unpredictable subsidiary characters. Cuba Gooding Jr is the only other actor to be rewarded with an Oscar nomination, but there are lovely performances from Renee Zellweger, Jonathan Lipnicki as her small son, and Bonnie Hunt as the kind of aggressively frank woman who prefaces her most cutting remarks with "I'm not going to say anything..."

Parts of the movie smack of conventional, cute comedy; but Crowe – who used to be a reporter on Rolling Stone magazine – retains a journalistic eye, and much of the talk and observation feels first-hand, not filtered through other movies. Crowe shows the world of businessmen with a clear-sighted attitude to what's right, as well as wrong, with them; he is both affectionate towards agents and appalled by them, much as Howard Hawks was by journalists in *His Girl Friday*, or Budd Schulberg was by producers in his great novel about Hollywood, *What Makes Sammy Run?*

It is that unresolved tension between cynicism and sentiment that makes *Jerry Maguire* a landmark picture about money and masculinity, not just another lightweight romance from Tinseltown.

JURASSIC PARK *(1993)*

Here's a valuable memo to Hollywood that summer blockbusters don't have to be stupid.

The hero (Sam Neill) is a dinosaur expert, a man who loves digging for fossils, and – like Robin Williams in *Hook* – is unsympathetic to children: "They're noisy, they're messy, they're expensive, they smell!" He and his botanist girl-friend (Laura Dern) are invited to pass judgment on a very unusual, secret theme park, built on an island by Hammond (Richard Attenborough), a Scottish entrepreneur.

On their first ride around it, they are accompanied by Gennaro (Martin Ferrero) who represents Hammond's investors, a sceptical mathematician (Jeff Goldblum) and Hammond's grandchildren (Joseph Mazzello and Ariana Richards).

Unfortunately, one of Hammond's employees (Wayne Knight) has, from motives of greed, decided to smuggle dinosaur embryos off the island. His treachery – together with a tropical storm – triggers off events which leave Neill and the two children stranded within inches of a Tyrannosaurus Rex, and everyone else in the park in jeopardy from other kinds of dinosaur, including Velociraptors – smaller, more mobile and intelligent carnivores.

From this description, you might be forgiven for thinking that *Jurassic Park* is just another Monster Movie – but

Spielberg's come a long way from the primitive mechanical shark he used to scare the trunks off us in *Jaws*. The dinosaurs here are wonderfully lifelike and used so three-dimensionally that you can see the interaction between real and artificial characters. They were the best special effects since another Spielberg production, *Who Framed Roger Rabbit?*

But really outstanding Monster Movies (such as *King Kong*) turn their monsters into more than mobile special effects. In *Jurassic Park*, Spielberg makes them individuals: he seems at first to be making a facile distinction between "goodie" dinosaurs (vegetarians) and "baddies" (the flesh-eaters), but the climax of the film entertainingly subverts that distinction, and proves that (as Neill observes) "they're animals – they do what they do", unfettered by human notions of right or wrong.

Through a series of telling visual images, Spielberg makes clear – as Neill and the children are nearly killed by a falling car, an electrified perimeter fence, a failed computer system – that the real monster is the modern technology which created the dinosaurs but is now out of control.

Nor is this just another Mad Scientist movie. The genetic engineers in this film are mere subordinates of Hammond, and he's a fundamentally well-meaning man whose aim is not to dominate the world, or even make a lot of money, but to entertain: he's a flea-circus proprietor who's bitten off more than he can chew. It would be easy to be cruel about Attenborough's performance – his Scottish accent comes and goes – but he endows the character with a warmth and visionary enthusiasm that make his character's folly even more chilling.

Most of all, *Jurassic Park* is a terrific action-adventure. Like Hitchcock, Spielberg knows how to build suspense, use humour to ease tension, and shoot heart-stopping action: he's already proved himself a master of the genre with the Indiana Jones trilogy. *Where Jurassic Park* is better than his previous pictures is that here he shows how adventure can change people. Sam Neill learns that he has paternal feelings which he never suspected, and Attenborough discovers the perils of even benevolent totalitarianism.

Action films are all too often "Boy's Own" adventures, but Spielberg has learned from his mistake in *Indiana Jones and The Temple of Doom* and given his female characters more to do. Laura Dern and Ariana Richards are not just screaming damsels in distress: Spielberg doesn't deny their femininity or vulnerability, but he shows that resourcefulness and courage are not exclusively male attributes.

Screenwriters Michael Crichton and David Koepp may have simplified the story of Crichton's best-selling book, but I think they have improved it. They have made it clearer, more dramatic, less lecturing. And they've removed its sadism – which may well have been done to placate a family audience, but also makes it a lot less meretricious.

Just as importantly, they have made the story more humorous. Jeff Goldblum as the sceptical mathematician gives one of his most likeably laid-back performances; the dialogue (though initially indistinct) is always in character and funny at the right, tension-releasing moments. The film even makes some affectionate, satirical sideswipes at Disney's Epcot Center, with its gung-ho attitude towards technology.

Finally, and most surprisingly, it's a Film of Ideas. Spielberg may have simplified Crichton's novel, but he's retained its most interesting concepts: about dinosaurs having much in common with birds, about scientific research falling into the hands of irresponsible commerce, about Chaos

Theory (which holds that life is too complicated ever to be totally controlled). And at a time when the old world order has disintegrated, a film which explains Chaos Theory in terms that a child can understand is extraordinarily well-timed.

One word of warning. This is a scary movie which could give children of any age nightmares. The violence is shocking (we see a man disappearing into a Tyrannosaurus's mouth, and one of the best sight-gags in the film features a disembodied arm), but there's no sadism, less delight in violence and destruction than you'd find in *Tom and Jerry*.

It's very exciting and entertaining, and genuinely a family film. Although the picture makes clear that not all adults are to be trusted, and that even the best have their limitations when faced with a pack of meat-eating dinosaurs, Sam Neill is the kind of father-figure which has often been missing from Spielberg's films. It will leave most children reassured that grown-ups are there to take care of them, and to that extent is less profoundly disturbing than *E.T.*

Jurassic Park won't move you to tears as *E.T.* did: it's a different kind of film. But it combines the best elements of this director's previous successes: the spectacle of *Close Encounters*, the suspense of *Jaws*, the excitement of *Raiders of the Lost Ark*, the wonder of *E.T.* It also contains things I haven't seen in Spielberg before: more of a delight in ideas, a dryer sense of humour, an absence of sentimentality.

THE KIDS ARE ALL RIGHT *(2010)*

Films about the stresses and strains of marriage don't come any better, or more entertaining, than this.

Nic is a workaholic doctor who's the breadwinner of the family, a disciplinarian with his two children, and a little too dependent for relaxation on red wine. He treats Jules, the scatterbrain he's been with for twenty years (that's Julianne Moore, never funnier) in a way that suggests he knows he's a lot brighter and more driven than she is. So she goes off and has an affair.

This could be the template for any number of triangular romances, and a similar premise has been used in everything from screwball comedy to Bergmanesque tragedy, but this time there are striking departures from the norm.

In the first place, Nic is a woman, beautifully played for laughs and pathos by Annette Bening. She's the kind of lesbian who's at ease with her own sexuality, but prickly if anyone challenges her seemingly libertarian, but in reality strictly controlled, universe.

Apart from her sexuality, Nic is comically conventional. She doesn't want her studious, Scrabble-playing daughter (Mia Wasikowska, recently Tim Burton's *Alice in Wonderland*) to risk her life on motor-bikes. Nor does she wish her son (Josh Hutcherson, last seen in *Cirque Du Freak*) to be friends with a yob who probably can't wait for the release next week of *Jackass 3D*.

Like a lot of high-flying males, Nic is privately dismissive of her wife's attempts to make money and attraction to fads, such as organic gardening. After Nic's had a glass or two, make that "publicly dismissive".

Into Nic's tightly controlled life steps a menacing male. That's because her teenage children have contacted their birth father. He's Paul (endearingly played by Mark Ruffalo), an easy-going, hippyish, organic restaurateur who's like an overgrown kid himself.

Superficially, he's anything but threatening. He's a kneejerk liberal who is only momentarily put out when he finds out how his sperm has been used – "I love lesbians!"

He thinks it's cool that his two birth-children want to meet him, and it's even cooler if their mom would like to redesign his garden, and if she wants to have sex with him, hey that's kinda cool too. I mean, it's not going to do any harm, and no one need find out about it, right?

Er, wrong. Needless to say, Paul and Jules's romance comes to light, with painful consequences for everyone concerned.

This film isn't as tough as it might have been. It is not a hard-hitting analysis of the differences between a heterosexual and a homosexual relationship. The children are so well-adjusted to having two mothers that they're arguably a little too good to be true.

The film is supremely uninterested in exploring any problems that same-sex partners might have bringing up children in a predominantly heterosexual society.

On the contrary, the central point of the piece is that a lesbian marriage is uncannily similar to a straight one.

That might strike some people as wishful thinking, and because of the film's raunchiness and relaxed attitude towards pornography, I wouldn't recommend it to, say, Ann Widdecombe.

However, just about anyone else should have a good time. This is that treasurable rarity: a Hollywood film filled with characters who have flaws but are thoroughly likeable and believable.

It is efficiently, unflashily directed by Lisa Cholodenko, and much more emotionally mature than her previous movie, the sudsy *Laurel Canyon*.

Apart from anything else, Ms Cholodenko seems to have grown out of thinking that all repression is bad, and all hedonism harmless. I wouldn't normally drag in directors' private lives, but it may be relevant that she has herself settled down to a monogamous relationship with her female partner, and given birth to a son conceived with the help of a sperm donor.

The piece has been co-written by Cholodenko with the assistance of Stuart Blumberg, a heterosexual who previously wrote *Keeping The Faith*, a refreshingly witty comedy about religion, starring his former roommate at Yale, Edward Norton.

The script has a lovely ear for Los Angeles prattle, as when Jules is trying to excuse her own vagueness ("We just talked *conceptually!*") or Nic is finding the right words to congratulate Jules on her planting ("It's so… *indigenous!*")

It's perceptive about the class nuances that most Hollywood screenwriters miss, or don't like to admit exist, in America. There's a wealth of condescension in Nic's reaction to Paul's news that he dropped out of college – she had chosen him because he was studying international relations

– and her icily polite inquiry "Did you always know you wanted to be in the food services industry?"

The achievement of the film is that it keeps the tone entertainingly light, but not at the expense of emotional depth. It pokes gentle fun at all the characters but makes sure we care about them too. Like the best of Alan Ayckbourn's stage plays, it combines civilised behaviour and good intentions with dark yearnings and unthinking cruelty.

The result is a highly intelligent, observant and compassionate study of modern family life – far more three-dimensional than those films you have to watch through silly spectacles.

Bening and Moore are superb at suggesting a relationship that has lasted over two decades. And the film sensibly emphasises just how much understanding, commitment and forgiveness are required to sustain any long relationship of genuine intimacy.

Liberals have predictably rushed to embrace the picture for its positive view of lesbian motherhood, but I suspect its appeal for mainstream audiences really lies in its underlying conservatism.

This is one of those all too rare Hollywood films where parental duties and children's feelings are given their proper weight, and adult irresponsibility is viewed with a clear and judgmental eye.

At the same time, it's pragmatic and compassionate. This is a moral tale, but with the humanity to acknowledge that we can't all be moral, all of the time.

KING KONG *(2005)*

Peter Jackson's splendid and often moving remake of his favourite monster movie will reward you with magnificent spectacle, terrific action, a droll sense of humour, and cherishable performances, though the 1933 version had one virtue that Jackson hasn't mastered – and that's economy.

The original King Kong ran a pacy 100 minutes. Jackson's version clocks in at around three hours. Whereas his masterpiece *The Lord of the Rings* had a multiplicity of characters and interwoven plotlines that justified its length, *King Kong* is a simple story that feels overextended when produced on this scale.

Any director who is being paid 20 million dollars to direct and is coming off the back of an achievement like *The Lord of the Rings*, is unlikely to find producers who will question his judgment; but Jackson is at fault for allowing too much unnecessary detail to accumulate.

There's an entire subplot about the relationship between a cabin boy (Jamie Bell) and a ship's First Mate (Evan Parke) that fails to do much except slow down the movie. And some of the action sequences, including the famous Empire State Building finale, play just that bit too long. By the end, I was willing the title character to die – and that's not good.

But should you see it? The answer's an emphatic "yes".

Not only are the consistently astonishing special effects worth the price of admission in themselves. Peter Jackson and his usual co-writers Fran Walsh and Philippa Boyens have remained laudably true to the story and spirit of the old movie. They have notably improved its script, fleshing out the central characters and giving them much sharper dialogue.

In Depression-era New York, an out-of-work actress Ann Darrow (delightfully played by Naomi Watts) steals an apple and is rescued from arrest by desperate filmmaker Carl Denham (amusingly portrayed as an irrepressible rascal by Jack Black). He's lost his leading actress for his next film and has to set sail before his producers can cancel his movie, which he wants to set partly in a place that may or may not exist: Skull Island, in the South Seas.

Also on board is an intellectual playwright Jack Driscoll (soulfully played by Adrien Brody), who is writing Denham's movie for ready money that never seems quite to be forthcoming.

When they land on Skull Island, they discover that it is inhabited by distinctly unfriendly natives (no concessions to political correctness here) who worship a mighty ape that lives on the other side of a great wall and abyss. When Ann is sacrificed and abducted by the aforementioned gorilla, Denham and Driscoll lead a search party to get her back.

That's when the adventure part of the movie really starts, interspersed with sweet and lyrical sequences of Kong and Ann finding they have a lot in common, especially a taste for romantic sunsets. The second hour is an amazing succession of exciting set-pieces, including a brontosaurus stampede, an all-in wrestling match between Kong and no fewer than three tyrannosaurus rexes, and some brilliantly choreographed attacks on the rescue party by Skull Island's spectacularly homicidal flora and fauna.

The third hour takes us and Kong to a lovingly recreated 30s New York, which Peter Jackson trashes with every appearance of enjoyment.

Jackson and his team have turned Kong's story into not just a thrilling adventure, but also a moving triangular love story. Watts enlivens her relationship with Kong by making Ann a much funnier, more resourceful and above all less wimpish character than Fay Wray could manage in the original.

The less satisfying love story is between Ann and Jack Driscoll. Until Kong appears, this is handled very sensitively. Afterwards, too much is left unclear. We never really know what Jack's view of Kong is, still less whether Driscoll resents that the woman he loves seems to prefer the amorous advances of a 25-foot gorilla.

King Kong is too long for most children, and probably too frightening for kids under 10. But, for the rest of us, it's a must-see. There is plenty here to entertain and involve us, and the film's a technological marvel.

The dinosaurs featured here may be only a slight improvement on monsters we've already seen in the *Jurassic Park* series. But Jackson's team has allowed its collective imagination to run riot with some memorably unpleasant creepy-crawlies, and Kong himself shows masterly use of the same kind of motion-capture effects used to animate Gollum in *The Lord of the Rings* (Andy Serkis once again plays the performance reference for the character and also has a small role as the ship's cook).

The 1933 Kong varied vastly in size from shot to shot, and the attempts to animate him were jerky and primitive. Thanks to modern special effects and first-rate production values, this most sympathetic of movie monsters has become real, terrifying and touching, all over again.

KING'S GAME/ KONGEKABALE
(2005)

Don't be deterred by the fact that *King's Game* is subtitled and set in modern Denmark. This is the most gripping and accurate depiction yet of the way spinning, leaking and lying to the public have come to dominate democratic politics in Britain.

When the leader of the major Centre Party in Denmark is injured in a car accident a week before a General Election, a power struggle breaks out between his two likely successors, a wily conservative and a reformer who's something of an ice-maiden.

A youngish, inexperienced and apparently ineffectual journalist (Anders W. Berthelsen) who has long lived in the shadow of his successful ex-politician father, is given a scoop by a spin-doctor. This earns our hero the instant glory of a story on the front page of his paper, but his pride is short-lived when he realises that he is being used as part of a smear campaign.

Sensing that something is rotten in the state of Danish politics – and journalism – he has to decide whether to take the sensible option, which is to collude with the power elite of politician, spin doctor, big business and newspaper editor, or expose the truth, which will undoubtedly cost him his job and probably won't have any lasting impact anyway.

Events unfold which bear uncanny similarities to recent shenanigans in the UK, involving Alastair Campbell and the tragically deceased scientist David Kelly. The detail comes across as extremely authentic (it's based on a novel by a former Danish spin-doctor) and it's expertly directed by Nikolaj Arcel.

King's Game is all the more impressive because it's convincingly plotted, avoids melodrama and always gives the devil his due. Every time the hero does something to hurt the establishment, those in power come back at him even more strongly, whether through insidious pressure or skilful character assassination.

Some will call the film cynical, but its power really comes from its underlying idealism. Not only does it wish to show the dirty nitty-gritty of how real politicians operate, it also transmits a sincere rage that the public lets them get away with it.

King's Game is so outstanding – and unique – that it cruelly exposes the lack of films coming out of Britain about the way we are governed, not only nationally but by the European Union.

The reason is, of course, that film-makers are – however unconsciously – reluctant to bite the hand that feeds them, and the vast majority of European film-makers are heavily dependent upon state or EU subsidy.

All credit to the Danes, then, for showing us the way. *King's Game* is an even more thought-provoking thriller about the interface between politics and journalism than *All The President's Men*, almost 30 years ago. Anyone interested in, and repelled by, the Blair regime's dependency upon first Peter Mandelson and then Alastair Campbell should rush to see this before it disappears. For all politicians and political journalists, it's obligatory viewing.

THE KING'S SPEECH *(2010)*

The rumours are true. The superlatives are justified. Colin Firth really does give the performance of his life as the Queen's father, George VI. But his is not the only stellar achievement in a wonderful British film that's certain to challenge America's finest at this year's Oscars.

The story of how the shy, sensitive, unambitious Albert, Duke of York rose above a crippling speech impediment to become King and a focal point of opposition to Hitler is so fascinating that you may end up wondering why on earth it has not been told before in the cinema.

Wisely, screenwriter David Seidler has chosen to centre the narrative on the unlikely friendship between the stuffy, frustrated Albert — or Bertie as he was known to his family — and the laid-back but autocratic Australian speech therapist Lionel Logue (Geoffrey Rush), whose less than deferential methods might have been calculated to make any royal's hackles rise.

"My castle, my rules," Logue loftily informs the future king, at the start of their long and far from untroubled relationship.

The sensationally well-played scenes between these two fine actors would be enough on their own to make the film a delight, but they are assisted by a supporting cast that must be among the best in the history of cinema.

Proving once again that in the right role she is an actress of genius, Helena Bonham Carter is certain of at least an Oscar nomination as the late Queen Mother, Bertie's loving, supportive and, when she needs to be, formidable wife.

She reluctantly takes on the mantle of monarchy when she would much prefer to have been just a wife and mother, and scarcely bothers to conceal her contempt for Wallis Simpson (played with a commendable lack of warmth by Eve Best) and Edward VIII, masterfully acted by Guy Pearce as weak, selfish and petulant.

Important cameos are supplied by Michael Gambon as Bertie's ferocious father George V, Timothy Spall as a sympathetic Winston Churchill and Derek Jacobi as a spikily officious Archbishop of Canterbury.

As Logue's wife, Jennifer Ehle (who last played opposite Firth in the *BBC's Pride And Prejudice*, and deserves to be on the big screen more often than she is) is terrific in a scene where she finds herself unexpectedly playing hostess to an unannounced home visit from the King and Queen.

As in his previous film about Brian Clough, *The Damned United*, director Tom Hooper trusts his actors to do much of the work, but he knows where to place his camera, when to move it, and when to keep still. Danny Cohen's cinematography is also quietly impressive, whether he is giving us grand occasions or intimate moments.

One of the most commendable aspects of the piece is that it doesn't over-dramatise. There is no miracle cure for Bertie's stammer. The friendship between the future King and his therapist never becomes sentimental. The story is all the more charming, moving and realistic for its restraint.

But this is, above all, the film for which Colin Firth will be remembered. It's no stretch for him to play a cold, stuffy

Englishman, but he's wonderfully complex as this reluctant monarch: tetchy, insecure, dutiful but resentful of duty at the same time. It's a technical *tour de force*, and tremendously raw and touching in its vulnerability.

Firth gave a sensational, low-key performance last year in *A Single Man*, but that film was never likely to be popular enough to win him more than a nomination as Best Actor at the Oscars. This one certainly is.

L.A. CONFIDENTIAL (1997)

Three L.A. police detectives find themselves investigating different crimes – a wave of gangland assassinations, a prostitution racket, a seemingly senseless massacre in a cafe – which ultimately lead to the same criminal.

It's a tough, detective thriller set in Los Angeles during the 1950s, so it was always bound to be compared with the Roman Polanski/ Jack Nicholson classic, *Chinatown*; but *L. A. Confidential* is even more stylish and gripping. And with three detective anti-heroes instead of just one, there's a lot more suspense about which, if any, is going to survive to the end of the picture.

The most obviously heroic of the three cops is Ed Exley (Guy Pearce), a crusading moralist and by-the-book prig who's cordially disliked by his fellow-officers. Pearce, the young Australian actor from *Neighbours* and *Priscilla, Queen of the Desert*, is wonderfully subtle and sympathetic as a humourless careerist who's scarcely aware of how lonely he is.

Then there's the defiantly unheroic Jack Vincennes (played by the excellent Kevin Spacey) a glib cynic who dresses smartly and enjoys the glamour of being technical advisor to a TV series, *Badge of Honor*, which presents an unrealistically rosy-tinted view of American law-enforcement.

Jack is less interested in justice than in receiving backhanders from a sleazy magazine editor (Danny De Vito, dependable as ever) who derives a voyeuristic kick from exposing the sordid side of Hollywood life.

And there's Bud White (played by New Zealander Russell Crowe) who is none too bright, unscrupulous when it comes to planting evidence on anyone he thinks is guilty, and given to brutal, pathological rages whenever he encounters violence against women.

The course of their investigation, immaculately adapted by Brian Helgeland and Curtis Hanson from the novel by James Ellroy (and greatly improved), does require effort to follow; but it is entirely logical, and I won't spoil your enjoyment by revealing more. There are plenty of shocks and nasty surprises, with an extremely thrilling show-down, as the forces of darkness are confronted by – well, the forces of a slightly less murky grey.

The astonishing cinematography is the best work yet by Dante Spinotti, whose credits already include *The Last of the Mohicans* and *Heat*. Though shot in colour, *L.A. Confidential* looks and feels like classic *film noir*, with shadowy lighting, very dark deeds and the obligatory femme fatale in the voluptuous form of Kim Basinger.

Spiritually, though, this is less a *film noir* – concerned with revealing the dark side of humanity – than a *film gris*. It takes the darkness of the world as its starting point, and gradually becomes more generous-spirited, as it investigates how, despite their squalid moral environment, most people do try to retain a measure of self-respect and find some form of personal salvation. Unlike traditional *film noir*, *L.A. Confidential* does, in the words of its Johnny Mercer theme tune, "Accent-tchu-ate the Positive."

The film's preoccupation with redeeming oneself through professionalism is similar to that which lay beneath Quentin Tarantino's *Pulp Fiction*; but it's a theme which has run through many of the great Hollywood movies about men, from Howard Hawks's *The Dawn Patrol* to Michael Mann's *Heat*.

Oddly enough in so male-dominated a movie, the actor most likely to win an Oscar is a woman. Kim Basinger is not only glamorous enough to convince as a high-class Hollwood call-girl, she manages to communicate an innate decency and perceptiveness about men that might enable such a person to endure the humiliations of her profession.

The rest of the cast (especially David Strathairn and James Cromwell) could hardly be better, and Curtis Hanson – long a polished director of impersonal films like *The River Wild* and *The Hand That Rocks the Cradle* – is so assured as to put one in mind of other great directors who chose to operate within the Hollywood system, like Howard Hawks and Michael Curtiz.

Just as modern Chinese directors often make period pictures which talk in coded terms about their own time, Hanson has made no cosy costume drama. His portrait of a racist, sadistic, profoundly corrupt Police Department has strikingly modern resonances, and not only in America. The movie exposes an exploitative, drugs-ridden, hypocritical side of the entertainment industry which still exists, and which West Coast film-makers are not usually keen to publicise.

There is plenty of brutality and revolting behaviour on display, and parts of this movie are as gruesome as anything in the best thriller of last year, *Se7en*. If you can cope with that (and a half-happy ending that savours of studio intervention), *L. A. Confidential* is a film that can be recommended with confidence. It's a detective movie on a par with such acknowledged classics as *The Big Sleep*. I think it's one of the best films Hollywood has ever produced.

LES MISERABLES *(2012)*

They dreamed a dream, and now it's come true. It's been a long time coming – 27 years since it opened in London – but it's worth the wait. This is a wonderful movie, an all-time-great musical. It's guaranteed – despite its title – to raise your spirits, as well as make you cry.

Superbly directed, brilliantly acted and sung with unprecedented emotional depth, this is a magnificent tribute to Working Title and Cameron Mackintosh, who produced it. It isn't just the most ambitious British film of all time, it's one of the finest.

Victor Hugo's classic story is about a prisoner Jean Valjean (Hugh Jackman) consumed by hatred after serving twenty years in prison for a pitifully minor offence – stealing a loaf of bread to feed his sister's starving child. He breaks his parole and is pursued by a remarkably determined lawman, Javert (Russell Crowe), who believes no criminal can ever reform.

Yet, reform Valjean does. Inspired by the gift of church silver from a bishop he was stealing from (a lovely cameo from Colm Wilkinson, who played Valjean in the original London production), Valjean becomes a factory-owner and mayor of a French town, and surrogate father to Cosette (Isabelle Allen), the orphaned daughter of Fantine (Anne

Hathaway), one of Valjean's factory workers who falls on hard times and turns to prostitution.

Pursued by the implacable Javert, Valjean flees to Paris, where – years later – the now grown Cosette (Amanda Seyfried) falls in love with a revolutionary student called Marius (Eddie Redmayne) just before he helps man the barricades against the repressive French government of 1832.

Comic relief throughout is provided by the Thenadiers (Sacha Baron Cohen and Helena Bonham Carter, both hilarious), dishonest innkeepers who mistreat the young Cosette as child labour, and then take their enthusiastic brand of thieving to Paris, where their beautiful daughter Eponine (Samantha Barks) falls unrequitedly in love with Marius' student revolutionary.

This is a revolutionary musical in more ways than one. Director Tom Hooper's stylistic masterstroke is to borrow a technique used previously in Peter Boganovich's catastrophic Cole Porter musical, *At Long Last Love*. Hooper's brave choice is not to pre-record his singers, but to record them as they sing on set. This adds hugely to the authenticity and emotional intensity of the singing.

The film does a stunning job of cramming Hugo's novel into just two and a half hours. The original stage version, which ran three and a half, brought out the emotional highlights of the book but felt rushed. Somehow, William Nicholson has made it leaner and speedier, without sacrificing anything important.

Tom Hooper was a brave choice to direct. His first two films, the Brian Clough biopic *The Damned United* and the Oscar-winning *The King's Speech* were excellent films, but offered few clues that he could direct anything on an epic scale.

Ably supported by casting director Nina Gold and a tremendous crew at Pinewood Studios, he succeeds magnificently, and makes marvellous use of cinema's two greatest assets over any other art form: the huge panorama – used with special brilliance in the dream finale – and the close-up.

The piece has much grittier documentary realism than I expected, but it also makes room for imaginative cinematography, sets, costumes and make-up, all of which I expect to see reaping their just rewards at awards ceremonies. The costumes and make-up for the villainous Thenardiers are a particular triumph.

But it is Hooper who deserves to attract rave reviews. Wisely, he goes to the other extreme from most fidgety, fast-cutting directors of modern musicals. He trusts the actors to excel in extended takes, often in intimate close-up, allowing them to build a performance and develop the emotional resonance of Herbert Kretzmer's heartfelt lyrics and Claude-Michel Schonberg's glorious music.

Virtually every song received an ovation at the world premiere, and rightly so. Highlights include Eddie Redmayne's beautiful tenor rendition of *Empty Chairs and Empty Tables*, and Anne Hathaway's raw, astonishingly moving version of *I Had a Dream*. But there isn't a dud song or performance in the film.

Jackman manages the vocally and emotionally challenging role of Valjean with such power and integrity that even Daniel Day-Lewis as Abraham Lincoln may find it hard to beat him to Best Actor at the Academy Awards.

Though the least powerful singer in the cast, Crowe does an impressive job of humanising Javert so that he becomes not a melodramatic villain, but a rounded human capable of redemption. The two scenes where he sings about his feelings are staged by Hooper with high intelligence, as mirror images of each other.

The very mixed reviews for the film will come as no surprise to those who remember that the RSC's original production received even more grudging notices on stage, in 1985. Underlying the antagonistic reviews then were some old-fashioned cultural snobbery about through-composed musicals being intrinsically inferior to opera, a belief that the RSC should be devoting itself to high art rather than populist musicals, and a feeling that *Les Mis* was a fusty period-piece with little relevance to the present day.

I saw the stage show when it was in previews and remember feeling that it did seem a bit old-fashioned. Student-led revolution had been tried and found wanting in 1968, and Trevor Nunn and John Caird's production, though set in 1832, felt like a romantic tribute to a much later group of European revolutionaries, Daniel Cohn-Bendit and his followers. But now, the idea of brave but potentially fatal resistance to authoritarian regimes is topical again, with the Arab Spring and resistance to President Assad in Syria. It packs much more emotional punch.

The stage musical has been seen by more than 60 million people in 42 countries. In its new, spectacularly cinematic form, with this remarkable array of performances, it's going to be seen and enjoyed by even more. I know these are times of austerity but, if necessary, beg for a ticket. Seeing a movie this terrific is a truly thrilling experience.

THE LION KING *(1994)*

Despite accusations of political incorrectness, this roaring success managed to recover its costs of 40 million dollars in its first weekend, and broke the 100 million dollar barrier in under a fortnight. So it's easy to forget that it started as an underdog – Disney's first film to come up from nothing. Unlike every other feature-length success by the studio, it is not based on an established fairy tale, fable or children's book. Instead, the Disney team has tried to produce a late 20th century myth of its own.

By far the most important contributor to the screenplay, which was worked on by at least 20 American writers, is an uncredited Englishman – William Shakespeare. For a start, there's an indecisive, Hamlet-style hero exhorted by the ghost of his murdered father to take revenge on the wicked uncle who has usurped the throne. The villain bears a striking resemblance to Iago in *Othello*, as he skilfully exploits the fears of the hero. And the young lion king makes unsuitable friends but learns his royal duty in much the same way as Prince Hal does in Shakespeare's History Plays. It may seem far-fetched or even pretentious to draw such parallels; but, like all the great Disney cartoons it teaches eternal truths about life and adult responsibility.

It is also very funny. The script is the wittiest ever written for a Disney cartoon, full of wisecracks and quick-fire gags. There may be no single figure as entertaining as Robin Williams's genie in *Aladdin*. Instead, the jokes are shared out liberally among a terrific cast.

Best of all are the two British actors. Jeremy Irons, who voices wicked Uncle Scar, hams it up royally and comes across as sly, smarmy and oddly likeable in his despicability. "Are you weird?" our young hero asks him at one point. "You have... no idea," drawls Irons, in a deliberate echo of his Oscar-winning performance as Claus von Bulow. The Disney animators have wittily used Irons's own facial expressions to add visual nuances to a sensational voice-over tour de force; here's the outstanding Disney villain since Cruella De Vil, way back in *101 Dalmatians*. Also excellent is Rowan Atkinson as Zazu, the Lion King's hornbill major domo.

The film has all that late 20th century sophistication which made *Beauty and the Beast* and *Aladdin* so enjoyable. The ecological message is cleverly balanced; it does not disguise the fact that lions eat antelopes and zebra, but points out that there is a balance to nature, a circle of life, that is disrupted at every creature's peril. The animals are as anthropomorphic as in any Disney cartoon, but more knowingly so.

Artistically, the animators have departed from the Disney norm and gone primitive. *Bambi* used more delicate, Oriental-style backgrounds; *The Lion King* goes for strong shapes and lurid colours, which are exactly right for the African subject-matter. There is marvellous detail in the half-human, half-animal mannerisms of as lively a collection of characters as ever graced a cartoon. The wildebeest stampede and the Nuremberg-rally march past Uncle Scar by the hyenas are great set-pieces of modern cinema.

The film predictably came under fire in America from the Politically Correct lobby. Gay pressure groups objected that Uncle Scar was obviously homosexual – which seems a shade fanciful, since his sexuality is left unclear (if anything, one suspects it might involve doing things too kinky to mention with his goose-stepping hyena friends). Ethnic groups objected that the three hyena muggers (led by Whoopi Goldberg) were racial stereotypes – but ignore the fact that two of the most sympathetic characters are played by black actors James Earl Jones and Robert Guillaume.

More damagingly, a few American parents objected that some passages (notably the first hyena attack and the wildebeest stampede) were too frightening for young children. In fact, the scenes are rather less upsetting than the Wicked Queen's death in *Snow White*, or the shooting of Bambi's mother. Even small children enjoy being pleasurably scared – as long as there is a reassuring grown-up voice to explain things, and an unscary life to return to, afterwards.

LITTLE MISS SUNSHINE *(2006)*

Little Miss Sunshine is a dark but defiantly feelgood comedy about that old Hollywood stand-by, a dysfunctional family. It's the funniest comedy of the year, by many a mile. It's also the most cleverly written – by unknown New York screenwriter Michael Arndt. Though shot on a low budget, it's very smartly directed by husband-and-wife first timers Jonathan Dayton and Valerie Faris, and brilliantly acted by the entire cast, especially Greg Kinnear and Steve Carell.

Kinnear is dad Richard, a peppy and annoyingly optimistic motivational speaker with a 9-step programme that he calls "Refuse to lose". It's too bad Richard hasn't noticed that his programme has only eight steps, and he himself is regarded as a loser by everyone around him, including his patient but stressed-out wife (Toni Collette).

Another reason she is under stress is that she has just offered space in her home to her suicidal brother Frank (Steve Carell). He's in a near-catatonic state, having just lost his gay lover, his academic post and his reputation as America's number one Proust scholar.

Needless to say, as a self-confessed loser who recently tried to slash his own wrists, Frank is extremely depressed by his brother-in-law's gung-ho insistence on winning. It may be just as well Frank is being kept away from sharp objects, or he might try to bury one in Richard's neck.

Frank is forced to share a bedroom with his nephew, 15 year-old Dwayne (Paul Dano), who may be even more depressed than he is. Dwayne wears black, has kept a vow of silence for nine months, and reads the German philosopher Nietzsche. His way of welcoming Uncle Frank to the house is to scrawl on his notepad "Welcome to Hell".

The only apparently normal person in the family, seven year-old Olive (Abigail Breslin) is, despite being a bit podgy, plain and bespectacled, addicted to beauty pageants and inexplicably managed to come second in a local under-10 contest. She is being trained in a new dance routine by her grandpa (Alan Arkin) who may not be her best choice of choreographer, since his main pastime is ogling women who look like strippers, snorting heroin and being thrown out of old people's homes.

The disqualification of the local beauty contest-winner after a diet-pill scandal means that little Olive qualifies at the last moment for the Little Miss Sunshine pageant in California. So the whole family embarks in a battered old Volkswagen camper van to make the trip.

The journey is very funny in itself, and leads up to a beauty pageant that is like everyone's worst nightmare of American competitiveness.

The movie covers some remarkably dark subjects with warmth as well as wit, sensitivity as well as satire. And it makes perceptive points about a culture that is abusive not only of young girls who wish to become beauty queens, but of family life in general.

It makes perceptive points about the modern obsession with winning, and asks pertinently who decides whether we win or not? What if these judges' standards are not our own? And what if, in attempting to win, we lose our sensitivity and respect for ourselves and those around us?

The whole story could be interpreted as an upbeat anthem to loserdom, but the reason I love this movie more than any other I've seen this year is that I think it's more realistic, yet positive, than that. It's a film that recognises the true glory of humanity as lying in our resilience and good humour in the face of our inevitable failures.

THE LIVES OF OTHERS/
DAS LEBEN DER ANDEREN *(2006)*

The Lives of Others won Best Foreign-Language Film at the Oscars – which was a disgrace. If there had been any justice, it should also have won Best Picture, Director, Screenplay and Actor (for Ulrich Muhe). This is by far the most memorable and perfectly crafted movie to have reached us so far in 2007: a classic that I'm sure will still be watched in 50 years time.

It's a very superior thriller and psychological drama, set mainly in 1984, about an East German playwright (Sebastian Koch) who thinks he is well in with the Communist authorities, and anxious to prevent his liberal-leaning theatrical associates from doing anything that might get them into trouble.

But a corpulent East German minister (Thomas Thieme) has eyes for the playwright's sexy girlfriend (Martina Gedeck). The minister wants the playwright out of the way and instructs the splendidly seedy, sweatily obedient Lieutenant Colonel Grubitz (Ulrich Tukur), who's the philistine Head of the Culture Department at State Security, or Stasi, to institute surveillance.

The Stasi operative given the job of bugging the writer's apartment is the stern-faced, hard-line interrogator Gerd

Wiesler (Ulrich Muhe). But the more Wiesler spies on the showbiz couple, the less comfortable he feels. The film traces the tense, moving and dangerous four-way relationship that develops between Grubitz, Wiesler, the playwright and his mistress.

Though clearly indebted to George Orwell's novel *1984* and Francis Ford Coppola's movie *The Conversation*, it's startlingly original. No film has done a better job of exploring the rising terror of retaining one's principles inside a police state.

A hugely talented first-time director, Florian Henckel von Donnersmarck, reproduces the minutiae of Stasi investigation with chilling accuracy. More importantly, though, he shows the effects on the human spirit of life under a repressive regime.

That may sound depressing; but the film-maker finds just enough hope of redemption to make a tragedy that ends up raising the spirit.

It has even been accused of being sentimental about the Stasi, though there is none of the nostalgia for East German Communism that made me uneasy about that highly acclaimed German comedy of 2002, *Good Bye Lenin*. I defy anyone to watch *The Lives of Others* and come away without feelings of the deepest revulsion for the Stasi, and a determination that nothing of its kind must ever happen here.

Apart from this picture's timely message about the need to preserve our liberties, it's gripping because its twists and turns arise from realistic characters, not from some hack writer's adherence to cinematic formula, or from producers' mercenary desire to please undemanding teenage Americans on the first weekend of release.

All the actors are marvellous, but the cadaverous Ulrich Muhe – last seen as Doctor Mengele in Costa-Gavras's undervalued *Amen* – is extraordinary. Almost as extraordinary is the fact that Muhe himself discovered from his Stasi files, released after the fall of the Berlin Wall, that he himself had been under surveillance not only by four of his fellow-actors in Berlin theatre, but also by his wife of six years. When asked about he prepared for the role, Muhe answered "I remembered".

Go and see this movie and you will remember how life felt in East Germany during the 1980s, just as clearly and almost as painfully as if you'd lived there yourself.

LONE STAR (1996)

John Sayles has made an outstanding thriller.

A skull and sheriff's badge are discovered on the land of a Texan military camp. They are the remains of Charley Wade (Kris Kristofferson), a corrupt, racist cop supposedly run out of town 40 years before by legendary lawman Buddy Deeds (Matthew McConaughey). Nowadays, the sheriff is Buddy's son, Sam (Chris Cooper), who lives in the shadow of his charismatic but long dead father, whom Sam remembers as a bully. Investigating the murder becomes Sam's way of getting his own back against Buddy, who is chief suspect.

Lone Star is also a bitter-sweet love story. For Sam is recently divorced, and anxious to remake contact with his Hispanic childhood sweetheart (Elizabeth Pena), from whom he was forcibly separated at the age of 15.

Racial tension is never far beneath the surface. The town has two mayors, one official and white (Clifton James), the other unofficial and black (Ron Canada). Whites are now in a minority, and the various ethnic groups bicker constantly about how historical events like the Alamo should be taught in school.

Lone Star is illuminating, heavenly to look at, and has a host of stellar performances. But it does take its time to get off the ground. The first half-hour introduces so many characters and plot lines that it's easy to feel confused: who are these people? how do they relate to each other? Be patient – this is a movie with riches in store, and all will be revealed.

Set on the border between Texas and Mexico, *Lone Star* is a story about divisions: not only between countries and races, but also between parents and children. It is anything but a parochial film about the Tex-Mex border. It raises issues which are every bit as relevant to the troubles in Northern Ireland or the racial turmoil in Britain's inner cities.

The film goes beyond the political, too, by inviting us to re-examine our deepest feelings about our cultural and family history: do we allow the past to embitter us? to give us pride? to avoid taking personal responsibility for our own lives?

Writer-director John Sayles made his debut with the cult hit, *The Return of the Secaucus Seven* (1981), and he's made decent movies since – romps like *Alligator* (1980) and more thoughtful pieces like *Matewan* (1987) *City of Hope* (1991) and *Passion Fish* (1992) – but this is the movie where he achieved his full potential.

Sayles shifts brilliantly and fluidly between past and present, with a fascinating mixture of nostalgia and scepticism. Cinematographer Stuart Dryburgh does even better work than he did on *The Piano* and *Once Were Warriors*. They shoot their mythical frontier town – Frontera – in mythic fashion. Many images, especially the final one of a deserted movie drive-in, linger in the mind.

Sayles has amassed a fine repertory of actors to work with him over the years; and here, inspired by excellent dialogue and colourful characters, the actors are, without exception, superb – with sensational performances in supporting roles by Joe Morton, Frances McDormand and, perhaps the greatest revelation of all, Kris Kristofferson.

Matthew McConaughey is ideally cast as Buddy, who is rarely on-screen but whose legend suffuses the film. He looks like a taller Paul Newman, more clean-cut and charismatic than anyone in the present day. Buddy's surname – borrowed from the hero of Frank Capra's *Mr Deeds Goes To Town* – hints that he is a symbolic idealization, not only of old, liberal certainties, but also of the days when whites were firmly in the ascendant.

Chris Cooper, an actor usually seen in supporting roles, seizes his chance to prove that he is a thoughtful, sympathetic leading man; Sayles cleverly uses his lack of movie-star good looks, to establish him as a decent, ordinary guy, flawed by envy of his father but also the inheritor of Buddy's ideals about justice.

Lone Star is a shining light in the darkness of modern American cinema, one of only a very few highly intelligent, humane films to be released in 1996. Sayles manages to put across his ideas without a hint of didacticism, with characters who have a life of their own, and a storyline that steadily gathers momentum and power. He interweaves his plot strands with a skill that compares with *Pulp Fiction* and *Four Weddings and a Funeral.*

The final twist is a tremendous storytelling coup: not only a shocking surprise, but a revelation that changes our perception of all that has gone before.

Lone Star was never going to be a commercial hit, but that reflects more on the dwindling attention span of modern audiences than on the film itself. This is a movie masterpiece which will repay seeing again and again. It's an initially demanding but very rewarding film – not to be missed by anyone who enjoys an excellent story, supremely well told.

THE LORD OF THE RINGS:
THE FELLOWSHIP OF THE RING
(2001)

A small, unassuming chap with furry feet goes on a quest to save the world from ugly guys with an unusual taste in costume jewellery.

Peter Jackson's adaptation of J.R.R. Tolkien's classic is as near to perfection as makes no difference. The decision to shoot wholly in New Zealand is inspired. Here is landscape photography of a grandeur and emotional resonance that we haven't witnessed in the cinema since John Ford revolutionised the western, and David Lean took to the desert in *Lawrence of Arabia*.

The movie has a mythic grandeur, and a profound understanding of human corruptibility, that makes the *Star Wars* movies look like kids' stuff. The epic battles and huge set-pieces are as impressive as anything in *Braveheart* or *Gladiator*, but the human dimension is never lost, nor a sense of humour.

The performances are flawless. Tolkien has been accused of writing one-dimensional characters, but the actors give the lie to that. Two of our most talented theatrical knights, Sir Ian McKellen (as Gandalf) and Sir Ian Holm (as Bilbo), are inspired by their roles to give their finest, most multi-faceted performances on film.

It comes as no surprise that Christopher Lee exudes magisterial menace as his rival, Saruman. But actors who have hitherto failed to take the critics by storm – such as Viggo Mortensen as Aragorn and Sean Bean as Boromir – also demonstrate an unexpected degree of nuance and intensity. These are the performances of their lives. Elijah Wood's English accent is excellent, but even more importantly every reaction of his as Frodo, the reluctant hero, seems full of truth and spontaneity.

Although I enjoyed the leading performances in *Harry Potter*, few are in the same class as the ones on offer here. Chris Columbus's film deserved acclaim as a magical experience for children, and solid entertainment for adults. But *The Lord of the Rings* is an altogether higher achievement.

A loving adaptation by Jackson, his wife Fran Walsh, and first-timer Philippa Boyens ensures that, although Tolkien's tale has been shortened (Tom Bombadil, for example, has bitten the dust), not a single major theme has been lost. Diehard Tolkien purists may object that the professor's archaic language has been toned down a little, but this strikes me as justified on grounds of clarity and accessibility. The books are not without their stilted passages and pomposities, and the movie is in some respects an improvement.

The two least Tolkienesque remarks – Gimli's indignant "Nobody tosses a dwarf!" and Aragorn's final cry for revenge "Let's hunt some orc!" – succeed in generating the biggest cheers from the audience, and don't detract from the film's essential grandeur and seriousness.

Even the most boringly obsessive of Tolkien nerds is likely to find little, if anything, to dislike; and even if you didn't care for the Professor's books, you should still thrill to the movie if you have any feeling for myth, narrative, landscape or cinema.

Peter Jackson's direction shows wonderful flair. It is his skill at moving the camera that makes a classic action sequence of the Ringwraiths' chasing on horseback of Arwen and Frodo.

The mines of the ruined dwarf kingdom Moria are awesomely designed to look like cathedrals of stone, but the directorial touch that really makes them stick in the subconscious is to send orcs – misshapen goblins with serious dental hygiene problems – scuttling down the pillars like cockroaches.

The effects are at their most special when they are least obvious – reducing Elijah Wood (5'6") to Frodo Baggins (3'6"), and shrinking Ian Holm to half the size of Ian McKellen.

Cate Blanchett as the elf-witch Galadriel is photographed with an ethereal glow that perfectly complements her finely judged, slightly threatening performance. Even smaller moments of awe, such as Gandalf's firework display at Bilbo's birthday party, are richly imagined and superbly realized.

The New Zealand tourist authorities must prepare their country to be invaded by the rest of the world, for every landscape is magnificent. Hobbiton in the Shire is cosy without being twee, the epitome of an English village yet just slightly strange. Some may find the elvish paradise of Lothlorien kitsch – it undeniably owes a lot to Busby Berkeley musicals and the *Midsummer Night's Dream* of Max Reinhardt – but it's as breathtaking in its way as the darker images which dominate the film.

The movie faithfully reflects the book, in that it does

contain scenes of extreme violence. Tolkien survived the trenches of World War I but saw virtually all of his childhood, teenage and university friends perish. Those images haunted him for the rest of his life, and contribute to the emotional power of his battle scenes.

The combination of horrible monsters and violence might well give young or nervous children nightmares, and I personally wouldn't encourage a child of under eight to see it. But I took two boys of ten to its first preview. Both sat riveted for its three hours, pronounced it infinitely better than *Harry Potter*, and asked immediately when they could see it again.

Though it contains all the traditional thrills of a "boys' film", the females are far from ciphers. Liv Tyler as Arwen makes an immediate impact as a heroine, with one of the movie's most exciting chases and the only love scene. Cate Blanchett is superb as the shimmering elf-queen Galadriel.

More than any other action-adventure I can recall, the film works as a movie about relationships. The grandfatherly bond between Gandalf and Frodo, the growing cameraderie between the four journeying hobbits, the racial enmity turning to mutual respect of Gimli the dwarf and Legolas the elf, all add texture and human interest.

There is a sense that these adventures are more than just a parade of awesome set-pieces. Each climax triggers the emotional growth of the characters. The movie does spectacular justice to Tolkien's love of landscape, which is more than just some vague nostalgia for a pre-industrial England: it also represents a deeply-felt disgust at environmental pollution, that marks him out as decades ahead of his time. The corrupted wizard Saruman's felling of trees and ruination of his own land for warlike purposes is marvellously depicted by Jackson, with the nightmarish grandeur of a Hieronymus Bosch painting.

Tolkien was famously modest about his intentions, claiming that he was more interested in the languages he had created than in his own story. But because he was so steeped in northern mythology, he himself became a master of gripping narrative. Although his trilogy was published in the mid-Fifties, he wrote the books over the pre-war and post-war period. Many of his concerns are the same that made George Orwell write two very different fantasy novels at much the same time, *Animal Farm* (1944) and *1984* (1948).

Tolkien was a conservative Catholic, not a Socialist; but he shared Orwell's fascination with the corruptibility of human nature, and the horrific attractions of totalitarianism. This is the ideological engine that drives the trilogy, and Jackson makes it admirably clear.

On the evidence of this first part, *The Lord of the Rings* is likely to become the most successful movie trilogy of all time, surpassing even *Star Wars*. But its achievement is artistic, not merely commercial. And there has been no more memorable rendering in cinema of that most uncomfortable and eternally relevant of truths – that power corrupts.

THE LORD OF THE RINGS: THE TWO TOWERS (2002)

In the first film, the narrative followed only one group of characters. Now the story divides into three: Frodo and Sam's arduous journey towards Mordor, guided by the potentially treacherous Gollum; Merry and Pippin's abduction by the Uruk-Hai and their close encounter with the inhabitants of Fangorn forest (a splendidly Arthur Rackhamesque creation); and the attempt by Aragorn, Legolas and Gimli first to rescue Merry and Pippin, and then to save Rohan and its bewitched King from the forces of Saruman.

The multi-million dollar question is: is *The Two Towers* up to the standard set by *The Fellowship of the Ring*? I have to tell you that the answer is: no. It's better – more spectacular, more exciting, more emotionally rewarding. Not only is this head and shoulders above the other films of 2002; it is going to inspire a whole new generation of moviegoers and film-makers with the magic that only the cinema can create. It's fabulous and fantastic, in the truest sense of those words.

No film is perfect, and I think director Peter Jackson made a mistake in casting John Rhys-Davies to voice Treebeard the Ent. This is too recognisably the same actor who plays Gimli the dwarf, with a strange accent that is midway between Scotland and Wales. While we're on the subject of dodgy accents, those of Sam (Sean Astin) and Frodo (Elijah Wood) are liable to turn American at times of stress. But this is nit-picking when set against the film's achievements.

The climactic event of *The Two Towers*, the seemingly hopeless defence of Helm's Deep against insuperable odds, is an outstanding, extended battle sequence that dwarfs any others on celluloid; but that is only the greatest of many wonders. Several other action sequences would have made spectacular climaxes for any other movie – especially the warg attack on the emigrants from Rohan, and the Ents' angry storming of Isengard.

One of the greatest services director Peter Jackson and his team have done to Tolkien is to grasp the importance of landscape. Most of Tolkien's finest writing lay in his descriptions of Middle Earth itself. The judicious use of digital technology has added to the natural, unspoiled marvels of New Zealand, and created a world that is at once fantastical and familiar. No directors – not even David Lean and John Ford – have used geography more effectively, to lend atmosphere and texture to their narrative.

One of the many excellent aspects of Jackson's script, co-written with Fran Walsh, Philippa Boyers and Stephen Sinclair, is that it supplies comic and romantic relief to go with all the action and grandeur. Neither comedy nor women were Tolkien's strong points; and these enhancements are part of the reason why the films are destined to reach an even wider and more appreciative audience than the books.

Especially astounding is Jackson's attention to directorial detail. Two of the moments which make the heart leap are when the elf Legolas (a) gets on a horse and (b) travels down a staircase. These events may not read like much on the page, but thanks to Jackson's imagination they amount to two of the most stirring moments ever seen.

Those killjoys who dismiss *The Lord of the Rings* as mere escapism should stop to consider whether its tale of racial hatred, genocide, the corrupting nature of power, the need to stand against evil and yet guard against the temptation of using extreme force, isn't of greater relevance to the world of today than most films of so-called realism.

Tolkien is often said to make too simplistic a division between Good and Evil. But characters here are torn between the two in a fascinating way. Theoden, King of Rohan (brought brilliantly to life in an Oscar-worthy supporting performance by Bernard Hill) has to decide between isolationism and involvement in a way that is relevant to several modern western leaders, especially those in France and Germany.

Treebeard the Ent (and an astonishing computer creation), must decide whether the evil-doing of Saruman warrants revenge or merely a shrug of resignation. Elrond, King of the Elves (superbly played by Hugo Weaving), has to resolve whether his people have any further responsibilities to the world they are shortly to leave behind. Gollum – a stunning breakthrough in computer animation, and wonderfully voiced by Andy Serkis – has to decide between his doglike devotion to Frodo and his feral determination to steal back his ring. The scenes where the good and bad sides of his nature compete are funny, touching and horrific, all at the same time.

These ethical dilemmas are treated with all the sensitivity and seriousness for which one might hope. Yet, as if by magic, the pace of the storytelling never flags. This is the speediest three hours in the cinema that I have ever experienced.

The quality of the acting is amazingly high, especially if you contrast it with the woodenness we have become resigned to in the *Star Wars* films. Viggo Mortensen as Aragorn easily dons the mantle of epic hero that used to be worn by Charlton Heston, and he's a lot sexier. The triangular love relationship between him, Arwen (Liv Tyler, acting better in Elvish than she ever has in English) and Eowyn, Theoden's niece (played by Mirando Otto) is deftly and delightfully done.

The rise of post-war cynicism and the decline of the Western and the war film have not diminished the huge need in the popular cinema for heroes. In the *Lord of the Rings* trilogy, there is a whole range of heroes for anybody to identify with.

I know a few people who felt distanced and bored by *The Fellowship of the Ring*, but I'm afraid the failure lies in their power to appreciate it, not in the film itself. (I, for my part, have a similar incapacity to appreciate Wagner). But even they should give *The Two Towers* a try, for it is an even more towering achievement.

Necessarily darker and more violent than its predecessor, it may be too overwhelming for those under eight. For the rest of us, it's an overwhelming experience, in a totally positive way. This is, I can say without fear of exaggerating, one of the great films of all time.

TOOKEY'S TALKIES

THE LORD OF THE RINGS: THE RETURN OF THE KING *(2003)*

Disappointing. Anti-climactic. Bungled. Overblown. These are just some of the adjectives I shall not be using to describe the third part of The Lord of the Rings. How about amazing, stupendous, jaw-dropping and overwhelming? For this is wonderfully imaginative cinema on the grandest possible scale, fabulously inspired but never restricted by Tolkien's original vision.

There are sights here unparalleled. If ever you questioned director Peter Jackson's ability to improve upon the battle for Helm's Deep, shame on you. The Battle of the Pelennor Fields is on such a colossal scale and so excitingly shot that it blows away every war scene ever filmed. If Gollum was the special effects achievement of *The Two Towers*, here it's the enormous war-elephants of Mordor, which have such mass and presence that it's impossible to believe they're merely special effects.

The integration of digital effects with live action is shattering: one sequence alone, where Legolas the elf (Orlando Bloom) demonstrates how to bring down one of these super-elephants, would be worth the price of admission in itself (and it's topped by one of the film's best jokes). But then so would the cavalry charge of the Rohirrim. And Aragorn's arrival with unusual reinforcements. And Sam and Frodo's fight with the giant spider Shelob.

One eternally memorable aspect of the series is the way Jackson has been inspired by Tolkien's masterly descriptions of landscape. The scene where Pippin lights a warning fire in Gondor, and answering beacons stretch across Middle Earth to Rohan, is breathtaking, as are the coming of the eagles and Aragorn's encounter with the mountain dead... I could go on, but you get the idea.

The quality of the action and visuals alone would make this a shoo-in for Best Picture and Best Director at next year's Oscars. But I hope some recognition is given to the cast as a whole, who – without exception – turn in immaculate performances under very difficult circumstances, often acting opposite creatures that most of them saw only on the movie's first night in New Zealand.

They are helped by the fact that there are more emotional scenes in this than in the other two films put together. Sean Astin as Sam and Elijah Wood as Frodo are outstanding as the balance of power shifts between them, but every leading character has his or her moment; and it's good to see the way the hobbits Sam, Merry and Pippin develop from amusing comic relief into moving, rounded characters.

Any criticisms I have are very minor. It's a pity that Denethor, Boromir's father and the lord of Minas Tirith, has been simplified so much from the book; he could have done with a touch more faded nobility – instead he's an out-and-out villain. I would have liked to see Faramir's love for Eowyn made a little clearer. And Tolkien might have winced at the way Sam becomes very nearly a conventional Hollywood action hero towards the end – though the sequences where he does are among the biggest crowd-pleasers in the film.

At three hours 21 minutes, the film feels (paradoxically) a little rushed. There's more that could, and doubtless will, appear on the DVD extended version, including the come-uppance of Saruman, who is summarily dismissed at the start of the movie without appearing.

But I can't remember a shorter-seeming epic. The number of tear-jerking false endings suggests that Peter Jackson is reluctant to say goodbye to these characters. And you will be too.

In some ways, Jackson proves himself in *The Return of the King* to be an even better storyteller than Tolkien. Through clever intercutting, Jackson and co-writers Fran Walsh and Philippa Boyens make the chronology of the final showdown and Sam and Frodo's journey to Mount Doom much more transparent and thrilling than it is in the book.

And though some of the dialogue is a bit plonky – there is inevitably an awful lot of plot explaining to do – there's also plenty of heart and passion, and a refreshing use of humour. John Rhys-Davies as the belligerent dwarf Gimli has several funny lines which weren't in the original novel; and the film is all the better for having a little light and shade.

So *The Lord of the Rings* has come to the most triumphant possible conclusion. For its scale, imagination and passion, this is, without doubt, the greatest cinematic trilogy ever – far surpassing its nearest competitors, *The Godfather* and the first three *Star Wars*.

The *Lord of the Rings* is a major cultural landmark, a masterpiece that will inspire future generations of filmmakers, and it will be watched with admiration for as long as cinema exists.

LOVE ACTUALLY *(2003)*

Love Actually may not be perfection, but it is two and a quarter hours of cinematic delight. In terms of ambition, range and entertainment value, Richard Curtis's first film as writer-director can stand alongside the great romantic comedies – and it's the most heart-warming Christmas movie since *It's A Wonderful Life*.

At least something good has come out of 9/11. Curtis establishes his Twin Towers-inspired theme in the opening moments, when he makes his alter ego, Hugh Grant, point out that, although fear and hatred sometimes appear to dominate our planet, the world is also full of love. When people knew they were about to die on September 11th, they didn't give vent to their hatred: they sent fond messages to their love ones. Love, as the song says, is all around.

As if this isn't enough to enrage melancholics the world over, Curtis enlarges on his theme by depicting the extraordinary variety, versatility and virulence of love. He does that by intertwining 9 short stories and 22 leading characters, with a skill I haven't seen bettered in any movie. The technique and self-discipline are staggering.

And the effect is magical. It's not often you can go to the cinema, look around at almost any point in the film, and see virtually the entire audience crying with joy.

This New Zealander turned quintessential Englishman first made his name in international cinema with *Four Weddings and a Funeral*, and his achievements since have included *Notting Hill* and *Bridget Jones's Diary*. So it is no surprise to find Hugh Grant in the leading role. Once again at the peak of his powers, Grant plays a new, highly charismatic Prime Minister. He enters Downing Street unencumbered by Blairite blandness, smarminess or marriage. "No nappies! No teenagers!" he promises the domestic staff. "No scary wife!"

He immediately, and inconveniently, falls for the Number 10 tea lady (Martine McCutcheon, showing us the Eliza Doolittle that most of us missed), but gets dispirited when he catches her being snogged by a visiting US President (Billy Bob Thornton, amusingly arrogant – and just a bit chilling – as a Clintonesque womaniser who takes British subservience too much for granted).

Love finally gets the better of the PM, however, and he decides to track her down on Christmas Eve – and he doesn't want a cup of tea.

December 24th is traditionally the moment when the year's Christmas Number One pop single is revealed, and one contender for this dubious accolade is clapped-out rock grandad Billy Mack (Bill Nighy), with an atrocious version of *Love Is All Around*, retitled *Christmas Is All Around*.

This narrative strand charts the love-hate relationship between Billy and his long-suffering manager (Gregor Fisher). Nighy builds upon the hilarious character he played in *Still Crazy*: someone who's been there, done that, but can't remember much of it. This must be one of the funniest performances ever, and – were everyone else not so tremendous – he would steal the movie. There was scarcely a moment when Nighy was on screen that I was not weeping with laughter.

In a darker strand of the film, Laura Linney has wonderful warmth as a woman entering middle age but still too nervous to date the best-looking man in her office (Rodrigo Santoro). Besides, she has a family responsibility of her own, arising from a very different kind of love, and it keeps getting in the way of her "love life".

The other tragic-comic story brings out arguably the finest performance in the film. Emma Thompson makes a triumphant return to the big screen as a middle-aged Wandsworth mum increasingly aware that her husband (Alan Rickman) is succumbing to the less than subtle advances of his gorgeous, predatory secretary (Heike Makatsch).

Thompson is terrific, whether faking joy at her daughter getting the role of First Lobster in her school's Nativity play but unable to disguise her incredulity ("There was more than one lobster present at the birth of Jesus?") or dispensing sage advice to a male neighbour who's grieving for his wife ("Nobody's ever going to shag you if you cry all the time").

With comparatively little time on screen, she's as moving as she was in *Howards End* and *Sense and Sensibility*. If you don't have a tear in your eye when she gets her Christmas present, there's something wrong with you.

I could also rhapsodise about the father-son strand, with Liam Neeson showing an unexpectedly light, charming touch as a widower resigned to a single life, unless of course Claudia Schiffer should suddenly become available, and coping with the sudden stroppiness of his 11 year-old stepson (played by a talented young newcomer, Thomas Sangster, who is Hugh Grant's real-life cousin).

Unrequited love is also on show, through the best man at

a wedding (Andrew Lincoln) who apparently resents the beautiful young wife (Keira Knightley) of his best friend (Chiwetel Ejofor). Another of the film's highlights is when he is made to show Knightley his highly embarrassing video of her wedding.

Lust is represented by the splendid Kris Marshall (the elder son in TV's *My Family*), playing sad sack Colin, disastrous at chatting up London totty but convinced that if only he can move to America and charm the girls with his English accent he will be transformed into a Love God. "Stateside," he assures his sceptical best friend, "I am Prince William without the weird family!"

We're also shown love flourishing under inauspicious circumstances – Joanna Page and Martin Freeman, trying to make personal contact while "standing in" for actors in a porno movie.

Finally, there's love across the language barrier, with Colin Firth back on form as a diffident thriller-writer who's crushed by his partner's infidelity but bounces back thanks to his Portuguese maid (Lucia Moniz).

Curtis weaves together these varied but complementary strands with sublime artistry. He knows just when to put in the big comic set-pieces, when to give us the romantic escapism we're hoping for, and when to bring us down to earth with a dash of realism.

Curtis is usually portrayed by his detractors as relentlessly optimistic, which he is if you haven't bothered to watch his movies with any care. There are spectacles here – especially those involving Linney and Thompson – which are far from rose-tinted.

Though a first-time director, Curtis hardly put a foot wrong. Even the dodgiest sequences – and I wasn't wholly convinced about the likelihood of the bar room scene involving Marshall, Firth's procession through the streets of Marseilles, or Neeson's cheerful disregard for airport security- all have a goofy charm.

Though Curtis will rightly scoop most of the plaudits, production designer Jim Clay and costume supervisor Joanna Johnston show the same fine eye for modern detail that they did in *About a Boy*. Nick Moore's editing has the energy that helped make *The Full Monty* a hit. Michael Coulter's cinematography is gorgeous, once again – as he did in *Notting Hill* – making London seem the world capital of romance. And the film is immaculately cast by one of the UK's most distinguished casting directors, Mary Selway.

Because of its unfashionable charm, humanity and generosity of spirit, a small but vociferous minority will condemn *Love Actually* out of hand. Most people, however, are going to love it, and – like me – will want to watch it over and over again.

MEN IN BLACK *(1997)*

A young, fit and extremely dogged New York cop (Will Smith) is surprised to find that the street punk he is chasing can run up the side of tall buildings, has four eyelids, and announces "your world is going to end".

Smith's athleticism impresses an older man in a black suit, black tie and shades (Tommy Lee Jones) who tests him for recruitment to his secret elite, then tells him the truth about aliens – not only are they "out there", they are here.

Some are innocent refugees. Like other immigrants, they are a mixture of good and bad. "There are about 15,000 aliens on the planet, mostly in Manhattan," Jones explains to Smith. "Most are just trying to make a living."

Smith thinks for a second, and the idea suddenly makes sense.

"Cab-drivers," says Smith.

"Not as many as you'd think," says Jones.

The aliens are being monitored by a secret group of immigration controllers, the Men in Black, who make sure the aliens obey regulations and keep their identities secret.

In the meantime, a flying saucer has crash-landed near a farmhouse, and a giant cockroach with a sweet tooth and a nasty temper has taken over the body of its owner (Vincent D'Onofrio), with the ease of Luciano Pavarotti cramming himself inside the skin of Jarvis Cocker. He sets about killing humans in the same spirit that humans exterminate cockroaches.

The story gets weirder from there, and involves a galaxy hidden inside a jewel, and another group of aliens threatening to blow up Earth if a deadline isn't met. But the plot is just an excuse for some very funny sketches built around the central premise. There are scenes here of inspired silliness, including one where Jones intercepts an illegal alien immigrant posing as an illegal Mexican immigrant ("Put up your hands," snaps Jones, "and all of your flippers!").

In a movie which could have easily been dominated by special effects, Tommy Lee Jones gives one of the funniest screen performances of all time. He is deliriously funny, simply by being humourless, matter-of-fact and world-weary. His air of bitter experience give credibility to the whole ridiculous plot.

Will Smith, a much better actor than this cartoonish character allows him to be (the script gives him no family or social ties whatever), brings the same freshness, vitality and cool he showed in *Independence Day*. Together, Smith and Jones make a terrific double-act.

A further delight is the look of the film. Director Barry Sonnenfeld (whose directorial credits include *The Addams Family* films and *Get Shorty*) shows why some of the best directors started out as cameramen (he worked on most of the Coen brothers' best films, including *Raising Arizona* and *Miller's Crossing*). He constantly chooses unfamiliar camera angles which seem at first to be pointless, but then reveal themselves to be telling the story in an original and offbeat way.

Production designer Bo Welch – whose excellent credits include *The Little Princess* – has devised a magnificently naff set for the headquarters of the Men in Black: a Kennedy-era, futuristic building that not only looks wonderfully dated but also carries overtones (as does the story) of *The Man From Uncle*.

The special effects are by George Lucas's company, Industrial Light and Magic, and are of *Jurassic Park* quality. The aliens, designed by Rick Baker, are marvellously funny. Baker is one of the under-publicised heroes of cinema, whose creations include *An American Werewolf in London* and *Gremlins*. Thanks to him and Lucas's team, the whole film has the inspired zaniness of the bar scene in *Star Wars*.

The story is, admittedly, thin, and the characters hollow. *Men in Black* is a romp – nothing more – but a hugely enjoyable one. It moves at a cracking pace, and doesn't outstay its welcome at 98 minutes. Everything about it has style, wit and humour – including the script by Ed Solomon, the under-appreciated author of *Bill and Ted's Excellent Adventure*.

And, though it's fast food for the brain, it's more than fun – it makes you look at things anew, as all the best Science Fiction does.

It's based on two inspired premises. One is that aliens are disguised as humans. The same idea permeated *Invasion of the Body Snatchers* and *They Live!* but this is the first film to appreciate the humorous, as well as horrific, side of the idea.

The other premise is that American supermarket tabloids represent the finest traditions of investigative reporting. It's the "straight" press that hasn't a clue what's really going on. All those headlines like "MAN AWAKES FROM 35-YEAR COMA" or " ALIEN STOLE MY HUSBAND'S SKIN" are true. A similar concept lies behind the cult TV series, *The X-Files*, but this film realises its comic potential.

The appeal of such ideas is obvious. The notion that the intelligentsia and opinion-formers are stupid and uninformed is enormously attractive to those who are not that intelligent themselves, or feel their intelligence is insufficiently recognised – which covers just about all of us.

And the idea that alien people are already among us is quite obviously true; the only question is how alien?

MIDNIGHT IN PARIS *(2011)*

Just when Woody Allen seemed to have written and directed himself out, he comes up with his biggest hit. *Midnight in Paris* arrives here as his highest-grossing movie, surpassing even *Hannah and Her Sisters, Manhattan* and *Annie Hall* – and it's one of his best.

The blond, laid-back, very un-Jewish Owen Wilson may seem a daft choice to play Allen's latest angst-ridden alter ego, but turns out to be ideal. His unpretentious charm takes the curse off the 75 year-old Allen's increasingly crotchety approach to characters he dislikes – which includes pedants, academics and anyone politically to the right of centre.

Wilson plays Gil, a Hollywood hack screenwriter with dreams of being a great novelist. He's revising the first draft of a book while visiting Paris with his practical-minded fiancée Inez (Rachel McAdams) and her stuffy, Francophobe parents (Kurt Fuller and Mimi Kennedy). As if they are not bad enough company, Gil runs into Inez's old friend Paul (Michael Sheen), an insufferable know-it-all who prefaces every statement with the mock-humble "If I'm not mistaken", and spends his time either contradicting the guide at the Rodin museum (Carla Bruni, adequate in an undemanding role) or trying to make Gil feel inferior.

Gil's holiday is hugely improved when, on the stroke of

midnight over a number of nights, he is miraculously transported back to Paris in the 1920s, where he meets a who's who of cultural heroes, starting with F. Scott Fitzgerald (Tom Hiddlestone), Ernest Hemingway (Corey Stoll) and Gertrude Stein (Kathy Bates).

Allen has a lot of fun with them, especially Hemingway, whom he makes an endearing mixture of artistic integrity and posturing machismo. Hemingway probes Gil for evidence of masculinity with the query "Have you ever hunted?" Gil parries this away with the quintessentially Woody one-liner "Only for bargains".

Gil also falls in love with the gorgeous Adriana (Marion Cotillard, so who wouldn't?). She's a high-class groupie, formerly involved with Braque and Modigliani, and currently shacked up with temperamental, up-and-coming artist Pablo Picasso (Marcial Di Fonzo Bo). She, of course, loathes the mediocrity of Paris in the 1920s and much prefers the *belle epoque* of the 1890s, when the arts scene was livelier, and you could have run into truly talented people like Gauguin, Degas and Toulouse-Lautrec.

Cynics might suggest that the reason *Midnight In Paris* is turning out to be Allen's biggest hit is it offers a superficial view of Paris, a name-dropping view of artists, and an ambivalence about nostalgia. The argument of the film is that you shouldn't live in the past; the underlying, and surely contradictory, message is that the past is infinitely more alluring than the present. And yet so harsh an analysis is to underestimate the film's attractions.

The opening shots (reminiscent of Allen's 1979 masterpiece, *Manhattan*) are at first sight a compendium of clichés – Notre Dame, The Louvre and the Eiffel Tower all put in appearances. No attempt is made to show the less attractive sides of Paris. But even in these opening shots, cinematographer Darius Khondji craftily prepares us with a sprinkling of rain and the coming of night for a return to the kind of magic realism Woody Allen explored cinematically in *The Purple Rose of Cairo*, and in short stories such as *The Kugelmass Episode*, where Madame Bovary visited present-day Manhattan.

Wisely, Allen does not waste time trying to explain time travel. He realises the audience doesn't care. We know the story isn't real, but go along with it because it's such a beguiling fantasy.

Woody Allen has made funnier films and a few deeper ones (here I'm thinking especially of *Crimes and Misdemeanors*), but he has never made one that glides by with such ease and confidence. While you are watching it, it has the lightness of a soufflé. It's only in retrospect that its more satisfying qualities emerge.

It's easy to see that it has a magic about it, a warmth and charm, and – above all – a yearning for romance, and values beyond the mercenary.

Less obviously, it shows a understanding of the value of criticism and self-criticism. Gil is uncertain whom to show his novel to for a sympathetic but honest critique. We see early on why he doesn't offer it to his fiancée, for she is uninterested in his talent except as a way of making money, and would be happiest if he stuck to Hollywood hackwork. On meeting Hemingway, Gil wonders if the great writer would criticise his novel, but Hemingway refuses, saying that if it's bad he'll be merciless because he's a rival, and if it's good he'll be vindictive because he's envious.

The ideal critic, Gil finds, is Gertrude Stein, portrayed here as a selfless, motherly soul and a fount of human and artistic sympathy. She does, indeed, lend Gil her support and gives him an insight – not hers, ironically, but Hemingway's – that fundamentally alters Gil's perspective on his novel and his life.

The real message of the movie is not the one that it seems to be labouring – that nostalgia is a trap – but that life and art are both worth the most meticulous re-examination, and a life without art or romance is one that's only half-lived.

Moreover, Allen argues – in an entrancing final scene – that lasting relationships are built not on lust or love at first sight, but on understanding based on shared tastes. That's a point rarely made in romantic comedies, and has much to recommend it.

Midnight in Paris is not only one of Woody Allen's most enjoyable films, it's also one of his wisest.

MILLION DOLLAR BABY *(2004)*

Million Dollar Baby comes on like a nice, polite, old-fashioned, boxing movie, jabbing away at its audience at arm's length, while showing us some fancy footwork. It waits until we are under its spell, lulled into a sense of feelgood familiarity. And then it delivers a sucker punch guaranteed to knock anyone out. This is a world-class heavyweight contender.

Coming after the almost as impressive *Mystic River*, it proves that, at the age of 74, Clint Eastwood is just entering the full glory of his maturity, helped no doubt by the steadying influence of Henry Bumstead, his 89 year-old production designer who, nearly a half century ago, helped Hitchcock out on *Vertigo*.

Million Dollar Baby is the outstanding movie of Eastwood's already glorious career, and deservedly won Best Picture at the Oscars.

Frankie Dunn (Eastwood) is an elderly gym-owner, trainer and manager who's ultra-conservative and past his prime. He's trained fine fighters but has grown over-cautious about putting them up for title fights, with the result that most abandon him before they reach the top. Maybe he feels too fatherly towards them – an irony, in view of the fact that he and his real daughter have been estranged for years, and she returns his weekly letters to him, unread. His only friend is his long-time employee Scrap (Morgan Freeman), a one-eyed ex-boxer. They bicker together like a long-married couple.

Into their well-ordered but dead-end lives comes Maggie Fitzgerald (Hilary Swank), determined to make it to the top in boxing, but inexperienced, seemingly too old at 31, and – to make matters worse as far as Frankie's concerned, "a girlie". But guess who takes her under his wing.

All this may sound cosy and over-familiar, and to some extent it is. The first two-thirds of the movie constitute an utterly conventional boxing movie, albeit presented with clarity and wit, and performances that aren't just faultless, but inspired.

The scene where Maggie finally browbeats Frankie into training her is among the best written and acted I've seen. Even though it's obvious what's coming and the scene delivers precisely what you expect, you won't be able to stop a tear from coming to your eye. It's similar in that respect to *Billy Elliot*, another movie that somehow managed to rise above its own clichés.

Throughout the movie, there's a marvellous air of authenticity. Paul Haggis's screenplay is based on a short story from the collection *Rope Burns* by F.X. Toole. Toole was himself a former "cut man", the member of a boxer's team whose job it is to patch him up so that he can continue to fight. The film reeks of experience and expertise.

The less revealed about the final third of the picture, the better. I saw it coming, for in this kind of well-crafted script there's always an element of foreshadowing; but it still carries an enormous emotional punch, and carries the movie on to another level.

Million Dollar Baby is one of those rare, courageous films that takes religion seriously. Frankie is an Irish-American Catholic who's disillusioned with his church and lack of relationship with his daughter. He's searching for his own roots by learning Gaelic, and he's searching for spiritual redemption, though he's not sure how. Eastwood plays him with wonderful dignity and depth, and a touching minimum of words.

Hilary Swank has already won one Best Actress Oscar for *Boys Don't Cry* (1999), and she's even better in this. She draws upon her own background – like the heroine, she was born poor and lived in a trailer – and she is utterly convincing as a world-beating welterweight boxer, even though before she was cast she had never thrown a punch.

It's no accident that actors in Eastwood's movies have a tendency to win Oscars. Sean Penn and Tim Robbins both triumphed last year, for *Mystic River*, and Kevin Bacon deserved at least a nomination.

Eastwood casts expertly, trusts the actors to do their job and shoots a minimum of takes. 20 takes or more are the norm on a Hollywood movie. Eastwood shoots between one and three. Not only is this highly economical as regards time and money: it clearly keeps the actors fresh, and concentrates their minds to a miraculous degree.

Like so many classic American movies, from John Ford's *The Grapes of Wrath* through to John Sayles's *Lone Star*, *Million Dollar Baby* shows huge respect for the common man and woman, their dreams and disappointments. Yet in Maggie's white-trash family it dares to paint one of the most deeply unsympathetic – and, I fear, realistic – portraits of the lumpenproletariat ever to grace the screen. This is a wise, humane but clear-sighted movie, made by a marvellous director at the height of his powers.

MINORITY REPORT *(2002)*

John Anderton (Tom Cruise) is a high-profile cop in Washington DC. He's supremely confident in his embrace of new technology. He stands before perspex screens, conducting crime data on and off them with the panache of Mickey Mouse in Fantasia.

Anderton is loyal to his elderly boss (Max von Sydow) who is responsible for a revolution in crime-fighting. He brought in the system whereby three uncannily gifted people – "pre-cogs" – can predict the future and enable the police to capture people on the point of committing a murder.

So what if those arrested haven't actually done anything wrong yet? The effectiveness of the "pre-cogs" is such that the murder rate in Anderton's home city of Washington, DC, has dwindled to nothing and stayed there for six years. Anderton has a personal interest in fighting crime efficiently, because of the disappearance of his young son, which has left him a user of drugs to stave off his loneliness.

But there's a catch. Anderton himself is seen by the "pre-cogs", murdering a man he has never met. From then on, it's a race between Anderton, a believer in the harsh new system of law and order yet with a vested interest in proving it fallible, and Witwer (Colin Farrell), an ambitious federal bureaucrat suspicious in principle of the new system but determined to catch a potential murderer.

Minority Report is one of the finest pieces of screen science fiction yet – more visionary than *2001: A Space Odyssey*, more gripping than *Blade Runner*, more hard-hitting and mature than Spielberg's previous sci-fi masterpiece, *E. T.*

It is also the most stylish *film noir* thriller since *LA Confidential*, the most exciting chase movie since *The Fugitive*, one of the most entertaining action flicks since Spielberg's own *Raiders of the Lost Ark*, and the most creative use of Tom Cruise's unique mixture of cockiness, vanity and machismo since *Jerry Maguire*.

And, for horror fans, there is one moment that will make audiences jump higher than they have done since Carrie's hand came out of the grave and grabbed the future Mrs Spielberg, Amy Irving.

Examine the ingeniously twisting plot in retrospect and you may be able to spot some flaws. Why, if Anderton is such a clever cop, does he not deduce the only conceivable reason why he might kill a man he has never met? Why does he have to be set up to commit murder in the first place? And surely someone would have noticed when the victim of a previous crime who was supposedly saved from her murderer, then disappeared?

But such objections are unlikely to bother you while you're watching. You're much more likely to be bowled over by the pace and invention of the story-telling by Scott Frank and Jon Cohen, based on a short story by Philip K. Dick – not to mention some of the most spectacular action sequences since movies began.

The technical daring and humorous detail in the special effects are as extraordinary as anything in George Lucas's *Star*

Wars films. They are used not only to entertain, however, but to create a very credible forecast of how the future really might be. This is not the antiseptic future that has become a cliché, but one in which people's leaking bodily fluids and ability to spread detritus remain unchanged and constitute an act of instinctive rebellion against the optimistic technocrats who hope to "clean up" humanity.

Spielberg's deep distrust of technology – ironic in a director who uses it so cleverly – runs through the whole of his career. *Minority Report* carries on this theme from *ET, Jurassic Park* and *AI*. Where it scores highly compared with all of them is that he never stoops to cuteness or easy sentimentality, and – unlike *AI* – the film never comes close to collapsing in its final quarter.

Though highly entertaining, *Minority Report* is unmistakably a work of art. The visual symbolism – mostly involving water and eyesight – is stunning and anything but clichéd. It underpins the whole story, ensuring that the imagery lingers in your subconscious long after the final credits.

Spielberg's film doesn't bring to an end the age-old debate of where free will ends and predestination begins, but it is visionary film-making by the world's greatest director at the height of his powers. So dark, stylish and confident is it that it resembles the best work of Stanley Kubrick, raised to a still higher level by Spielberg's greater ability to manipulate his audience's emotions.

Take, for example, the astonishing sequence where Cruise has to hide from mechanical spiders that are being used to hunt him down. You'll experience not only brilliant use of set design and a moving camera but also state-of-the-art special effects that create a wonderfully Hitchcockian blend of suspense and black humour.

Some will distrust the serious credentials of any film that is this entertaining. I've seen it dismissed as emotionally cold and little more than a glorified chase movie. That's because it doesn't wear its heart on its sleeve or indulge in lengthy, soul-searching speeches that express the film-makers' liberal beliefs.

Instead, it wisely allows us to share in the leading characters' hopes and anxieties, and leaves us to reach our own conclusions. Though not didactic, it has at least as much seriousness and passion as Spielberg's previously most acclaimed films, *Schindler's List* and *Saving Private Ryan*.

Many thinking people across the political spectrum have worried since September 11th about the threat to liberty that a crackdown for the sake of security necessarily involves. *Minority Report* explores and expresses those fears better than any other film.

It's uncannily topical, at a time when the American authorities are imprisoning people without trial for potential crimes they haven't actually committed, and most of the world is eagerly supporting them. Either Spielberg is incredibly lucky, or he's more tuned in to the spirit of our times than his critics. My guess is that he's both, but principally the latter.

MOULIN ROUGE (2001)

A young Scottish poet called Christian (Ewan McGregor) comes to Montmartre in the Summer of Love (that's 1899, in case you didn't know) – to pursue his literary dreams in a photogenic garret that's a mere *pierre's* throw away from that hotbed of nightclub decadence, the Moulin Rouge.

Through his ceiling fall some dodgy Bohemians led by the artist Toulouse-Lautrec (John Leguizamo). Thanks to Christian's ability to improvise verse (actually, the opening lines of *The Sound of Music*) he gets a job as chief writer.

Yes, that's right. A gang of free-thinking, avant-garde Parisians are bowled over by lines from the most critically-maligned, bourgeois, all-American musical of the subsequent century. Maybe Luhrmann is making a satirical comment that this year's *avant-garde* may be tomorrow's middle-of-the-road entertainment, and vice versa. That's a worthwhile point to make, in these far too fashion-led times. But let's not get side-tracked.

Our penniless poet is understandably staggered by the Moulin's principal artiste and courtesan, Satine (Nicole Kidman), who first appears on a trapeze singing a prophetic medley of *Diamonds Are A Girl's Best Friend* and Madonna's *Material Girl*. In her dressing room (which is, *naturellement*, inside a fantastically bejewelled, three-storey, papier-mache elephant) Christian bowls her over with his ability to improvise Bernie Taupin's lyric for *Your Song*.

She seduces him under the impression he's a wealthy duke, which gets right up the nose of the real wealthy duke (Richard Roxburgh) who's deciding whether to invest in the Moulin's first ever musical comedy, which is being mounted by the Moulin's ebullient, showbiz-crazed proprietor (Jim Broadbent, never knowingly underacting).

Will beauty, freedom, truth and love conquer commerce? Will the show go on? And will our leading lady's cough turn into something like the death scene from Camille restaged by Danny La Rue? You betcha.

Moulin Rouge is stunningly spectacular, dazzlingly dizzy, a cascading cornucopia of colour, camp and Kidman. Following up his triumphs with *Strictly Ballroom* and *Romeo + Juliet*, Baz Luhrmann has produced an even more sumptuous visual and aural feast.

He provides course after course of seemingly clashing ingredients – Bowie, Busby Berkeley, Bolan and Bollywood, to name but four – and comes up with something truly different. I can't honestly predict whether you'll love it or hate it. It will be too rich – much too rich – for some tastes. But I loved it.

The story is simple to the point of banality, and some would say well beyond, but memorable images abound. I may have been hallucinating but I'm pretty sure I saw Jim Broadbent performing *Voulez-Vous Coucher Avec Moi* while doing backflips in a red wig, and singing *Like a Virgin* in a way that Madonna could never have imagined in her worst nightmares.

The medleys are so bizarrely eclectic that it's a miracle they combine into anything that's musically coherent, but they do. Two new songs, *Come What May* and *Fool To Believe* – performed mainly by Kidman – deserve to be in contention for Oscars as Best New Song. And there are two treasurably extravagant production numbers, built around *Roxanne* by the Police and *The Show Must Go On* by Queen.

What has all this to do with 1899, I hear you cry? Well, the idea is to show that universal notions of love and romance run through the whole of popular music and opera.

For those who care to explore the film's visual metaphors, there are echoes of Puccini's *La Boheme*, Offenbach's *Orpheus in the Underworld*, *Les Enfants du Paradis* and many greats of the silent and downright noisy cinema.

Ewan McGregor achieves the same puppyish naivety that Dick Powell had in the great Busby Berkeley musicals. Nicole Kidman is lusciously beautiful, elegant and decadent as she embodies the screen sirens of more innocent days, especially Marilyn Monroe in *Gentlemen Prefer Blondes*, Rita Hayworth in *Gilda* and Martine Carol in *Lola Montes*.

Kidman's physique is a fine advertisement for conspicuous consumptiveness, and her performance will be a revelation to those who weren't able to catch her on stage in *The Blue Room* – versatile, nuanced (in a not noticeably nuanced production) and sensationally sexy. And, like Ewan McGregor, she reveals a surprisingly pleasant singing voice.

Some viewers will be overwhelmed by the Niagara of musical and cinematic references, and feel that Luhrmann is bludgeoning them with his own cleverness. The bravura camerawork and frenetic editing will inevitably attract charges of flashiness and, unlike Luhrmann's *Romeo + Juliet*, there isn't a classic text to fall back on.

Especially towards the end, the romantic dialogue between the leads strays perilously close to *Pearl Harbor*-style cliché, and another polish of the screenplay might have saved the film from some distancing moments of caricature and non-working slapstick that defy even these talented actors.

The tone is operatic rather than subtle, but deliberately so. Luhrmann employs fabulous production values (by courtesy of his wife, Catherine Martin) and melodramatic overkill (by courtesy of everyone else), to achieve the kind of direct, innocent emotion that you see in the best moments of modern Indian musicals, and that was such a part of western musical culture until the late Sixties.

What is Luhrmann trying to accomplish? I think he is trying to capture the glamour, romance and heart that cinema has largely lost, and combine it with the more jaded, sexual knowingness of the present. To my mind, he does it brilliantly.

Moulin Rouge may be too offbeat to be a mainstream hit, but it's obviously destined to become a cult classic. And though it's camp and kitsch at times (most of the time, actually) it doesn't settle for the kind of cool ironic amorality that pervades so much of post-modern art.

It is post-modernist in the way it plunders the culture and attitudes of the past, but has the good sense to suggest that for too long film-makers have avoided the core values of art and entertainment. These are – as the film never tires of telling us – beauty, freedom, truth and love. In many ways, it's the antidote to Quentin Tarantino and his imitators.

Moulin Rouge is one of those rare movies that is really beyond criticism. Good taste doesn't enter into it, though bad taste certainly does. It is what it is. It achieves what it sets out to do. And if we can't appreciate its glamour, wit and exuberance, that's our loss.

MUCH ADO ABOUT NOTHING *(2012)*

Summer in the cinema is normally all about expensive blockbusters. So it's especially refreshing in June to see a high-quality, unhyped entertainment that was made on a shoestring by someone who really loves what he's doing.

It's even more endearing when the film does justice to the finest writer in the English language.

William Shakespeare's *Much Ado About Nothing* is one of his most popular comedies, and no wonder. It contains some of his best banter, a couple of involving love stories and comic relief that actually succeeds in being funny.

In the theatre, I've seen great productions starring Maggie Smith and Robert Stephens, Judi Dench and Donald Sinden, and Kenneth Branagh and Samantha Bond. The 1993 film Branagh made with his then wife Emma Thompson wasn't bad either. But I've never before laughed as much as I did at this version.

Some Shakespeare purists may be suspicious that it's by the Hollywood populist who created *Buffy The Vampire Slayer*. Writer-director Joss Whedon is not the first person you'd expect to come up with the finest production of Shakespeare in many years.

Whedon is hardly a household name, but he's the hottest property in Hollywood right now. His Summer blockbuster of last year, *The Avengers Assemble*, was a monster hit, the highest-grossing movie since Avatar. His script for *The Cabin in the Woods* was the wittiest in the horror genre since… well, ever, actually. *Toy Story*, which he co-wrote, is one of the best-loved family pictures Pixar has produced.

One thing not well known about Hollywood's new favourite son is that he's an Anglophile. As a boy, he attended one of England's best schools, Winchester College, and one of his A-levels was in English Literature. It made a lasting impression. His 10 year-old son is called Arden, in honour of Shakespeare's mother's maiden name, the publishing house for Shakespeare plays, and the forest in *As You Like It*.

Whedon's new version of *Much Ado* is charming, funny and wonderfully entertaining. It even appeals to those who would normally reach for their gun at the mention of Shakespeare.

Seeking relaxation after his blockbuster production of *The Avengers Assemble*, Whedon and his wife Kai Cole shot the movie in 12 days in their own home and garden in California, with actors Whedon cherry-picked from his TV hits. They speak the original words but with American accents. They wear modern dress but carry cellphones, drive cars and scoff cupcakes. It ought not to work, but it does.

English teachers are going to weep with gratitude at the way it makes Shakespeare not only accessible to the young, but also funny and sexy. It's also a welcome reminder of just how much Shakespeare has contributed to our entertainment culture.

Probably created in 1598 or 1599, *Much Ado* established the template for romantic comedy. It features a pair of lovers, Beatrice and Benedick, who apparently can't stand each other and can't chat without exchanging insults.

What their friends realise is that these sharp-tongued, defiantly unromantic adversaries are ideally suited. So their male friends stage a conversation they know Benedick will overhear, in which they talk of Beatrice's love for him. The women convey exactly the same misinformation to Beatrice about Benedick.

This merry war of wit between the sexes has influenced every other romantic comedy, from Tracy and Hepburn's classics through to the Woody Allen, Nora Ephron and Richard Curtis films of our own time.

It even underpins some entertainments outside the genre, from Hitchcock's thriller *The 39 Steps*, with an apparently incompatible man and woman literally manacled together until they fall for each other, through to Whedon's horror series, *Buffy the Vampire Slayer*, in which the tough-guy heroine gradually succumbs to the much-maligned Spike.

One of Whedon's many achievements with his new production is to show that *Much Ado* is the inspiration for screwball comedy. This genre started with Frank Capra's *It Happened One Night* and developed with movies such as *Bringing Up Baby* and *Some Like it Hot*. It's still with us in the form of *The Hangover*, *Silver Linings Playbook* and *Desperate Housewives*.

Merely by leaving a lot of empty wine bottles around, Whedon cleverly establishes why the characters in *Much Ado* do ridiculous things and experience violent mood swings: they're all, ever so slightly, drunk.

Most of the play is romantic comedy, but it takes a dramatic turn when the heroine's best friend Hero is unjustly accused of infidelity by her fiancé, Claudio, and believed by some of the characters to be dead.

When the tone darkens and Beatrice instructs Benedick

to "Kill Claudio", the unexpected transition makes perfect sense in the light of her alcohol intake – as does Benedick's dismay.

Just as central to the way romantic comedy has developed is the kind of sparkling repartee that Shakespeare invented in *Much Ado*, all beautifully performed here, whether Benedick is insulting his future bride as "my lady Disdain" or she is pretending not to listen while he is yammering on: "I wonder that you will still be talking, Signor Benedick: nobody marks you".

Their war of words has helped to inspire innumerable film romcoms, from *You Can't Take It With You* and *The Front Page* through to *Juno* and *Midnight in Paris*.

There are two more ingredients that Shakespeare pioneered in this particular comedy. One is the Malapropism – the misuse of English by characters too dumb to know they're making fools of themselves. The word is named after Mrs Malaprop, who appears in R.B. Sheridan's eighteenth century comedy *The Rivals*, but Shakespeare invented the breed two hundred years earlier, in head of security Dogberry, brilliantly played by Nathan Fillon as an accident-prone bumbler who's convinced he's smarter than Colombo.

The other innovation in *Much Ado* is the incompetent police force. There isn't a single one of Dogberry's security men that isn't a bungler. They're the ancestors of innumerable progeny, from the Keystone Cops through to the students in *Police Academy*.

Arguably, the most delightful innovation in Shakespeare's *Much Ado* lies in his creation of Beatrice, the archetypal strong woman, ready to make her way in the world alone if necessary, and sharply critical of lesser specimens of the masculine gender.

She's a pre-feminism feminist, the antecedent not only of all those smart but abrasive women played by Katharine Hepburn, but of action stars like Ripley in the *Alien* Movies (one of which, *Alien Resurrection*, Whedon wrote before he was fashionable) – and indeed Buffy.

Many intellectuals look down on romantic comedy as an inferior form of drama, but *Much Ado* covers identical themes – alleged infidelity, pretending to be dead, the thirst for revenge, the need for reconciliation – to the ones Shakespeare covered in his tragedies, *Othello, Romeo and Juliet, Hamlet* and *King Lear.*

The difference in *Much Ado* is that Shakespeare looks for happy endings and emphasises the power and desirability of love and marital commitment. Although he drops hints that the multiple marriages at the end of *Much Ado* may not all be plain sailing, they still have the powerfully feelgood effect on an audience that they did in the sixteenth century.

Of course, there have been great productions of *Much Ado* before. Whedon's unique achievement is to go in a diametrically opposite direction from the one you'd expect from someone whose last film was a Hollywood blockbuster. He has gone for an endearingly domestic-scale approach that clarifies the text and quickly makes you forget that the characters are speaking in sixteenth century English.

He and an excellent cast not only succeed in doing justice to Shakespeare's talent. They make the Bard look bright, funny and fresh. They allow us to appreciate Shakespeare's genius with new eyes, and it's a wonderful sight.

MULHOLLAND DRIVE (2001)

A perky, blonde Canadian actress (Naomi Watts) arrives in Los Angeles to make her name, and borrows a conveniently central apartment from her aunt, an older actress who has gone off to make a film. But our heroine unexpectedly discovers a beautiful woman (Laura Elena Harring) with that good old stand-by affliction of *film noir*, amnesia, hiding out in the apartment. Together, they try to work out the latter's identity, with the blonde acting as girl detective and the beauty as the mysterious *femme fatale*, and they fall in love, as detectives and *femme fatales* so often do.

Meanwhile, a smart-alecky director (Justin Theroux) is pursued by the Mob for his refusal to cast an actress they want in his latest picture. His marriage, credit rating and career are shot to pieces, until he gives in.

There is a nightmarish quality to David Lynch's *Mulholland Drive*. That's because it really is a nightmare – dreamed by one of the leading characters, who displays an astonishing facility for imagining a more-or-less coherent storyline in the style of David Lynch.

In this picture, all is not remotely as it seems. Sharp-eyed film buffs will notice quite early on that the characters and situations conform to old Hollywood stereotypes, and may suspect that this dark, sinister view of modern La La land is a skewed one, by somebody with a movie-influenced vision of him or herself.

Eventually we discover that these events are in fact the fantasies of one of the central characters, trying to justify a horrible act of revenge against an ex-lover and her director fiance, but unable to do so, and now on the verge of suicide.

That's my solution, at any rate, and I'm pretty confident it's the one Lynch has in mind. But the film is an elaborate puzzle that each member of the audience has to work out. Many won't bother, put off by some critics telling them (erroneously) that it's a meaningless mess, and by its chequered history: it began as a pilot for a TV series, which ABC rejected, so Lynch resolved the mystery with some late, explanatory scenes and turned it into a movie.

There are plot-lines that seemingly don't lead anywhere, and the effort of deciding what's real and what's fantasy, what's past and what's present does demand an attention span of much more than ten minutes. It does all make sense, but you'll have to work at it, however clever you are.

My big criticism is that there are too many false trails, and that some of the more pretentious passages – such as a largely pointless scene in a theatre infested by posers and performance artists – could be cut. The film is too long, at almost two and a half hours.

Even so, I loved it. Throughout, there is the sense of a great director at the height of his powers. *Mulholland Drive* is undisciplined and infuriating at times, yet Lynch conjures up an unforgettable atmosphere of unease, suspense and passion. He does for Hollywood what he previously did for rural America, in *Twin Peaks*.

At the heart of this analysis of how the Dream Factory

has distorted our dreams is a marvellous central performance by Naomi Watts.

This film isn't for everyone, and Lynch shows his old inability to know when to stop. But much of it is tremendous. This is a unique achievement by a colossal talent, and it deserves to join *Blue Velvet* and *The Straight Story* at the top of the list of Lynch's best movies.

THE ORPHANAGE/ EL ORFONATO
(2007)

Did you ever play "grandmother's footsteps" as a child and remember that frisson as someone touched you on the shoulder? *The Orphanage* contains two versions of that game: the first childish and innocent, the second grown-up and terrifying.

You might think that haunted house stories have been done to death and beyond, but this one rises above the clichés of the genre to be terrific. It's brilliantly written, directed and acted.

There are welcome echoes of Guillermo del Toro's work, particularly *Pan's Labyrinth* and *The Devil's Backbone*, and he is the film's producer. Like both of those movies, this is a story about children but too scary for anyone except adults. *The Orphanage* is the classiest, most suspense-packed horror film since *The Others*, in 2001.

The picture takes place almost entirely in an old, extremely creepy orphanage, which has become a private house owned by a doctor (Fernando Carlos) and his wife (Beluen Rueda). She is herself an orphan who is eager to turn her childhood haunt into a home for her adopted seven year-old son Simon (Roger Princep) and perhaps five or six other children.

But young Simon talks of having child-friends, who may or may not be imaginary. One of them wears a disturbingly grotesque mask.

Then Simon – after a row with his mother – disappears. Nine months later, his adoptive parents are still looking for him, and desperate to know what has happened.

Perhaps a sinister, old woman (Montserrat Carulla) who turns up calling herself a social worker can help. Or a skeletal medium (Geraldine Chaplin), who thinks that the house holds a grisly secret. Or are the grieving mother's troubled visions merely inside her head?

Director Juan Bayona prolongs suspense to a well nigh unbearable degree, culminating in some nasty shocks that deliver in ways which are far from conventional.

Congratulations are also owed to screenwriter Sergio G. Sanchez for coming up with a story that so expertly merges a feeling for the supernatural with a solution that is, in fact, capable of rational explanation. The integration of J.M.Barrie's Peter Pan myth is both clever and emotionally satisfying, without – miraculously – being fey or literary.

To appreciate this movie, you will need an attention span of considerably more than ten seconds. In return for your efforts, you will get a unique atmosphere, a central character you can care about, and that prickling feeling you get on the back of your neck when you just know you're about to see something really, really horrible.

Terrible events do indeed reveal themselves, but the climax is – in a curious way – upbeat. This is a great little film, but not for the faint-hearted.

THE OTHERS *(2001)*

We're in the Channel Islands towards the end of World War II. The initially unsympathetic heroine is a young, austerely Catholic mother called Grace (Nicole Kidman).

She is raising her young daughter and son (Alakina Mann and James Bentley) in a cavernous Gothic mansion while she awaits the return from the war of her husband (Christopher Eccleston), who is missing, believed dead. Three mysterious servants (Fionnuala Flanagan, Eric Sykes and Elaine Cassidy) arrive and seem like the answer to Grace's prayers. Her principal concern is that the two women care for her children, who are allergic to sunlight. To that end, she demands that curtains must always be drawn in the rooms where they are, and that doors to those rooms must remain locked.

The new servants are weird, bordering on spooky, but things weren't right even before they arrived. The previous set of retainers left suddenly, without explanation. And the daughter has visions – first of a little boy named Victor, then of a wizened crone, then of a man and woman… We, like Grace, don't see them at first, but we seem to glimpse them out of the corner of our eyes, and we certainly hear them. Who, or what, are these intruders?

Kidman turns in a mesmerising and beautifully judged psychological study that transcends the horror genre, and carries this into the realm of tragic drama. Those who look beyond movie stars should also note the name of the film's Chilean writer-director-composer Alejandro Amenabar, one of the brightest talents to emerge in cinema since Kidman's previous director (in *Moulin Rouge*), Baz Luhrmann.

The Others is a reminder of the days when a first-rate director could make an audience yelp with communal terror without the aid of expensive special effects, slashing blades or gallons of gore.

Like all the best directors, Amenabar makes the audience imagine things that are worse than anything he can show. Don't be lulled into a sense of security by the 12 certificate. This one is really scary, all the more so if you have a fertile imagination.

It creates the kind of very English, understated yet spell-binding unease that pervades the masterpieces of those two doyens of supernatural fiction, M.R. James and Algernon Blackwood.

The master of cinematic mystery and suspense, Alfred Hitchcock, would have admired, and probably even envied, the first-rate writing, camerawork, design, editing and acting. *The Others* makes other recent efforts at horror – even such successes as *The Blair Witch Project* and *The Sixth Sense* – look crude.

The director skilfully plays with our worst fears and blithest certainties, by making the audience see different points of view at different times. The little boy doesn't want to see the intruders, and reminds us of a time when all of us were too frightened to look under our bed, and convinced there was something nasty hiding behind the curtains.

The little girl accepts the intruders as a fact of life, and she is resentful and rebellious when her mother punishes her for lying. She wants to make the intruders appear, to show that it's not she who is going mad.

Most of all, and increasingly, we identify with Grace's fierce determination to protect her children. We share her stoicism turning to fear, and fear turning to panic, as her old certainties collapse and the terrifying fact emerges not just that her children are telling the truth, but that everyone else is concealing it...

Kidman rightly attracted rave reviews, but Fionnuala Flanagan is also excellent as the housekeeper, expertly steering a course between homely helper and Mrs Danvers-style harbinger of doom. The previously inexperienced child-actors are wonderful, too; and, in an unaccustomed serious role, Eric Sykes as the gardener adds a kind of world-weary quirkiness, which keeps the audience guessing as to just how well-meaning, or profoundly sinister, the new servants really are.

We live in a supposedly ironic, post-modernist age, where even children often appear unshockable, so it's refreshing to see a movie that still has the power to make our spines tingle, and the hairs on the back of our necks stand on end.

The scene when Kidman enters a room where all the furniture is shrouded in white sheets is sheer perfection, and requires nothing more hi-tech than a roving camera and a fine actress to create an atmosphere of almost unbearable terror.

Even more importantly, there is in this movie a cumulative power, a mounting dread reflected in Kidman's increasingly pale features and terrified eyes. Masterful pacing rises to a memorably outrageous conclusion that may beg a few logical questions about the veil that divides the living from the dead, but undeniably packs a punch. The final, tremendously sad, powerful image must rank with the great ones of recent cinema.

There are not many classic films about ghosts. Until this, the best were probably Jack Clayton's *The Innocents*, Robert Wise's *The Haunting* and (if you stretch the notion of ghosts a little) Hitchcock's *Rebecca*. *The Others* is a work of equal skill and intelligence, with a central performance that's as good as any there's ever been in a thriller. This deserves to be called a modern classic, and if you let it creep into your subconscious it could stay with you for a lifetime.

THE PAINTED VEIL *(2006)*

Here is high romantic drama of the kind you may have feared they didn't make any more. Not only is it based on one of W. Somerset Maugham's finest books; it actually improves upon it. David Lean in his prime would have been proud to have made this.

Co-produced in China with the local authorities – no mean feat in itself – it is superbly written, sensitively directed and brilliantly acted.

Kitty (played by the film's co-producer Naomi Watts) is an upper-class young flapper in the 1920s, with the exaggeratedly lackadaisical air of a girl fully aware of her effect upon men. She is beautiful and vivacious, but also selfish and spoilt, with more than a touch of Scarlett O'Hara about her.

Even though she is offhand to the point of rudeness, she is wooed and won by a stiff, diffident microbiologist called Walter (played by the film's other co-producer, Edward Norton). They marry without really knowing each other – he because he admires her looks and needs a wife to accompany him to Shanghai, she because she can't wait to get away from her stuffy, domineering parents (Maggie Steed and Alan David).

"I think I improve greatly on acquaintance," he assures her, and she's prepared to take that on trust.

Unfortunately, they discover in China that they have

nothing whatever in common – he's an intellectual, she's a party girl – and she embarks on an affair with a splendidly oily, smooth-talking British diplomat called Charlie (Liev Schreiber, who in real life is Watts' boyfriend and father of her forthcoming baby).

When her husband discovers her infidelity, he politely gives her the option of marrying her lover. When, to nobody's surprise except Kitty's, Charlie lets her down, Walter demands that Kitty accompany him to a remote, cholera-infected area of China.

This appears to be either a punishment for her adultery or a bizarre form of joint suicide. But a marriage that appears to have perished beneath several layers of frost comes to hesitant life again, partly because of political events, partly because of two westerners: Toby Jones as the kind of seedy diplomat-gone-native you'd expect to find in a Graham Greene novel, and Diana Rigg as a doughty old nun with a pragmatic approach to the Almighty.

But mainly it's because – just as Lizzie Bennet comes to love Mr Darcy in *Pride and Prejudice* – Kitty learns to appreciate Walter's finer points. And he starts to accept her as she really is, not as he would like to be. This is the best but most difficult kind of love story to pull off – unsentimental and painfully truthful about how difficult true love can be.

Writer Ron Nyswaner won an Oscar for *Philadelphia*. His work here is far tougher and less sentimental, and his feeling for period dialogue is excellent. Maugham's claustrophobically intense novel has been expertly opened out, to make China an important supporting character. Not only is the scenery breathtaking; there is a real sense of the benefits and dangers of colonialism, and the racism that westerners often encounter in a foreign country.

Director John Curran's previous film was a well-acted chamber-piece called *We Don't Live Here Anymore* (2004), which also starred Naomi Watts. This is far more ambitious, but he does not allow the epic landscape to dwarf his equally magnificent cast.

There is no more luminous actress around than Watts, and she is admirably fearless in showing us Kitty's spiky, dislikeable side. Rightly, she realises that this makes Kitty thoroughly human and believable, and makes her redemption all the more moving.

A lesser actress would have sweetened the role. Watts makes her a marvellous, timeless anti-heroine. She's the kind of young woman you would be even more likely to meet in today's selfish, superficial society.

Edward Norton has a virtually flawless English accent as Walter, and uses his one weakness as an actor – an almost total absence of warmth – to startling effect. Like Ralph Fiennes's underrated performance as a suspicious, undemonstrative Englishman finding how much his wife loved him in *The Constant Gardener*, this is a superbly sensitive portrayal of a man who might be dismissed as a "cold fish" by those who don't know him.

In a master-class of subtle screen-acting, Norton makes us realise that his cruelty towards his wife, and his recklessness about dying from cholera, emanate not just from bruised pride, but from deep unhappiness and a kind of heroic selflessness.

Norton has been impressive before in showier roles – notably in *Primal Fear* and *Fight Club* – but here he shows a maturity and subtlety that confirm he is among the great actors of his generation.

Diana Rigg and Toby Jones are excellent in important

supporting roles, but I was particularly struck by Maggie Steed and Alan David as Kitty's parents. Even though they are allowed a minimum of screen time, they conjure up a world of pettiness and privilege.

Actors such as these may never command big fees or have celebrity features written about them and their "lifestyles". They are, nevertheless, far more talented and valuable performers than most who do get that kind of money and acclaim.

Stuart Dryburgh, a New Zealander born in Britain and one of the world's best cinematographers, here surpasses his work on *Lone Star* and *The Piano*.

Also of Oscar-quality are the costume designs of Brit Ruth Myers, whose clothes for Kitty sympathetically mirror her state of mind as she changes from callow egocentricity to a sadder, wiser maturity,

All too often, costume dramas are genteel, over-civilised affairs that leave the viewer on the outside. It's a tribute to everyone involved with *The Painted Veil* that this is a thoroughly involving film – handsomely mounted, to be sure, and remarkably faithful to its period, place and source material, but first gripping, then involving and finally deeply moving.

PAN'S LABYRINTH/
EL LABERINTO DEL FAUNO *(2006)*

Like Lewis Carroll's *Alice In Wonderland* and the Oscar-winning cartoon *Spirited Away*, *Pan's Labyrinth* is about a young girl being drawn into a fantasy world that's alluring but life-threatening.

A fairy – or is it really only an insect that the little girl thinks is a fairy? – lures Ofelia (touchingly played by Ivana Baquero) into an ancient labyrinth of stone, where an ugly, gaunt and distinctly mangy faun (Doug Jones) – who's not noticeably related to that nice Mr Tumnus in *The Lion, The Witch and the Wardrobe* – tells her she's a Princess of the Underworld. In order to gain her birthright she must accomplish three tasks before the moon is full, in a few nights' time.

These tasks are intercut with the girl's real life, set against the background of the Spanish Civil War, which is no less menacing than the fantastical creatures she must confront. Her mother (Alex Angulo) is heavily pregnant but seriously ill with pre-natal problems.

Ofelia's super-sinister stepfather (Sergi Lopez from *Dirty Pretty Things* and *Harry, He's Here To Help*) is a captain in Franco's fascist army, and likes nothing better than to bludgeon the local peasants to death, torture suspected traitors and shoot softies repeatedly in the head, to make sure that they're dead.

At first, he looks like a laughably melodramatic villain – the kind that Ken Loach might create when in uncompromisingly didactic, agit-prop mode. But Lopez, a terrific actor, finds surprising depth in the man, and through sheer force of personality turns him into a convincing yet mythic metaphor for authoritarian masculinity.

His austere cruelty is offset by the caring femininity of one of his servants (exquisitely played by Maribel Verdu) who becomes a surrogate mother to the captain's stepdaughter, and is at the same time feeding (both literally and information-wise) the anti-fascists in the woods.

Pan's Labyrinth is a fantasy film, but it's emphatically not for children. It's as savage as the grimmest of Grimm's fairy tales. Like Terry Gilliam's last picture, *Tideland*, this is a grown-up attempt to dissect the uses and limitations of our fantasies. The brutality of reality is shown in unflinching, and even sadistic, close-up.

Be warned that there are beating, slashings and torture scenes that will make many an adult flinch. This is not a film for everyone. But if you have a strong stomach, it is one of the most ambitious and original pictures of the year, with sights that may haunt your nightmares for years to come.

I'm not sure how popular it will be. It's far too brutal, bloody and disturbing for small children, and it's lucky to have escaped the censors with only a 15 certificate. At the same time, its baroque visual style and fantastical subject-matter are unlikely to appeal to prosaic adults. Early on, Ofelia's mother inveighs against fairy-tales, telling her "You're too old to be filling your head with that nonsense". Many grown-ups will agree. If you hated *The Lord of the Rings*, you should probably give this a miss.

The fantasy sequences might have been more imaginative and less under-populated. Despite some memorable special effects, it is possible to see that this has not had the budget of, say, a Peter Jackson movie or the Narnian Chronicles. But I sympathise with del Toro's desire to reclaim fantasy from the realm of the twee, the comforting and the Disneyfied. Many old fairy-tales have a violent subtext.

Pan's Labyrinth reveals why people need fantasies, whether or not they are true, in order to survive the realities of life. And del Toro makes the point effectively that monsters do not only exist in our dreams. Lopez's stepfather may seem exaggeratedly wicked, but the newspapers every day bring us more evidence of man's inhumanity to man, and to child.

Del Toro's commercial reputation rests on two comic-inspired movies he made in Hollywood: *Blade 2* and (by far the better of the pair) *Hellboy*. *Pan's Labyrinth* is an attempt to marry the production values of a mid-level Hollywood movie with the more subversive, intellectual streak del Toro showed in his Spanish-speaking movies, *The Devil's Backbone* and his debut, *Cronos*.

Pan's Labyrinth confirms that del Toro is one of the few genuinely visionary, and original, directors working today. And his best may still be to come.

THE PERKS OF BEING A WALLFLOWER *(2012)*

I won't be alone in loving this. It is, quite simply, one of the best coming-of-age films ever made. No film-maker has captured with more sensitivity the hell and heaven of being a teenager. It's sweet but not sickly, cute but not sentimental.

The movie contains an Oscar-quality performance by Emma Watson and a wonderfully astute one by Logan Lerman as the film's 15 year-old hero, Charlie.

Writer-director Stephen Chbosky has adapted his own "young adult" novel from 1999 with remarkable skill. For many teenagers I'm sure that it will be a landmark movie in their emotional development. But it will also strike chords of memory with many who are way over the target demographic.

The story is set in 1991-2, when the Smiths were cool, David Bowie's *Heroes* was exotic, and the ultimate thrill for a teenager was to dress up and mime along to the *Rocky Horror Picture Show.*

Charlie (Lerman), a 15 year-old with an initially unexplained history of psychiatric illness, goes to a new school, where he conspicuously fails to fit in. He's a wallflower, always on the sidelines, observing but never participating.

The first friend he makes is – depressingly – his English teacher, played with marvellous sensitivity by Paul Rudd, taking a very welcome rest from demeaning gross-out comedies and reminding us what a fine, intelligent actor he can be.

But then unassuming Charlie is adopted as a friend by the school's only "out" gay, Patrick (beautifully played with both ebullience and depth by Ezra Miller), who recognizes a fellow outcast. Patrick introduces Charlie to his beautiful step-sister Sam (Emma Watson).

Charlie falls hopelessly in love with Sam, but she's at least two years older than him, and going out with a young man who's at college. So Charlie settles for having an unreciprocated crush until... well, I won't spoil the story.

Suffice it to say that the film delivers on why Charlie has psychiatric problems. But the aspect that makes the film memorable is the relationship that develops between Charlie and Sam – one of the most touching I have ever seen on screen.

Lerman – unrecognisable from the boy who delivered lacklustre leading performances in *The Three Musketeers 3D* and *Percy Jackson and the Lightning Thief*, plays his part well, and makes something sweet out of what could have been an infuriatingly passive character.

But most of the heavy lifting, acting-wise, is done by Emma Watson, whose experience on the Harry Potter films has done her a world of good. Although the Potter films suggested she had the makings of a fine actress, she could be uneven from scene to scene and was visibly learning her craft; this is a major leap forward in terms of quality and consistency. Here she's a revelation, with the transparency and power of a young Kate Winslet. She has learned not to do too much, but just be. And she has the gamine beauty of the young Audrey Hepburn. If she were not so well-known already, I would be hailing this as a star-making performance.

The film isn't flawless. It's light on story, and hints at some things it doesn't follow through, notably Sam's bulimia. One of the bravest elements in the novel, concerning an abortion, has clearly been excluded in order to placate Middle America.

However, it's no exaggeration to say that this is *The Catcher in the Rye* for a later generation. There are many sharp lines, most of them given to Patrick as he challenges his friends to dislike him. There's a clever little section that shows how easy it is to drift into the wrong relationship merely because it would seem churlish to refuse. The movie covers such clichéd topics as homophobia, drugs, bereavement and abuse, and makes them all feel freshly observed.

Its effortless humanity reminded me a lot of Cameron Crowe's earliest movies, especially *Singles, Jerry Maguire* and *Almost Famous*.

The emotional honesty on display is very rare indeed in any form of cinema, let alone the traditionally dumbed-down genre of high school movies. The film visits dark areas of life, yet there's a joy in it which is quite uplifting. It captures the moment in all our lives when anything and everything seemed possible.

PHILOMENA *(2013)*

Wry, thought-provoking and touching, *Philomena* is a superb film with an Oscar-quality central performance by Dame Judi Dench. Even if, as I suspect, she loses at the Academy Awards to Cate Blanchett for *Blue Jasmine*, that will be no reflection on Dench's excellence. Here, she is as transparent, delicate and affecting as she has ever been.

Philomena is a fine example of the kind of movie critics routinely disparage as a "crowd-pleaser". In other words, it will involve your emotions and make you cry, more than once – which is most people's idea of a terrific time in the cinema.

Stephen Frears, noticeably less grumpy than he used to be and still on top form at 72, is always great with actors, and this is his finest film since he directed Helen Mirren in *The Queen.* He's well served by Steve Coogan and Jeff Pope's clever screenplay, based on Martin Sixsmith's non-fiction book, *The Lost Child of Philomena Lee.*

There's nothing stylistically innovative about the film, and that may earn it the familiar critical jibe of being "middlebrow". But the script has a rare, distinctly upmarket ability to combine laughter with tears.

And it has an even more unusual quality: right up until the end, it's carefully ambiguous about which of the two leading characters is the film's moral centre.

As the picture is called *Philomena*, you might expect it to be from her point of view. Dench splendidly and unpatronisingly captures the essence of a simple Catholic soul, eager to see the good in people and gracious even to the nuns who separated her from her illegitimate son, Anthony, when he was only three years old.

The central narrative is about her quest for that missing son, which leads to unexpected revelations that I would not dream of divulging.

You might expect such a story to be anti-Catholic. One of the film's strengths is that in its title character, it offers a complex, nuanced vision of religion. Philomena's belief in God enables her to survive the cruel depredations of people claiming to act in his name. Dench's own faith (she's a Quaker) helps her to portray such a character with impressive depth of understanding.

The other storyline, skilfully interwoven with Philomena's quest, is the humanisation of Martin Sixsmith, the BBC journalist turned Blairite spin doctor. He is portrayed with more than a hint of malice by Steve Coogan, whose lack of affection for journalists has been exhaustively documented, not least by himself.

When Sixsmith is first approached by Philomena's daughter (the consistently admirable Anna Maxwell Martin) he grandly dismisses the tale of her mother's 50-year quest for her lost son as "a human interest story," adding that these kind of stories are written both for and about the "weak-minded, vulnerable and ignorant".

But when he can't interest anyone in publishing his projected heavyweight tome about Russian history, he goes back to the story and pitches it to a magazine editor with an unashamedly populist agenda. The script wittily makes the point that in the morally topsy-turvy world of journalism, bad things are "good", i.e. marketable. For Philomena, good and evil are absolutes. But for Sixsmith and his journalistic ilk, they are commodities.

A legitimate criticism of a movie that's strong on irony is that it's unwilling to examine its own hypocrisies. The screenplay mocks Sixsmith for packaging human tragedy as entertainment, while simultaneously doing precisely the same itself.

Despite the film's eagerness to portray Sixsmith as exploitative, it is he who turns out to be its true moral centre. With all his faults, his reactions to the outrages inflicted by the Catholic church are easier to empathise with than Philomena's stoicism. His shock is our shock.

Frears' film is every bit as indignant about Roman Catholic injustices as Peter Mullan's powerful 2002 melodrama *The Magdalene Sisters*, but Frears' willingness to see them from multiple points of view makes his the more sophisticated movie. He shows not only the extent of the cruelty and bigotry involved, but enables us to understand how they were allowed to go unchallenged for so long.

This is a fine film, well up there with Frears' best, and the remarkable story it has to tell is certainly worth 98 minutes of your time.

PULP FICTION *(1994)*

A boxer (Bruce Willis) is supposed to take a dive in a fight but kills his opponent instead, then tries to escape with his wife (Maria de Medeiros).

The other chief protagonists are a pair of hit-men : ageing pretty-boy Vincent (John Travolta), rapidly running to seed on a diet of junk food, pop culture and heroin, and his black sidekick (Samuel L. Jackson) who sees himself as an instrument of Biblical vengeance.

Along the way, these two run into a smooth-talking dope dealer (Eric Stoltz) and his wacky wife (Rosanna Arquette). Uma Thurman gives the performance of her life as a gangster-boss's cocaine-addicted spouse – and the world's worst date. And there's a super-cool trouble-shooter (Harvey Keitel, who else?) who has the job of cleaning up after the two hitmen have accidentally blown a man's head off in the back of their car.

Inevitably, many reviews concentrated on the blood, bad language, drugs and depravity; but the ingredient which lifts this black comedy thriller to greatness is the storytelling. Although the dialogue has the bite of an Elmore Leonard novel or a David Mamet play, it is Quentin Tarantino's sheer delight in spinning a yarn which makes him the Spielberg of splatter.

But whereas Spielberg pictures are about Good versus Evil, Tarantino is interested in the palpable friction between Evil and Much, Much Worse. On display here is the kind of lowlife which makes the underside of a stone look salubrious. There is scarcely a character who is not motivated by greed or self-indulgence. Perhaps the most shocking moment is when a wife bursts into tears of relief at her husband's blood-soaked return; it's virtually the only sign of normal human concern in the whole movie.

Bookending the film is an episode where two petty crooks (Tim Roth and Amanda Plummer) hold up a fast-food joint. The narrative connection between them and the rest of the picture only becomes clear at the end; but their role is morally crucial. For they are young people who, lacking any roots or morality, are contemplating a life of crime. They fancy themselves as a latterday Bonnie and Clyde. The rest of the film charts that descent into a Dante's Inferno which they risk entering. The denouement delivers them from the worst consequences of their stupidity, and looks likely to dissuade them from trying anything like it again.

There will always be those who argue that *Pulp Fiction* trivialises violence and glamorises crime; but what clearly fascinates Tarantino is a world where bloodshed can become trivialised, where crime really does confer glamour, where greed and depravity are disguised beneath a veneer of cool professionalism. As surely as Martin Scorsese in *GoodFellas*, Tarantino exposes the banality of evil, but he does so with the clinical detachment of French New Wave film-makers such as Jean-Pierre Melville or the very early Jean-Luc Godard. He – and they – know that you can't hope to understand criminality without appreciating its attractions.

The numerous movie references within *Pulp Fiction* should not be construed as mere Post-Modernist affectation, or showing off for the benefit of critics; they reflect a recognition that films help create the role-models for our society. It was often said of the Kray Brothers that they imitated the Hollywood gangsters they had seen (though, of course, they chose to ignore those movies' moral lessons). Tarantino doesn't disguise the fact that Cinema forms part of criminal culture.

When Bruce Willis escapes in a cab from his fatal fight, for instance, the back-projection behind him is black-and-white. This reminds the audience that his story is part of a boxing movie tradition which runs from *Body and Soul* through to *Raging Bull*. At the same time, the colour foreground reveals that this is all taking place very much in the amoral present, with his cab-driver gaining a perverted pleasure from the knowledge that her passenger has just killed a man.

In another memorable scene, Travolta's hit-man enters a dance competition which knowingly sends up his big-screen debut in *Saturday Night Fever*. The sequence is richly comic because Travolta's character evidently fancies himself as a John Travolta; and the reason why his dancing partner is attracted to him is just as obviously that he looks like Travolta, though a bit fleshier, older and not quite as quick on his feet.

In perhaps the most nightmarish episode (and one which some people will find homophobic), Willis finds himself in a stylized, sado-masochistic situation which combines the worst moments of *Deliverance* and *The Silence of the Lambs*.

Such references might have been clever-clever or distancing; in Tarantino's hands, they are arresting. How many times have people said of reality, especially at moments of danger, that it was like being in the movies? Here is the film which, more cleverly than any art-house classic like *8 1/2*, explores that symbiotic interaction between movies and life.

The question remains as to whether Tarantino has made a film about desensitisation, or has merely made a desensitised film. It is hard to see *Pulp Fiction* without the uneasy feeling that modern audiences may – like the Krays with those old gangster movies – respond to the style, violence and sleaze without perceiving the moral underpinning. And there are moments when Tarantino's intention is clearly to gross out the audience. But then Shakespeare did the same with the eye-gouging in *King Lear*, the decapitation in *Titus Andronicus*, and the murder of Macduff's family in *Macbeth*.

This is not a film for anyone who is easily offended by bad language, or who thinks that all screen violence is "unnecessary". Do see it, however, if you enjoy a cracking story, lively characters, sparkling dialogue and bravura cinematic talent. For once, the Grand Jury at Cannes – under the timely Chairmanship of Clint Eastwood – came to the right decision in awarding *Pulp Fiction* the Palme d'Or. For this is the film in which Tarantino fulfils the promise of *Reservoir Dogs* and lifts himself immediately into the class of Scorsese. Not only is this among the best films of the 90s; it is also the most 90s film of the 90s.

QUEEN OF HEARTS (1989)

These unreliable memoirs of a child (Ian Hawkes) growing
up in London's Italian community turn out to be a
magnificent film about a boy's childhood, and in my opinion
one of the most magical movies ever made. It's a modern
myth, a fantastic fairy-tale about the importance of family
and forgiveness, movingly written by first-time screenwriter
Tony Grisoni, and beautifully directed by Jon Amiel. Italians
are here portrayed with the same quirky affection which
Scottish villagers received from Bill Forsyth in *Local Hero*.

The film which it most resembles, however, is Frank
Capra's 1946 masterpiece, *It's A Wonderful Life*. In both
movies, the plot revolves around suicide and miraculous
survival. But it is also reminiscent of *The Godfather*, for it is
also about that most Italian of emotions, revenge. The villain,
Barbariccia (Vittorio Amandola), and our child-hero both
attempt acts of revenge; but neither is successful, and it is
only when Eddie's father, Danilo, renounces revenge in
favour of forgiveness that the story can end.

The film is openly emotional, with an almost operatic
feel. The opening, Italian sequence is worthy of Visconti in
its over-the-top romanticism and pictorial lushness. Even
when the story moves to London, the lighting could have
been designed by Zeffirelli; and director Jon Amiel, though

Jewish rather than Italian, exhibits a Fellini-esque flair for photographing the human face.

At the same time, there is a distinctively British irony and sophistication. Immediately after the picturesque, opening account of how our child-hero's parents escaped certain death, we become aware that the sequence we have just watched is probably not the literal truth. We hear a child's voice narrating the tale, and we realise that the story may have grown in the telling. Uniquely and brilliantly, the film hooks us on the narrative and the characters, yet keeps us subtly distanced at the same time.

Throughout the rest of the film, there are constant visual hints that what we are seeing may not be the literal truth. *Queen of Hearts* has a particular affinity with *The Ladykillers*, in the way Jim Clay's production design creates a fantastical, cinematic landscape in a stylised corner of London. The set – supposedly in the Italian quarter of Clerkenwell – is deliberately and charmingly phoney.

Queen of Hearts draws its visual style mainly from the 1950s; but little anachronisms constantly appear, to remind us that this is not reality, but romance. The Beatles, D-registration cabs, an anti-AIDS poster, all lurk around the corner, in the outside world of the present. Such anachronisms are not, as some critics assumed, mistakes. They are central to the movie. The film is a child's unreliable memoirs, not a faithful history; poetic, not literal, truth. One of the messages is that it is folly to try to turn the clock back and recreate the past in the present; and the style of this lovely little picture – a unique mixture of nostalgia and irony – imaginatively reflects its content.

QUIZ SHOW *(1994)*

In mid-Fifties America, Charles Van Doren (Ralph Fiennes) was the egghead Elvis. A college academic from a respected literary family, he became an unlikely TV star through his ability to answer trivial General Knowledge questions on a popular quiz show, *Twenty-One*. His intelligence, unpretentiousness and Ivy League charm brought him $129,000 in prize money, and over 500 marriage proposals. Van Doren's picture appeared on the cover of Time and Life magazine. Pop-culture pundits latched on to his success, hailing him as an emblem of America's thirst for knowledge.

But then things started going wrong. Allegations of question-rigging came from a former champion, Herb Stempel (John Turturro), angry and vindictive at being dumped in favour of the more telegenic, patrician Van Doren. As evidence mounted against him, America's favourite intellectual confessed he had been fed the questions and answers in advance. He retired in disgrace from academia and public life. In reality, though not in Robert Redford's new film about him, there was at least one happy ending – he married the young woman he had hired to answer his fan mail, and they have been together ever since.

Robert Redford's excellent study of the Quiz Show scandal didn't set the box office on fire. Nineties audiences may have found it hard to see what the fuss was about. Ethical standards have slipped to the point where most of us assume (quite rightly) that game shows such as *Blind Date* or *Celebrity Squares* are partially scripted. Concepts of ethics, shame and disgrace are clearly foreign to many of our politicians, captains of industry, and football managers... Why should we expect them of showbiz personalities?

As an audience-grabber, *Quiz Show* also suffers from a lack of suspense. It is obvious from the start that Van Doren will be seduced into selling his soul, and then get found out. Why else bother to make a film about him?

Fortunately, *Quiz Show* is not intended to be a thriller. It is in part an evocation of an era. It takes us back to more trusting, innocent times, and does succeed in capturing a moment when America first lost faith in its establishment.

Like the Profumo affair in Britain, the quiz show scandal lifted society's backdrop for a moment, and showed people a little of what was going on behind the scenes. For better and for worse, it helped pave the way for the cynicism and anti-establishment attitudes of the 1960s.

Quiz Show is also a human drama about conflicting characters – and a vivid array they are, written with wit and intelligence by the former film critic for the Washington Post, Paul Attanasio.

British actor Ralph Fiennes was marvellous as the Nazi commander in *Schindler's List*, and is just as impressive as the less spectacularly flawed Charles Van Doren. He explores all the character's weakness, yet enabling us to sympathise with his fascination with the new medium of TV, his need to escape his own bloodlines and establish his own identity, his eagerness to believe that his own celebrity was doing good for the cause of education.

With less to work with, Paul Scofield gives an even more miraculous performance as Charles's father Mark – a fascinating study in cultural aloofness, paternal pride and dignified disappointment.

The two Van Dorens could so easily have been caricatured as privileged and out of touch; instead, they are portrayed as clinging desperately to cultural standards which since then have virtually disappeared. Every scene between father and son is riveting. It is impossible to watch the film without feeling sorry for both men, and nostalgic for the loss of what they represent.

Equally splendid in a more cartoonish way are David Paymer and Hank Azaria, as the two producers of the quiz show, both obviously Jewish yet blithely anti-Semitic. Martin Scorsese is icily sinister as the unnamed representative of the show's sponsor, Geritol; and John Turturro gives his best performance yet in what could easily have been an offensively sterotyped role, as the whistle-blowing Herb Stempel, a neurotic nerd with bad glasses, worse teeth, and a brain like flypaper.

Quiz Show was rightly nominated for four Oscars, and the wonder was that it was not nominated for more. Fiennes and Turturro, in particular, were unlucky.

Redford's film has a few weaknesses. It is easy for filmmakers to blame TV for society's ills, when perhaps they could do with examining their own motives and practices a little more carefully.

Redford's movie plays just as fast and loose with characters, truth and chronology, in order to maximise its dramatic potential and therefore its audience, as those less than ethical TV executives did back in the 1950s.

It also suits Redford to exaggerate the degree to which

the quiz scandal "robbed America of its innocence". America has lost its innocence so many times in the movies that it's hard to avoid wondering if America was ever that innocent in the first place.

Organized crime was rampant in the 1950s. The practice of feeding answers to chosen contestants took place on virtually all prime-time game programmes of the era, including the even more popular quiz show, *The $64,000 Question.*

Perhaps the most shocking fact about the case – not brought out by the film – is that many of the 150 contestants and TV executives who testified before a grand jury must have perjured themselves in saying that they were not in on the fraud.

Van Doren was very much a scapegoat, and the film fails to bring that out fully. Even so, this is a gripping story, a superbly acted drama and by far Robert Redford's finest film.

RATATOUILLE *(2007)*

Rats have been blamed for numerous disasters, ranging from the bubonic plague to breakfast television. Rats are badmouthed for deserting sinking ships, yet no one bothers to say what happens to them afterwards. (Presumably, they drown.) Politicians have been known to rat on their principles and, heaven forbid, scavenge other parties' policies. Max Clifford would be the first to tell rats that they have an image problem. But no more. A movie starring rats – and lots of them – is about to become one of the most popular movies of the year.

Ratatouille, which celebrates a rat called Remy as a newer, nicer, less rodent-like Gordon Ramsay, is a tremendous animated comedy. In terms of visual panache and confident story-telling, it's second to none.

The only areas in which it falls short of perfection are that there aren't quite enough laughs, and some sequences are allowed to drag on for too long. Maybe the film-makers were enjoying themselves too much.

With a few more gags and slightly more ruthless editing, it would have been on a par with writer-director Brad Bird's previous masterpiece, *The Incredibles*. But it's still one of the finest movie achievements of 2007, a certainty for next year's Oscar as Best Animated Film and, whatever your age or attitude to vermin, a must-see.

Remy (charmingly voiced by comedian Patton Oswalt) is a rat with an unlikely taste for *haute cuisine*. His father (Brian Dennehy) warns him not to get too close to humans, and his tubby rat sibling Emile (Peter Sohn) is shocked to discover that his brother can read cookery books. "You read?" exclaims Emile. Remy is modest: "Well, not excessively."

Arriving in Paris via sewer, thanks to some brilliantly kinetic animation, Remy falls in love with the city's views and smells (as do we – the film finds time to be charmingly lyrical).

After being chased around a kitchen by its greedy, diminutive and disreputable chef (hilariously played by an unrecognisable Ian Holm), Remy finds an unlikely ally in Linguini (Lou Romano), an awkward lad who becomes – under guidance from Remy – a chef whose dishes wow the whole of Paris and attract the attention of a very suspicious restaurant critic named Anton Ego (Peter O'Toole masterfully recapturing the sneering majesty of George Sanders).

The well-crafted story goes through a number of delightful twists, and covers with refreshing intelligence the ideas that artistic genius can be found in the most unlikely places, that it's tempting but wrong to take credit for others' efforts, and – I must admit this notion was an especially pleasant surprise – that good, honest, informed criticism should be valued far more highly than it is.

REQUIEM FOR A DREAM *(2000)*

What's the film about? In a word, addiction. When we first see Harry Goldfarb (Jared Leto), he's persuading his frightened, widowed mother (Ellen Burstyn) to let him pawn her TV set, in order to pay for his drug habit.

He and his best friend Tyrone C. Love (Marlon Wayans) see drugs as an easy way to feel good and make money. And Harry's not such a bad boy. As soon as he has made a few dollars out of drug-dealing, he wants to buy his mother a new TV set.

Harry has an attractive new girl-friend (Jennifer Connelly), whom he genuinely loves and whose dreams to become a dress designer he wants to encourage. They use drugs to iron out any arguments that may arise in their relationship, and cushion themselves from painful memories.

Harry may not look after himself too well – there's a nasty sore on his arm where he keeps injecting himself – but he cares enough about others to try to persuade his mother to stop using diet pills.

Gradually, however, all four of the leading characters plunge into nightmare. The mother starts hallucinating that she is being attacked by her refrigerator, wanders the subway and ends up in a mental hospital. Her son and his friend end up disfigured and imprisoned respectively, while the girl-friend loses her self-respect and ends up selling herself to pornographers.

Not every great film is easy to watch. *Requiem for a Dream* contains scenes that are as harrowing as any I've seen, but they're there for a purpose. You could describe it as a cautionary tale about drugs, but that's a bit like saying that *My Fair Lady* is tuneful, or Albert Einstein knew a thing or two.

The film may sound very depressing, and it certainly doesn't pull any punches. But the film gets inside each of the character's mind so skilfully that you really care for these people.

Early on, Aronofsky makes drug-taking look quick, cool and even funny, through montages of advertising-style close-ups. But as the film goes on, we see more of the gruesome reality behind the ritual, in scenes that make one feel almost physically sick.

This is a film with wonderful visual creativity, a rare ear for sound and music (Clint Mansell's score, a blend of string quartet and modern electronics, is itself a masterpiece) and an emotional power that mark out Darren Aranofsky as one of the most exciting writer-directors working today.

He has the expressionist ability of the great German silent directors, coupled with the flair behind the camera of Martin Scorsese and David Fincher. And although his directorial style makes much use of distorting lenses and variations in camera speed, he can also draw the best out of his actors.

When much younger, Ellen Burstyn won an Oscar for *Alice Doesn't Live Here Any More;* and she was a major reason why *The Exorcist* was so successful – her performance as Linda Blair's anguished mother grounded the horror in believable behaviour.

Her performance here is only one of four central roles, but it makes every other performance by an actress in the last few years look superficial. This is the most affectionate display of motherhood since Brenda Blethyn's in Mike Leigh's *Secrets and Lies*; but she also presents the cinema's most memorable depiction in years of a soul spiralling downwards into madness. And it is because we care about her that the mental hospital scenes at the end make the ordeal that Jack Nicholson went through in *One Flew Over The Cuckoo's Nest* look tame.

The script, by Aronofsky and *Last Exit To Brooklyn* author Hubert Selby is so cleverly crafted that each step towards Hell appears grounded not in the moralising of the authors but in the weaknesses of each character. All the actors descend into their own particular form of degradation, without having to resort to overwrought posturing.

Burstyn will deservedly win the lion's share of the rave notices; but Jennifer Connelly deserves special praise as well.

I remember spotting her as a marvellous child actress in *Once Upon a Time In America*. 17 years on, she emerges here as a brave and considerable talent. Her sensitive study of self-hatred is never showy, but it's finely observed and deeply felt; and she courageously submits herself to scenes at the end that give the lie to the comfortable notion that one man's pornography is another person's harmless fun.

A lot of credit should go to the director. There's none of the cruelty and voyeurism that made me so uneasy about Lars von Trier's studies of female breakdown, in *Breaking the Waves* and *Dancer in the Dark*.

This film is not for the faint-hearted. Like Todd Solondz's *Happiness* and David Fincher's *Fight Club*, it dares to examine areas that are undoubtedly shocking. Yet non-exploitative

Requiem for a Dream   **333**

films should be able to tackle such topics in a responsible manner.

Aronofsky's film is not only a remarkable advance on his first, *Pi* ; it's the best movie I have seen about addiction, capturing both the allure of drugs and their direst consequences. It is the definitive film about drug abuse that *Trainspotting* tried and failed to be.

The horrific sights and the occasional use of foul language made an 18 certificate inevitable; but there's a side of me that believes this exceptional film should be shown to every 13 year-old, so that they can see what drug addiction really involves.

SAVING PRIVATE RYAN *(1998)*

American soldiers are sent behind enemy lines in World War II to retrieve a young man (Matt Damon) who is the sole survivor of four brothers, three of them killed on the same day in different theatres of war.

Steven Spielberg's film begins with an old man visiting a war cemetery with his wife and children. It sets up the question that will be in the back of our minds for the next two and a half hours: who is he?

Even by the end of this prologue – which is virtually silent – Spielberg is making the audience's eyes prick with tears. Within seconds, our eyes are widening with horror, as we are catapulted into what must be the most savage, and probably also the greatest, battle scene in movie history.

The first half-hour alone, a sickening re-enactment of the Normandy landings in all their deafening confusion and brutal carnage, should be enough to convert anyone with lingering doubts about Spielberg's genius as a director.

Even more than in Oliver Stone's Vietnam Oscar-winner, *Platoon*, there is a visceral sense of being in the thick of the action. It is exciting, suspenseful and horrific, all at the same time – even though Spielberg breaks one of the cardinal conventions of "serious" cinema, presenting heart-stopping action before we have a chance to know any of the people involved.

It is a brilliant piece of story-telling through visual montage. We hardly hear any words in the heat of battle, and scarcely any of the faces except Tom Hanks's, is familiar. The effect is disorientating.

As the camera alights on some new face, we think: could this be one of the stars? But no, a bullet penetrates his skull. Unforgettable images burn themselves into the memory: of a man searching for his own arm, of entrails pouring from a stomach, of half a man being dragged across the field of battle.

In the story which follows, Tom Hanks is the team's captain, Tom Sizemore his second-in-command. Both they and their men know that they are on at best an errand of mercy, at worst a public relations exercise. All would prefer to be back home – or, failing that, prosecuting the war to the best of their abilities.

Superficially, Robert Rodat's script is nothing special, with dialogue that rarely rises above the commonplace.

It relies heavily for its impact on three fine performances: from Jeremy Davies as an idealistic but nervous interpreter who has never seen action, from Tom Sizemore as Hanks' loyal second-in-command, and – crucially – from Hanks as a former English teacher whom war has changed into a tough leader under whose command 94 young men have died.

Like Gary Cooper of old, Hanks stands out as a beacon of decency in the film; yet he never seems too good to be true, or too perfect to be incapable of making a horrible mistake. Hanks is a great screen actor, and never more authoritative than here.

Damon has less time to impress as Private Ryan, but his

callowness as an actor suits a character who has not yet undergone the tortures experienced by Hanks and Sizemore.

Less likeable is Edward Burns as the most rebellious of Hanks's men, with a performance that struck me as rather mannered and modern.

John Williams' grandiose score has a tendency to overegg the pudding. Those of us who are not American may wonder why Spielberg has made it seem that the Yanks re-conquered Europe on their own. The British are conspicuous by their absence from *Saving Private Ryan*, and there's an unfair jibe at Field Marshall Montgomery. I could have done with a little less of Abraham Lincoln and the American flag.

But then there have been fine British-made war films which have more-or-less ignored the role played by Americans – and especially Russians – in defeating Hitler.

Spielberg's moments of stars-and-stripes jingoism are surely preferable to the defeatist miserabilism of so many European film-makers, whose attacks on their fellow-countrymen are routinely rewarded with prizes at major festivals, before plummeting equally predictably to box-office extinction in their country of origin.

Europe's film-makers and cultural apparatchiks have all done their bit to contribute to the current wave of anti-nationalistic propaganda that is threatening to bring European nations including Britain under the control of non-elected, non-accountable bureaucrats from an alien culture, thus bringing about one of Hitler's most cherished aims by stealth.

Far too many war films – even some of the most celebrated, such as *La Grande Illusion* and *All Quiet on the Western Front*, have taken the easy way out by blaming wars on nationalism.

Spielberg clearly understands the elements in human

nature which make nationalism understandable and even attractive, such as a wish to be ruled by one's own kind, and have them controlled and replaced by democratic means.

In *Saving Private Ryan* and his other wartime masterpiece, *Schindler's List*, Spielberg communicates something that very few makers of war films have done – why it is that people fight in defence of freedom, and are prepared to put duty above self-interest.

To his credit, Spielberg refuses to toe the guilt-ridden pacifist line that dominated Hollywood's output up to and including the presidency of Jimmy Carter, and probably encouraged Saddam Hussein to invade Kuwait, by leading him to underestimate America's will to fight.

In the decades after Vietnam, Hollywood reacted to such embarrassingly inept pro-war propaganda from the Sixties as John Wayne's *The Green Berets*, and the *Boys' Own* heroics of hits such as *The Great Escape*, by self-consciously propagandising for peace.

In film after film, especially those by Oliver Stone, American military involvement abroad was denounced as disastrous for the local population, and brutalising for the soldiers themselves. Virtually all the top Hollywood stars took turns in playing demoralised veterans returning home.

Saving Private Ryan is a return to an older tradition, since it acknowledges that war – though hellish – can be preferable to appeasement, and that war brings out the best as well as the worst in people.

Spielberg has never been on better form, visually. So graphic is his imagery that one would come away from this movie with near-total understanding of it, were one unable to comprehend a word of the dialogue.

The hand-held camerawork in the battle scenes by Janusz

Kaminski is as powerful as his work on Schindler's List. Some of the quieter moments have the poetic quality of a verse by Wilfred Owen.

Though simple enough on the surface, this is a film of moral complexity. Parts of it make you weep over the wastefulness of war; yet it's no fatuous anti-war tract.

You get the feeling that these people are fighting for something worthwhile, with enormous courage and heroism – something that has tended to be forgotten in anti-war films since the Sixties.

Spielberg's experience of action films has made him a master of suspense. The way he works up tension as tanks approach for the final showdown owes plenty to the Tyrannosaurus Rex attack in *Jurassic Park*.

Most endearingly Spielbergian, however, is his faith in common decency, which seems genuine rather than sentimental.

Do we need another war film? I think we do, especially at a time when violence is portrayed so casually on our screens, and most young men have no practical experience of war, beyond shoot-'em-up arcade games.

This film brings home the realities in the most shocking fashion, but also leaves room for old-fashioned notions like duty, loyalty and selflessness – rare in modern cinema, but here very much present and correct.

The message – that war is hell, yet at the same time a theatre for astonishing heroism – is, I suppose, unexceptional. The execution of the film, and its emotional effect upon an audience experiencing the truth about warfare for the first time, is very exceptional indeed.

SCHINDLER'S LIST *(1993)*

One thing that's often forgotten in times of "back-to-basics" Puritanism, is that flawed people can achieve great things. The hero of Spielberg's film is an inveterate womanizer, an exploiter of slave labour, and a Nazi – yet still a hero, who saves more than 1100 Jews from the Holocaust. Where Thomas Keneally's Booker prize-winning novel was obliged to describe him with words, Spielberg shows us Schindler through a montage of visual images. He is a hedonistic dandy: his first, dressing-up scene is reminiscent of Richard Gere going to work in *American Gigolo*. He fraternizes with Nazis in a club, like a more corrupt Humphrey Bogart in *Casablanca*. He wheels, deals and threatens, like a Germanic Godfather.

His first act of rescue – when he saves his hapless accountant Itzhak Stern (Ben Kingsley) from a train leaving for a concentration camp – is for selfish, business reasons. "What if I'd got here five minutes late?" Schindler demands. "Then where would I be?" But he happens to be riding on a hilltop on March 13th, 1943, when he sees beneath him the brutal clearing of the Cracow ghetto: people being shot, children running for cover. He finds himself sympathising with a Jewish workforce which he had intended only to exploit. His moment of truth is not accompanied by angst-ridden soul-searching: instead, we see him starting to change through his deeds.

Neeson plays Schindler convincingly as a big man of impulsive appetites and actions, someone whose force of character, bonhomie and ability to turn nasty enabled him to bluff his (and others') way out of danger. He has an expert foil in Ben Kingsley's more calculating, self-effacing right-hand man. But the most stunning performance comes from another British actor, Ralph Fiennes, as Amon Goeth, the murderous commandant of the Plaszcow forced labour camp. Fiennes plays this monster with such understanding and black humour that he becomes comprehensible and even pitiable – while Schindler's attempts to dupe him with bribes and flattery become doubly scary.

One of the worst side-effects of modern cinema is that it has partly anaesthetised us to scenes of violence; but the casual shootings here – many of them by the demented Goeth – have the immediacy of today's news. Jews are dispatched as casually as pigs being slaughtered. This is how it must have been; and it is horrible to watch.

Yet this is not a depressing picture – so much so that Spielberg was even accused of making a "feelgood" film out of the Holocaust. It is true that he is eager as always to see light in the darkness: the striking of a match is his opening image. But he is not guilty of prettification, as he was in *Empire of the Sun* and (most damagingly) *The Color Purple*, which lost impact through Spielberg's constant pursuit of the perfect, backlit shot, and his seeming inability to contemplate the uglier sides of life.

Here, he seems a different and far superior director. At no point does he sanitise history, and he achieves a much harder-edged, black-and-white, hand-held style of shooting which (though as perfectly lit as ever) has the rough immediacy of real life.

He is unable to resist one vulgar, Hollywood touch: a schmaltzy, over-theatrical farewell where Schindler breaks down and expresses the wish that he could have saved more Jews. But perhaps Spielberg and screenwriter Steven Zaillian may be allowed one crass scene in three and a quarter hours.

Schindler's List has been called Spielberg's *Citizen Kane*, but in its vitality, style and quality it is more like John Ford's *Grapes of Wrath*. Spielberg gives a similar impression of huge numbers of people on the move: his amazing sense of scale and shot composition (first revealed in his worst ever flop, 1941) comes into its own with the enormous, hellish set-pieces, such as the exhumation and incineration of massacred Jews; the loading of children on to cattle trucks and the chase by their screaming mothers; the entrance into Auschwitz. Spielberg is not afraid to take us into the heart of darkness, and many of his images are unforgettable.

Most astonishingly of all, he achieves this epic scale without sacrificing any humanity – and without allowing himself to be sidetracked into the easy pathos of soap opera. Some have complained it is impossible to keep track of every individual Jew in the film, but that is one reason why it will bear re-seeing. Their stories are going on in the background, but their behaviour is shown in wonderful detail and variety – and every now and again (there is one staggering moment about a girl in a red coat) Spielberg brings us face to face with some moment of salvation or personal tragedy.

Schindler's List was bound to win the best Film Oscar for all sorts of bad reasons – in recompense for the one he should have won for *E.T.*, as a way of saying thank you for the box-office success of *Jurassic Park*, because its portrayal of a wheeler-dealer capitalist with a heart was bound to appeal to voters in Hollywood. But it is a masterpiece – a brilliantly made, richly textured and profoundly moving picture which does more than any other film to illuminate one of the central events of the twentieth century.

SEABISCUIT *(2003)*

Fancy seeing a film about horse racing? I thought not. All the same, I would urge you to give this one a try. Like every truly great sports film, *Seabiscuit* isn't primarily about sport at all: it's a tale of underdogs overcoming adversity, giving people (and animals) a second chance, and not letting bad luck grind you down.

The reason why the real racehorse *Seabiscuit* caught the imagination of the American public in the Depression era was that he was an undersized, bad-tempered, not particularly handsome horse that was keener on eating and sleeping than racing. He was written off as a loser by two trainers, but became a champion thanks to three men, all in their different ways making a comeback after terrible reverses.

One was jockey Johnny "Red" Pollard (Tobey Maguire from *Spider-Man*), an intelligent but aggressive part-time boxer whose spirit had seemingly been broken by his family losing everything in the Wall Street Crash.

The second was embittered, washed-up horse trainer Tom Smith (Chris Cooper from *Adaptation*), who had seen his wild west lifestyle disappear with the advent of the motor car.

The third was flamboyant businessman Charles Howard (Jeff Bridges from *The Fabulous Baker Boys*) a charismatic car dealer who had lost his millions, his son and his wife but still had an eye for talent and determination, and a self-deprecating charm that made him an instant hit with the public.

As Bridges puts it with a happy beam on his face, "Our horse is too small, our jockey is too tall, our trainer is too old… and I'm too dumb to tell the difference!"

All three of these excellent actors give performances that are as likeable, subtle and multi-faceted as any they have achieved. A fourth top-quality performance is given by the great character actor William H. Macy as a motormouth radio commentator who brings comic relief to the film just when it's in danger of becoming a little too emotional.

The picture has the old-fashioned virtues you would associate with the Golden Age of Hollywood: characters it's impossible not to root for; an emotive story that gives you everything you want but not quite in the way you might anticipate; a big, stirring score in the style of Aaron Copland (by the splendidly versatile Randy Newman); and enough social and political background to make you appreciate that the true hero of the movie is not jut one horse, nor the men who saved it from the knacker's yard, but America itself – here celebrated with a welcome lack of post-modernist irony as the greatest land of opportunity that the world has ever seen.

The fact that writer-director Gary Ross can put his patriotic, slightly left-of-centre message across without indulging in offensive flag-waving or mawkish sentiment makes this a film that everyone who isn't a paid-up member of Al Quaeda should enjoy. Ross has fulfilled the promise he showed as the screenwriter of *Big* and *Dave*.

As a sports movie that will entrance people with

absolutely no interest in sport, I'd rate it on the very highest level alongside *Field of Dreams* (about baseball), *Rocky* (boxing), *The Hustler* (pool) and the great basketball documentary *Hoop Dreams*.

It's a crowd-pleaser, but it doesn't patronise its audience; and John Schwartzman's cinematography is sensational – the best I have seen at transmitting the excitement and danger of horse racing. You feel you're right in there, among the horses and galloping as though your life depends upon it.

I went in with lowish expectations, imagining this would be a superior children's film, along the lines of *Black Beauty* or *Free Willy*, but it's much better than that. This is one of the great mythic tales about the making of America. Even though it's two hours twenty minutes long, it never drags for a second. And the extraordinary thing is that, in essence, it's all true.

SEARCHING FOR SUGAR MAN

(2012)

Searching for Sugar Man tells a tale far too incredible to be true. But this most gripping of musical detective stories is, indeed, a documentary. It tells the life story of a rock figure so insignificant that you're very unlikely to have heard of him. But it's riveting – and easily the most exhilarating music doc since *Standing in the Shadows of Motown* (2002), the splendid tribute to the Funk Brothers, Tamla Motown's in-house backing band.

Sixto Rodriguez was a singer-songwriter of Mexican-Native American descent, born in 1942. He sang in Detroit bars, but was so shy he kept his back to the audience.

He released two albums in 1970 and 1971, *Cold Fact* and *Coming From Reality*. The records didn't sell, and Rodriguez's career failed to take off.

The story went that after one particularly humiliating gig he committed the most grotesque onstage suicide in rock history. Some claimed he dowsed himself in lighter fluid and set himself on fire, like a Tibetan monk. Others said he responded to another evening of audience apathy by putting a bullet in his head.

The irony is that he was utterly unaware that in South

Africa he was hailed as a rock god. More famous there than Elvis or the Beatles, he became the voice of white revolt against apartheid. Curiously, no money from his albums nor news of his success reached Rodriguez.

The money trail ends abruptly at the door of one Clarence Avaunt, the belligerent and not terribly communicative gentleman who ran Sussex, the record company that fired Rodriguez a few years before it went bust in 1975.

But Swedish director Malik Bendjelloul, inspired by a couple of Rodriguez's most devoted South African fans, a rock journalist and a record-shop manager, isn't interested in laying blame or exploring the murky side of the pop industry.

His aim is twofold: to find out what happened to Rodriguez, and to show how talented he was. He succeeds in both aims.

Rodriquez's voice is strong and distinctive, like a less reedy James Taylor or a more robust Donovan, and his songs are soulful, melodic folk-rock with literate lyrics and a blue-collar protest edge that led some critics to call him the Hispanic Bob Dylan. For my money, he's closer in feel to Bruce Springsteen, but that's not a bad thing.

The movie sticks close to its structure as a musical detective story, and is coy about some intriguing aspects of Rodriguez, especially his love life, his degree in philosophy and his popularity in Australia, New Zealand and Zimbabwe. But it tells such a gripping yarn that none of that truly matters.

Over a fast-paced, economical 85 minutes, the search for Rodriguez unfolds like a thriller you can't put down.

I'm not going to spoil your enjoyment by telling you more. But the surprise twist in the tale helped *Sugar Man* win two prizes at the Sundance Festival, the World Cinema Special Jury Prize and the Audience Award. The film is an inspiring celebration of the human spirit and one unjustly forgotten talent. It makes you wonder how many other stories like this are out there.

THE SECRET IN THEIR EYES/ EL SECRETO DE SUS OJOS
(2009)

This Argentinian thriller was a surprise winner of last year's Oscar as best Foreign Language Film, defeating a couple of critical favourites in *The White Ribbon* and *A Prophet*. I can see why it appealed to the Academy electorate. It certainly impressed me.

Ricardo Darin is superb – hangdog, watchful and battered by experience, like a less shouty Al Pacino – as Benjamin Esposito, a retired investigator for the state criminal courts. Grey, dejected and lonely after the failure of his marriage, he is trying to write a first novel about a case that has dogged his memory for 25 years.

It gives him an excuse to revisit his boss, Irene (Soledad Villamil), with whom he has been hopelessly in love for the last quarter-century. She is now a respected judge, with a husband and children. Now, as she has always been, this beautiful, elegant and reserved woman is way out of his league.

We see the case and their relationship unfold in flashbacks, following the younger Esposito and his goofy, alcoholic sidekick (a funny, touching performance by comedian Guillermo Francella) as they try to find the killer of a beautiful young woman, whose devoted husband (Pablo Rago) is agonisingly unable to come to terms with his loss.

Writer-director Juan Jose Campanella is a master of camerawork and editing. He is also wonderful with actors. There isn't a false performance here.

The thrillerish high point is a tremendously crafted, exciting set-piece at a soccer stadium. The low point is an unconvincing interrogation in which Irene uses bullying tactics that seem out of character and would be extremely unlikely to have the effect that they do here.

The pace may be too slow for modern youth, and I never believed that one of the characters would be willing to read Esposito's novel with him hovering expectantly over their shoulder, let alone two.

Even so, the film is an extraordinary achievement. The central themes – of love and loneliness, missed opportunities, authority abused, and the question of what is the just penalty for murder – reveal themselves with cumulative power.

This is an unorthodox movie in that it works on at least three levels, as love story, social commentary and suspense – although we know the identity of the killer early on, we can't be sure if he will escape punishment.

This is an intelligent, humane film that makes a refreshing change from most Hollywood thrillers. In the context of this year's summer blockbusters, I felt pathetically grateful to be seeing it. It's a rare treat to watch any movie that doesn't seem to be made for pre-teenagers.

SECRETS & LIES *(1996)*

A young, black optician, Hortense (Marianne Jean-Baptiste) decides after the death of her adoptive parents to trace her "birth mother". She is shocked to discover that she comes from a white family. Head of that family is Maurice Purley (wonderfully played by Timothy Spall, who gives a touching, fully rounded portrayal of a figure usually ignored or derided in British cinema – the aspirational, self-made businessman). Maurice's pretensions to art are kept firmly in their place – he's a suburban photographer specialising in weddings and family portraits – but he is talented, responsible and good at his job.

Though they are childless, Maurice and his sharp-tongued, Scottish wife Monica (Phyllis Logan) have recently moved into a six-bedroom detached house which is a shrine to upward mobility. The numerous loos are in every shade of pastel, and it is hard to see the walls for the stencilling. Monica's pride in her possessions make her seem the villain of the piece (and in previous Leigh films she would have been) but Logan's powerful performance ensures that the part gains throughout in character and pain. We come to realise that she and Maurice are living a nightmare designed by Jocasta Innes.

Maurice's admiring female assistant (Elizabeth Berrington) says that he "has it all", but he is starting to use alcohol to cope with Monica's monthly moods, and losing contact with his roots – especially his older sister Cynthia (Brenda Blethyn) who complains that she hasn't seen him in a year.

Cynthia brought Maurice up as a son and now lives with her own, illegitimate, 21 year-old daughter in a run-down terrace. Cynthia has a dead-end job and none of Monica's taste for home improvement (the mangle is still in the yard, and she hasn't even got round to organising an inside loo). She's running to fat, a fact emphasised by excruciating dress sense. Her one leisure activity is smoking, and she's scarcely on speaking terms with her daughter Roxanne (Claire Rushbrook) a grumpy roadsweeper with a scaffolder boyfriend (Lee Ross) barely capable of speech.

All the mother and daughter do is grumble at each other. "You've been sitting there for a month with a face like a slapped arse," snaps Cynthia. At which Roxanne makes a sour face. It's clear that mum is an embarrassment. What Roxanne doesn't realise is that she is just as big an embarrassment to her mother.

For there's more to Cynthia than being a single mother and a more than usually lumpy member of the lumpen proletariat – and it's her credible revelation of those redeeming qualities which gives the film its power. Brenda Blethyn, always a marvellous actress, turns a revue turn into one of the most moving characters ever on film.

It is no secret that jury decisions at film festivals are often bizarre, but the movie which won the 1996 *Palme d'Or* at Cannes is a glorious exception. This is Mike Leigh's greatest achievement. His ability to satirise social pretension is as sharp as ever it was in *Abigail's Party*, but gone is that unattractive tendency to sneer at those who live by different values from those of North London writer-directors. Also gone is the depressing nihilism which made his last film, *Naked*, so hard to enjoy.

Mike Leigh's improvisational, actor-centred, low-budget style of working means that his films are never going to have the gloss or visual flair of Hollywood product. But that doesn't matter here.

Secrets & Lies is as uplifting as any feelgood comedy from Tinseltown, but with the truthfulness of great documentary.

Leigh's theme is the central importance to the human spirit of family and roots. In case we haven't got the point, there's a late appearance by a photographer (Ron Cook) who sold Maurice his business and has recently returned from Australia bereft of family, job and self-respect, reeking of alcohol and well on his way to becoming a dosser. "There but for the grace of God..." says Maurice.

Secrets & Lies is full of memorable characters, with virtually all of Leigh's past actors making cameo appearances, and – for the first time in his oeuvre – Leigh has worked out a story which makes the fullest possible use of them. The plot is worked through to a climax with the skill of Alan Ayckbourn at his best, but without the slightest sense of artificiality.

These are the kind of people who don't normally appear on a cinema screen. Watch them and you'll wince in recognition. But do please make a date to see this wonderful movie, which far transcends anything Leigh has done before and says so much about how real people struggle to cope with the cruel injustices of life. Funny, moving and true, this is a great, great film.

SENSE AND SENSIBILITY *(1996)*

It's about two sisters. Elinor (played by the film's screenwriter, Emma Thompson) is "Sense", pragmatic, conventional and emotionally repressed, while her younger sister Marianne (touchingly played by Kate Winslet) is "Sensibility", recklessly romantic and outspoken. They are at the poor end of aristocratic society, and confined to a dilapidated house in Devon, cheated of their inheritance by their older step-brother (James Fleet, wonderfully weak) and his mercenary wife (Harriet Walter, delightfully devious).

The sisters proceed to encounter more than their fair share of romantic problems. Elinor falls for an amiable, tongue-tied young chap (Hugh Grant) who seems at first to reciprocate but then abruptly leaves for London, never to be seen again – or so it seems.

Marianne, meanwhile, is being courted by neighbouring landowner Colonel Brandon (Alan Rickman, in a marvellously nuanced, brooding performance), who is as stiff as he is honourable. Marianne can't see beyond a younger man, Willoughby (Greg Wise, too handsome for his own good, and much too good to be true). Willoughby sweeps her off her feet, first literally and then metaphorically, before also leaving for London under mysterious circumstances.

When I first saw this, I was expecting just another worthy, picturesque and probably slow rendition of a classic novel. Inside, I found myself enjoying the paciest, wittiest, most entertaining romantic comedy since *Four Weddings and a Funeral* – faithful in spirit to Jane Austen's novel, but not in the least literary, cobwebby or outmoded: a sublimely funny film, which also moved me to tears on at least three occasions. The events which unfold are proof that Jane Austen could spin a rattling yarn, and Emma Thompson's screenplay actually enhances the original. making the men more interesting and pointing up the underlying darkness of the story – which hinges on greed and betrayal – without ever losing sight of its fun, high spirits and romance.

It has been objected that, at 36, Thompson is almost twice the age of Elinor (Austen mentions that she is 19), but oddly enough this helps a modern audience, which might well find it incredible that in Regency England a girl of nineteen could be considered "on the shelf".

Besides, it is impossible to imagine that any younger actress would be able to equal Thompson here. She is simply miraculous, moral but not priggish, extracting every bit of merriment and pathos from the role, while apparently playing second fiddle in almost every scene.

The moment when she learns of her own happy ending, and almost expires with great sobs of joy and long-suppressed anguish, is one I shall always remember. I doubt whether anyone watching it will be able to restrain the tears.

Hugh Grant is equally charming, and even more blissfully funny. With his air of incipient apology and head sinking ever deeper between hunched shoulders, like a tortoise in anticipation of a crushing tax demand, he suggests a man both emotionally retarded yet possessed of an underlying maturity which might easily be underestimated. It's an extraordinarily skilful, playful performance in a challenging role, and a welcome return to the form which deservedly made him a star in *Four Weddings*.

The rest of the supporting cast is better than faultless, with three admirable couples as light relief: Harriet Walter and James Fleet, Elizabeth Spriggs and Robert Hardy, and Hugh Laurie and Imelda Staunton. Perhaps Imogen Stubbs might have made a little more of Elinor's vixenish rival in love, and the script might have made her mercenary calculations clearer, but that's my only quibble, and a very minor one.

The young Taiwanese director Ang Lee has already made two highly enjoyable films in *The Wedding Banquet* and *Eat Drink Man Woman*. This is even better, and his subtlety is ideally suited to this very English story. Whereas Martin Scorsese might have shown off with over-elaborate camera moves or James Ivory might have dwelt too long on the background detail, Lee is rightly content to trust the screenplay, find the perfect framing and let his wonderful cast act within it.

Although Lee shows himself to be a profound, humane film-maker with exquisite taste and discretion, he is helped enormously by top-class creative support from Brits Michael Coulter (cinematographer on *Local Hero* and *Four Weddings*), Luciana Arrighi (production designer on *Howards End*) and Jenny Beavan and John Bright (costume designers on *A Room With a View* and *The Remains of the Day*). Patrick Doyle's music is as excellent here as it was on *A Little Princess*.

Sense and Sensibility combines some of our best home-grown cinematic talent with the unashamed emotionalism of a big, Hollywood movie. It will come as a splendid surprise to anyone who thought that any adaptation of a classic novel has to be dry, talky or outdated. It is quite the best ever transference of Jane Austen to the small or large screen, as fresh and entertaining as if it had been written yesterday.

Its central arguments – that love should conquer avarice, and duty and loyalty are beyond price – are timeless truths, expressed here with elegance, eloquence and refreshing intelligence. If you have any sense, you'll see it.

SEPARATE LIES (2005)

There aren't many films aimed at the intelligent and middle-aged, and even fewer of them are British. So heartfelt gratitude is owed to Julian Fellowes for his brave and astonishingly successful directorial debut. He won an Oscar for his *Gosford Park* screenplay, and *Separate Lies* is an even more expert piece of storytelling.

It starts out as a mystery thriller – who caused the death of a cyclist in a sleepy English village? – but deepens into an insightful, wonderfully acted study of marital conflict.

Tom Wilkinson was Oscar-nominated for *In The Bedroom*. Here, he's even better. At the beginning of the film, he is the model of a successful, pin-striped, buttoned-up executive. Others, including his wife, revolve around him, fulfilling his commands, trying to make his life easier; while he responds with the tetchiness of a man who's too stressed out to contemplate a social life, still less "quality time" with his wife.

Emily Watson plays that wife with the same heart-breaking sensitivity that rightly won her Oscar nominations for *Breaking the Waves* and *Hilary & Jackie*. You can sense her feelings of inferiority in her angular body language, her unspoken resignation at being treated by her husband as a slightly less efficient version of his PA at work (Hermione Norris, excellent).

Nothing is said, or needs to be said, about their sex life. You know how that's going from a line Watson utters while watching her husband batting in a game of village cricket: "He's always in for hours but he never scores any runs."

Little inconveniences in their relationship loom large (just watch Wilkinson's aghast expression as he contemplates one of his wife's undercooked boiled eggs). And it isn't hard to see why she becomes attracted to Rupert Everett, as a languid, sublimely arrogant aristocrat who's just moved into the neighbouring pile owned by his aged father (John Neville, so splendid that you wonder why he's been so underused in cinema).

The central marriage unravels in the wake of a hit-and-run traffic accident. A threat of manslaughter charges leads to a series of nasty ethical questions and compromises, increasingly uneasy brushes with the suspicious local constabulary, and revelations that eventually make the aggrieved Wilkinson offer three alternative "performances" to his wife: "you can have suicidal, bitter, or glad to be rid of you!"

There will be few people of 35 and upwards who will not recognise something of themselves or their friends in this study of modern marriage, which is as searching as anything by Ingmar Bergman but is lightened and humanised by a very English determination to do the decent thing, make the best of a bad job, and put a brave face on disaster.

The result is that the film is never depressing; you really come to care about these people, as they try to work their way through increasingly impossible circumstances.

Separate Lies is highly civilised and likely to appeal most to those of average intelligence and above, so it is certain to be condemned by some as "bourgeois". In reality, it's pretty universal.

The master-stroke is that, although it's the husband who's the "wronged" partner, the audience feels sympathy for both sides. There's an agonising moment when Wilkinson – out, literally and metaphorically, in the cold – spies on Watson and Everett in a Paris restaurant, and sees for the first time that they really love each other. You feel deeply sorry for the husband, but simultaneously pleased for the wife.

The film does hit a false note when one character is supposed to be suffering from a fatal illness and looks far too hale and hearty. It's hard to know if the actor or the make-up department is more at fault, but this scene is the only one that does not carry total conviction.

However, Julian Fellowes's screenplay is outstanding in its subtlety, profundity and freshness of observation. It's a miracle of understatement, yet also hugely powerful.

His direction of camera and actors – though not earth-shatteringly original – is a model of taste and economy, and he is rewarded with extraordinary performances throughout the cast. You can sense the care, commitment and love that went into the making of this film, and it is one that anyone with an interest in quality cinema should hurry to see. All together now: for he's a jolly good Fellowes...

SE7EN *(1995)*

An elderly, orderly detective seven days away from retirement (Morgan Freeman) is forced to work with a loutish younger cop new to the city and anxious to make his name (Brad Pitt). Though they don't get on, they have to trail a serial killer who seems to be on a personal crusade against the Seven Deadly Sins, beginning with Gluttony and Sloth.

With two corpses down and five to go, this may sound like the neat but contrived plotting of English detective fiction, but the treatment here is much more up-to-date and horrific – imagine an autopsy from a Patricia Cornwell novel, filmed by Quentin Tarantino.

This is an elegantly constructed film full of disgusting images, very gruesome in its portrayal of torture and depravity, and emphatically not for the squeamish. Oddly enough, it is not violent by the standards of modern thrillers; we see hardly any of the crimes being committed. The images are more of their shocking aftermath. This is not one of those Hollywood films which glorify violence – rather the reverse, since it concentrates on its grisly effects.

Andrew Kevin Walker's first screenplay is never corny or predictable, or clever-clever. The film delivers loads of suspense and some extremely nasty shocks. The scene where a "corpse" comes suddenly to life can rank alongside that moment when the dwarf turns round in *Don't Look Now*.

The film is lifted further towards greatness by exceptional performances from Morgan Freeman and Brad Pitt. The script helps by making them constantly surprising, and gradually feeding us new insights and astute little observations about them.

The killer is just as convincingly played by another fine actor, and the film succeeds – as have so many of the best horror films, like *Psycho* – in taking us inside his mind, and persuading us that his acts have a kind of single-minded logic.

Visually, *Se7en* is a *tour de force* – the finest exercise in *film noir* style since Ridley Scott's *Blade Runner*. Director David Fincher, whose only previous feature was the not noticeably promising *Alien 3*, shoots his fictitious American city in washed-out shades of brown and grey which make it look like a decomposing corpse, teeming with human maggots.

One traditional element of *film noir* – the *femme fatale* – is apparently missing; but in her place, there is Gwyneth Paltrow as Brad Pitt's sweet wife trying to make peace between the two cops and agonizing over whether the city is a proper place for her unborn child. As she wonders whether or not to have an abortion, the film gently points out that the city is helping to turn even this nice young woman into a potential killer.

This is a moral film which gazes disgustedly into the abyss. Its vision of the city owes something to *Chinatown*, but is essentially of a modern Dante's Inferno (allusions to which abound), where society no longer prizes "civilisation", experience, morality or literacy (even the most civilised character in the film, played by Freeman, doesn't know the difference between "contrition" and "attrition").

After a decade in which America's respectable people have increasingly abandoned the cities to drug-dealers, pimps and an under-educated, lawless underclass, *Se7en* asks pertinent questions about the consequences of such apathy. In an understandable concession to political correctness, the film-makers have chosen Morgan Freeman, a black actor, to voice those concerns.

The central question which the film poses is about how to react to the New Barbarism. Is it preferable to shrug and walk away, as Freeman initially intends, or stand and fight it – as the less civilised Pitt feels impelled to do, and as the killer also does in his own, much sicker way?

The visual style is contrived – this is another noir city where it never rains but it pours, and there are times when any real cop would simply turn on a few lights and ruin the atmosphere; but this is a terrific thriller, wonderfully directed, written, acted and produced with an excellent, atmospheric score by Howard Shore.

It succeeds because it creates a world that is a distorted but recognisable version of our own. It is not an easy film to watch. A few may walk out of it in disgust, and others will call it bosh, but really it's a modern equivalent to Hieronymus Bosch – unpleasant, over-the-top, riveting.

SHAKESPEARE IN LOVE *(1998)*

William Shakespeare (Joseph Fiennes), a young playwright and occasional actor with a failed marriage behind him and a bad case of writer's block on his latest effort, a comedy provisionally entitled *Romeo and Ethel, the Pirate's Daughter*, is wooed for the manuscript by two rival theatre managers, Burbage (Martin Clunes) and Henslowe (Geoffrey Rush) but unable to deliver.

He is angry at the way the actors mangle his lines – Will Kempe (Patrick Barlow) even has the temerity to turn his *Two Gentlemen of Verona* into a dog act. Most of all, Shakespeare is jealous that everyone thinks more highly of the handsome and talented playwright Kit Marlowe (Rupert Everett) than they do of him. No sooner does Will enter a boat than the ferryman, the 16th century equivalent of a cabbie, is informing him tactlessly "I had that Christopher Marlowe in my boat once".

Will needs a muse, and along she comes in the shape of a rich merchant's daughter called Olivia (Gwyneth Paltrow) who has acting ambitions, even though acting is a man's profession and her parents wish her to wed the dashing but awful Duke of Wessex (Colin Firth). Olivia infiltrates Shakespeare's company in drag, Will and she fall in love, and she becomes his inspiration; but their love is not to be, since the establishment, personified by Dame Judi Dench as Queen Elizabeth I, decrees otherwise.

How weary, stale, flat and unprofitable will seem so many films, after you have witnessed *Shakespeare in Love*: an Anglo-American romantic comedy that is in love with words, theatre, Shakespeare – and the pain and pleasure of overwhelming love. Director John Madden's follow-up to *Mrs Brown* is a far more lavish affair, and infinitely more cinematic. It is blessed with a marvellous screenplay by Tom Stoppard and Marc Norman – well-structured, witty and wise. Running throughout is a profound love of theatre and a huge though far from uncritical affection for actors. Even the moneyman who is suing Henslowe for debts (played by Tom Wilkinson) becomes stagestruck and is roped in to play the apothecary in Will's new production.

Personifying this very commercially-minded theatre is Henslowe, a wily, incorrigibly optimistic impresario miraculously played by the great Geoffrey Rush as a cross between Arthur Daley and Bill Kenwright.

"Let me explain about the theatrical business," he tells Wilkinson with glee. "The natural condition is one of insurmountable obstacles on the road to imminent disaster." "So how does it end well?" he is asked. "I don't know," he shrugs, "it's all a mystery".

Even Henslowe's optimism is shaken as Olivia's muse turns piratical comedy into a commercially dodgy tragedy.

"Well," says Henslowe sarcastically as Shakespeare recounts the double-suicide ending, "that will have them rolling in the aisles."

The two central jokes of the film, reworked ingeniously numerous times to wonderful effect, are that writers turn their personal experiences into fiction, but not in predictable ways, and that show business is pretty much the same through the ages.

"Who's that?" Wilkinson asks about Shakespeare, as he passes.

"Nobody," says the impresario. "He's the author."

Another thespian (Jim Carter) who plays the nurse is asked what *Romeo and Juliet* is about. "Well," he starts off, "there's this nurse…"

It will come as no surprise after *Emma* and *Sliding Doors* that Gwyneth Paltrow speaks with an impeccable English accent and is radiantly beautiful in a way reminiscent of Audrey Hepburn.

Less predictably, her fellow-American Ben Affleck turns in an effective performance as Henslowe's leading actor, whom Shakespeare attempts to placate with the role of Mercutio, having given the role of Romeo to Paltrow.

The film starts as a romp and continues in great good humour and with oodles of charm; but there are moments of pathos and depth, superbly played by Fiennes and Paltrow. Rush gives one of the scene-stealing performances of all time. Judi Dench, in three brief scenes, gives another.

Her exit line – "Too late" as various courtiers cast their cloaks on a puddle through which she has just splashed – gets the biggest laugh, and she conveys a lifetime of being Elizabeth in fewer than ten minutes of screen time.

A passing knowledge of *Romeo and Juliet* will help your appreciation, and there are allusions to *Macbeth, Twelfth Night* and several other plays; but the screenplay wears its learning lightly. It would be hugely enjoyable if you were coming to Shakespeare's writing for the first time.

Special praise is owed to Sandy Powell's costume designs, but this film is not content to be easy on the eye. It pulsates with energy. *Shakespeare in Love* begins as a bawdy romp in the tradition of Dick Lester's *The Three Musketeers*; but it deepens into a touching love story. It isn't quite like any other film. There have been few more affecting romances on screen in recent years. This is a classic romantic comedy.

SHREK *(2001)*

A curmudgeonly ogre (with a Scottish accent, by courtesy of Mike Myers) finds that his comfortable if insanitary swamp is being taken over by immigrants. These include three very blind mice, a trio of homeless pigs, not to mention a transvestite wolf in his bed.

Shrek travels to confront the local bad guy, a dead ringer for Olivier's Richard III called Lord Farquaad (John Lithgow), who has ethnically cleansed nursery characters from his kingdom, so that it resembles a squeaky-clean, more openly fascistic version of Disneyland. But Lord Farquaard's talking mirror (evidently liberated from the Wicked Queen's castle in *Snow White*) reminds him that he's not a King yet. To become truly royal, he must marry a princess.

Three suitable candidates are presented to Farquaard on his personal production of *Blind Date* – Cinderella (but he's warned that she's damaged goods, having been abused in childhood), Snow White ("she lives with seven men, but she's not easy") and a redhead called Princess Fiona. He chooses the one who hasn't taken the title role in a Disney picture.

However, Farquaard is far too cowardly to go on a quest for the maiden himself. He prefers to amuse himself by torturing gingerbread men and, in true Hollywood executive style, humiliating anyone who is taller than he is (which means just about everyone).

So he strikes a bargain with Shrek, whereby the swamp will be cleared of nursery characters if the ogre and his sidekick, a won't-stop-talking cowardly donkey (Eddie Murphy), will rescue Princess Fiona from the castle where she is held prisoner by a dragon.

This all-digital animation from Dreamworks follows in the footsteps of their own *Antz*. Fast, funny and technically brilliant, it's another step forward for the studio.

At first, I was a little disappointed. There's a second-rate rock soundtrack drawn from too many sources. And, as if to rub in how un-Disneylike the film is, too much of the humour early on dwells obsessively on bodily functions. The first lavatory and flatulence jokes occur within sixty seconds, and you don't want me to describe the earwax gag, especially if you're eating.

The malign influence of adolescent "gross-out" comedy can certainly be felt, and lets down the tone. However, the raunchier humour will sail over most children's heads. Inventive sight gags, high-quality jokes (even Eddie Murphy is funny) and some inspired mickey-taking of Disney and fairy tale conventions come, gradually, into their own. Such is the profusion of gags, in fact, that a second viewing would probably be even more rewarding than a first.

Although there is an irreverence about the movie, it's not jaded or over-cynical. There's just enough magic and warmth, to stop it from being too clever (and politically correct) by half.

Shrek didn't strike me as quite on a par with the *Toy Story* movies. Its subversion of myth and fairytale isn't on the same high level of wit or sophistication, but adults will find plenty to laugh at. Children will love it.

SHREK 2 *(2004)*

The Oscar-winning, record-smashing *Shrek* was an easy act to follow. Just put together any old rubbish, call it *Shrek 2*, and it would have cashed in on its first weekend. To their credit, DreamWorks haven't done that.

They've fused plenty of verbal wit with more sight gags than in the rest of this year's movies combined. They've hired inventive actors – many of them English – as vocal talent. And they've honed a script that is expertly structured with a neat twist. The result is a movie that succeeds in being superior to the original. It will appeal as much to sophisticated adults as to very small children, and looks certain to become one of the top five box-office hits of all time.

Princes Fiona (Cameron Diaz) and Fairyland's answer to John Prescott (Mike Myers) are now happily married ogres, and their idyll is only slightly marred by the fact that Donkey (Eddie Murphy) seems determined to move in with them, following the collapse of his short-lived relationship with a dragon.

But then word comes from Far Far Away, the Hollywood-like fantasy land ruled by Fiona's parents, tetchy King Harold (John Cleese) and straight-laced Queen Lillian (Julie Andrews), that they wish to give the happy couple their blessing.

Shrek is rightly pessimistic about how his parents-in-law are going to react. Their daughter's marriage flies in the face of a promise made by King Harold to a Fairy Godmother (Jennifer Saunders) that Fiona was to be awakened from her enchanted sleep by a kiss from the Fairy Godmother's vain son Prince Charming (Rupert Everett).

So, regretfully, King Harold hires an assassin to rid him of his unwanted son-in-law. The hitman is Puss-in-boots, a Zorro-type giant-killer (Antonio Banderas). Confronted by Shrek's superior strength, Puss cannily changes sides and becomes Shrek's second sidekick, even though – as Donkey haughtily informs him – "The position of annoying talking animal has already been taken".

It would be tempting to say that Banderas steals the movie with his wondrously over-dramatic send-up of Hispanic machismo, but that would be to undervalue the rest of the cast.

Julie Andrews and John Cleese have an ease together, especially when bickering, that suggests they really are a long-married couple. Murphy is at his best making an ass of himself. Myers and Diaz find both the humour and the pathos of married people suddenly realising that Living Happily Ever After isn't just something that happens, but has to be worked at.

The animation is tremendous, with a lot of funny background detail that will make the film worth seeing at least twice.

As in the first movie, the film is full of playful sideswipes at the squeaky-clean, Disney view of the world, not least at the start when Shrek and Fiona are embracing on a beach (in a shot which older moviegoers will notice is the Burt Lancaster-Deborah Kerr clinch in *From Here To Eternity*).

The tide washes in, and Shrek is discovered trying to free himself from the over-enthusiastic kisses of The Little Mermaid (clearly her marriage to Prince Eric isn't going so well).

Whereupon Princess Fiona, in time-honoured Posh Spice style, wrenches the Little Mermaid out of Shrek's arms and throws her back into the sea, where doubtless even now she is calling up Max Clifford to sell her Memoirs.

Another cheeky movie reference comes when Shrek, Donkey and Puss are shackled in a dungeon, and various fairytale characters come to their rescue, including Pinocchio, in a splendidly malicious satire on Tom Cruise attempting to appear butch in *Mission Impossible.*

For those adults who care to examine the film closely, there are camp overtones (such as when Queen Lillian rebukes her anxious husband with the words "Stop being a drama King!") and a weird obsession with cross-dressing (maybe someone at DreamWorks has misconstrued the meaning of Fairytale). But these references are saucy rather than sleazy, and will sail harmlessly over children's heads.

The film even points a wholesome moral: that interior beauty is more important than the external kind That is, admittedly, the same message as the first Shrek carried. But not many films these days are well-intentioned – and there hasn't been a movie this year that has been half as funny. There's enough here to please the most demanding ogre.

SHUTTER ISLAND *(2010)*

Scorsese's most entertaining film won't attract universally favourable reviews, but that is not because it is bad. It's just unusual, outrageous and made with a splendid disregard for "refined" critical taste. Maybe it's unrefined of me, but I loved it. It's a wonderfully inventive, visceral horror film, one of Scorsese's most enjoyable pictures, and right up there with *Taxi Driver* and *GoodFellas* as a waking nightmare.

It's a thrill to see one of the world's finest directors returning to top form at the age of 67. It's as if, now Scorsese has finally won Best Picture for *The Departed*, which I found polished but conventional, he can make the much more daring, idiosyncratic films he really wants to create.

It's 1954, and World War II veteran and US Marshal Teddy Daniels (a jowly and suddenly mature Leonardo DiCaprio) travels with his deferential new partner Chuck Aule (Mark Ruffalo) across Boston Harbour to the rugged and downright sinister Shutter Island.

They're on their way to Ashcliffe Hospital, based in an austere Civil War fortress. It now serves as a jail for 66 of the most dangerously insane prisoners in America.

Teddy and Chuck are investigating the disappearance from her cell of Rachel Solando, a multiple child-killer who leaves behind a cryptic note suggesting there is a 67th prisoner somewhere in the facility.

As a hurricane confines the marshals to the island, it becomes evident that Teddy and Chuck are receiving less than wholehearted co-operation from the strenuously polite doctor running the facility (Ben Kingsley) and his spooky, German-accented colleague (Max von Sydow).

It doesn't inspire confidence that the warden is played by Ted Levine, who was serial-killer Buffalo Bill in *The Silence of the Lambs*, and his deputy is the equally menacing John Carroll Lynch, chief suspect in another memorable serial-killer movie, *Zodiac*.

Like many a tough-guy noir detective before him, Teddy is a former alcoholic with a short temper, and none too impressed when people refuse to tell him the truth.

Teddy's also a widower plagued by memories of his beloved wife (Michelle Williams) and flashbacks to his traumatic experiences as a soldier liberating the concentration camp at Dachau, and he suspects more and more that the island is the scene of Nazi-style experimentation on prisoners.

Teddy has a series of meetings with nightmarish characters, expertly played by (among others) Patricia Clarkson, Jackie Earle Haley and Elias Koteas, which persuade him that the authorities will stop at nothing to prevent him from uncovering the truth.

Every scene is superbly written by Laeta Kalogridis, who has done a sensational job of adapting the complex novel by Dennis Lehane, also responsible for *Mystic River* and *Gone Baby Gone*.

From the earliest moment of a ferry appearing out of fog, Scorsese creates a sense of creeping unease, helped by one of the most terrifying scores I have heard, put together by Robbie Robertson.

Production designer Dante Ferretti turns Shutter Island into the most frightening environment since the hotel in *The Shining*. Scorsese, with the help of cinematographer Robert Richardson and veteran editor Thelma Schoonmaker, plays with our sense of geography and scale to keep us discombobulated.

One reason some people won't like this film is that it is a long way from the naturalistic norm. This is an uncompromisingly stylised example of expressionism, in which we see reality through the prism of a leading character's consciousness.

I love films that put us inside the heads of unusual characters, which is why I like movies as apparently different as David Fincher's *Fight Club*, David Lynch's *Mulholland Drive*, Hitchcock's *Vertigo* and Fritz Lang's *M*. It's a tradition as long as cinema itself, stretching back to silent classics such as *The Cabinet of Dr Caligari* (1919).

Just as most critics on the release of *Psycho* lambasted Hitchcock for making a slasher film, some will condemn Scorsese for making something as artistically disreputable as a horror flick.

Open-minded filmgoers will acknowledge that there are good horror films and bad ones, and *Shutter Island* is one of the finest, with numerous nods to previous masters of the genre, and the creepiness dial turned up to 11.

It's even more stylish and scary than Scorsese's previous venture into the genre, the much-maligned but exquisitely crafted *Cape Fear*.

Anyway, this isn't just horror; it's also an excellent conspiracy thriller. I've seen DiCaprio's performance severely criticised; but he is at his best, especially in the moving climax. Kingsley and Ruffalo's elegantly ambiguous performances are just as immaculately judged.

I found *Shutter Island* both emotionally involving and an interesting film of ideas. It explores Scorsese's favourite obsessions: guilt (never forget that Scorsese once wanted to be a Catholic priest) and mankind's capacity for evil and violence.

Shutter Island is particularly pertinent to the present, because it's about man's tendency not merely to "spin" the truth, but to rewrite history in order to escape unacceptable realities.

Anyone who has witnessed the evasions of, say, Tony Blair and Gordon Brown at the Iraq Inquiry or read the self-serving memoirs of political and military leaders will know just how pertinent an exploration of this topic is. *Shutter Island* is a wonderfully perceptive dissection of denial.

THE SILENCE OF THE LAMBS *(1991)*

Murderous psychopath Hannibal Lecter (Anthony Hopkins) helps FBI trainee Clarice Starling (Jodie Foster) track down a serial killer Buffalo Bill (Ted Levine), so named because he skins his female victims .

This is a terrific, though melodramatic, thriller with a frightening view of humanity – especially men. Jonathan Demme directs with Hitchcockian flair, but less of the old master's voyeurism and misogyny. Jodie Foster and Anthony Hopkins, both on top form, play some of the most memorable scenes in cinema history.

The film was much criticised for glorifying the serial killer. The author of the original, million-selling novel, Thomas Harris, was once a crime reporter and could undoubtedly have written a more realistic mass-murderer than Hannibal Lecter. However, the extent to which Lecter acquired a mythic status – and won Hopkins an Oscar as "leading actor" when really he was in a supporting role – suggests his decision not to was a shrewd one. Lecter is really a variation on an old cinematic theme: the evil genius, also known as Count Zaroff, Dr Frankenstein and the Phantom of the Opera.

Although Lecter is the most courteous, civilized and intelligent person in the film, he is not so clever that he understands what drives him: the result is that he also has something about him of the noble savage. There are moments when, trussed and restrained, he has the pathos of the Man In The Iron Mask or Frankenstein's Monster. His escape from custody is as ingenious as that of a James Bond, and the audience increasingly feels a sneaking sympathy for him as a free spirit. The film ends with him stalking his old jailer, and few members of the audience will not wish him "bon appetit".

Lecter is also the sexiest man in the film. He can recognize the heroine by her walk and the smell of her skin-cream. He draws romantic pictures of her. The moment when she ventures too close and Lecter chooses just to brush one finger across hers is erotically charged, precisely because we (and she) are aware of what he could do to her. The film is, in a perverse way, a romance.

The scenes between Hopkins and Foster won Oscars for the actors because they are so well written as love-hate sparring matches, with each punching deep into the other's psyche. The key speech in the film is Hopkins's, where he compares Clarice's childhood failure to save lambs from slaughter, with her feeble attempts as a member of the FBI to fight the dark side of humanity. That such attempts are ultimately doomed is never in doubt, for both Harris's novel and Ted Tally's screenplay are steeped in a sense of original sin.

In the film, however, the sin is specifically masculine. Director Jonathan Demme goes to great lengths to emphasise Clarice Starling's femininity. She is dwarfed physically by the men around her, and patronised or chatted up wherever she goes. Her boss chooses her to approach Lecter because she is young and pretty; and it is only because she is sexually humiliated in his presence that Lecter offers to help.

The Silence of the Lambs 379

Ironically, she finds the serial killer Buffalo Bill first because of her knowledge of dressmaking.

But Miss Starling, like her ornithological namesake, is also a mimic, in her case of men. When we first see her, she is sweat-stained and on an assault course. She is mechanically adept, and knows how to use a car jack. And she's no wimp: unlike your traditional heroine, she doesn't scream when she discovers the occasional severed head or decomposing corpse.

The reason why a lot of women found this the scariest film since *Psycho* lies in the way the external threats to Clarice reflect the conflict within her (and so many modern women) between masculine ambition and feminine vulnerability. The strength and luminous sincerity of Jodie Foster's performance allows the film-makers to get away with an almost comically extreme paranoia about the male sex.

In style, director Jonathan Demme wisely takes a more populist approach than Michael Mann did in his acclaimed but too self-consciously artistic 1986 flop *Manhunter*, based on Harris's previous million-seller, *Red Dragon*. Demme acknowledges the influence of his old mentor, Roger Corman, by allowing him on screen, briefly, as Head of the FBI. Demme's film – easily his most polished and self-assured – echoes Corman at his best, in its boldness of colour, texture and pace: two hours pass in a flash.

There are times when it is too frenetic: I would have liked more of Starling's relationship with her boss (who is, in the book, a moral counterbalance to Lecter), and more of that FBI procedural detail which makes Harris's novels seem so grounded in reality.

The film is not as frightening as you might expect, and its view of men is more fashionable than convincing. Still, it is a masterpiece of the horror genre, and explores the dark side of humanity and humanism to an extent rarely seen in the commercial cinema. The editing (Craig McKay) and sound (Tom Fleischman, Christopher Newman) were Oscar-nominated.

S1MONE *(2002)*

This little-regarded movie is one of the sharpest satires yet on Hollywood, and among the most topical and important comments ever made on the power of celebrity.

Its New Zealand-born writer-director-producer Andrew Niccol leaped to prominence with two films I thought overrated, *The Truman Show* and *Gattaca*. So I suppose there is a poetic justice in the fact that this far superior work is being so short-sightedly trashed.

Al Pacino is typically exuberant as Viktor Taransky, a film director who hasn't had a hit for ten years. His last chance of a comeback is scuppered when his egotistical leading actress (played with hilarious scariness by Winona Ryder) walks out after making a series of demands that border on the insane (but are, in fact, real demands made by equally crazed actresses over the past few years).

The departing star offers to cite "creative differences". At which Viktor becomes incandescent. "Creative differences? The difference is: you're not creative!"

Driven half-bonkers by Hollywood actors' insistence on placing themselves above "the work", by which Viktor means at least partially himself, he suffers the further indignity of being fired by his studio boss and ex-wife (Catherine Keener).

Whereupon opportunity knocks, in the off-putting form

of Hank (Elias Koteas), a one-eyed nerd who may be Viktor's one remaining fan, and who wants the director to use some new software he has designed. Viktor wants nothing to do with Hank, who is clearly just another failed Hollywood whacko.

A few weeks later, Hank has been killed by a brain tumour incurred from sitting for eight years solid in front of his computer screen; and Viktor inherits Hank's software anyway. It provides Viktor with the perfect leading actress (played in part by Rachel Roberts), one who combines the best qualities of all previous screen goddesses, and who is photogenic putty in a director's hands. Hank called her Simulation One, but Viktor shortens her to the catchier S1mone.

Hank's creation is, in fact, not so far ahead of modern technology. We've already had a digital actress starring in *Final Fantasy: The Spirits Within*, and she was no more artificial-looking than some of her living counterparts.

There is something of Garbo and Audrey Hepburn about S1mone – hardly surprising, since their faces and voices have been programmed into her. Her glamour makes Viktor's next two movies into hits; and her fellow actors, used to working with stars who make unreasonable demands, don't worry overmuch that they have to act their scenes without her physical presence.

Such is the power of her celebrity that everyone wants to claim that they've met her, even though they haven't; and this enables Viktor to cover up the fact that she doesn't exist.

Viktor makes it seem as if S1mone and he are having an affair, partly for his self-esteem, partly in order to make his ex-wife jealous, and he thoroughly enjoys his new reputation as a Svengali. Unfortunately, he soon becomes aware that

S1mone's celebrity is outshining his own. And when he tries to get his own back by diminishing her image, he finds that nothing he can force her to do or say makes the slightest difference.

He can't harm her even when he makes her appear, smoking and spaced out, on a chat show and she speaks out in favour of guns for schoolchildren ("I just think all elementary schools should have shooting ranges") and fur coats ("God invented furry animals to be worn"). She gains a reputation as being outspoken, and becomes more popular than ever.

And when he manufactures a pretentious art-house flick that pretends to be S1mone's directorial debut, in which she wallows in pigswill, feeds from a trough and proclaims in the title "I am pig", the starstruck critics rise to applaud her fearlessness.

Desperate measures are called for, but even these do not have the results that Viktor anticipates...

S1mone is funny, sharp and beautifully written, with a leading character in Viktor who has just the right comedic blend of making the audience like him, yet enjoy his come-uppance when his attempts at control-freakery go awry.

S1mone does require the same suspension of disbelief that you needed when reading *Alice in Wonderland* or viewing *Being John Malkovich*. Not only do you have to take the user-friendliness of the technology that created S1mone on trust; you have to believe that Pacino's wily director could really keep his project secret from prying journalists and entertainment executives.

I can see how this might be too big a stretch for some. However, it's part of Niccol's point that Pacino's lie becomes powerful because so many people wish it to be true. This is a world so obsessed with "image", it simply isn't interested in the reality.

S1mone is bound to be unpopular within Hollywood because beneath the obvious exaggerations there is truth. Robert Altman's much-praised "satire" on Hollywood, *The Player*, actually avoided insulting those people upon whom Altman depends, especially the actors. Niccol goes in with both fists.

Catherine Keener is terrific as a quintessential movie executive, totally corrupted by money and power yet blissfully unaware of the fact, and indeed morally patronising to anyone who doesn't subscribe to her miserable values.

S1mone is the Hollywood equivalent of *To Die For* – another movie disliked by entertainment moguls, because it showed the grasping ferocity of showbiz culture, and the grinning skull beneath the smiling face of celebrity.

Niccol bravely doesn't let the public off the hook either, for their appetite for mindless hero-worship. And he is at pains to show that journalists, as well as entertainment executives, collude in the process – a truth which is hardly likely to endear him to critics, who are after all just journalists who spend too long in darkened rooms.

A final reason *S1mone* won't become a commercial hit is that a lot of people simply don't understand irony. All the same, this is a fresh and brilliant comedy. And I can't help but be enthusiastic about any film that captures the mindless idolatry, the grotesquely distorted values, the collective lunacy that have just elevated Princess Diana to the Top 10 Britons of all time, at the expense of such clearly insignificant figures as Charles Dickens, J.M.W.Turner and Jane Austen.

SKYFALL *(2012)*

Skyfall takes the Bond franchise to a new pinnacle of quality. Nine times nominee Roger Deakins (*No Country For Old Men, The Shawshank Redemption*) should win his first Academy Award for his stunning cinematography, equally magical whether it is among the iridescent skyscrapers of modern Shanghai or the bleak, ancient moorland of Scotland.

One of the world's most talented yet least known composers Thomas Newman (*American Beauty, Road to Perdition*) must also be a good bet after 10 unsuccessful nominations to achieve his first Oscar for best score, finally emulating his famous cousin Randy. The score is matchlessly atmospheric, and makes witty use of old Bond themes while adding a few of its own.

Disgracefully for a series that has brought us such great numbers as *Goldfinger, Nobody Does It Better* and *Live and Let Die*, Bond has always failed to win best song. Adele should at least win a nomination.

And who would have thought that *Skyfall* would be a strong contender for Best Original Screenplay? John Logan (a previous nominee for *Gladiator, The Aviator* and *Hugo*) has teamed up with previous 007 scribes Neil Purvis and Robert Wade to come up with a script that has qualities rarely seen in action-adventures: topicality, wit and intelligence.

Perhaps most significantly, *Skyfall* is the first Bond film to have a realistic chance of winning the major awards: Best Picture, Director (Sam Mendes, who has already won for *American Beauty*), Actor (Daniel Craig) and Supporting Actors (Judi Dench, Javier Bardem).

That's how good this film is. A second viewing persuades me that this is not just the best Bond movie, it's up there with the top action-adventures of all time.

It tells a refreshingly simple story and succeeds because of consummate craft, marvellous action set pieces and a cast that looks like the National Theatre at play.

In the pivotal role, Judi Dench as M gets more to do than ever before in a Bond movie, and endows her role with a lifetime of experience and authority. She won an Oscar for *Shakespeare in Love*, and she's even better here.

There are juicy roles for Ralph Fiennes as M's deviously bureaucratic new boss and Albert Finney as an entertainingly violent gamekeeper, plus strong supporting parts for Rory Kinnear, Helen McCrory and especially Ben Whishaw as a new, modernizing Q.

In Javier Bardem, Bond gets his creepiest adversary ever: a man not – for once – bent on world domination but with good reason to hate MI6. Helped by astonishing special effects and a spectacularly demented hairstyle, Bardem exudes a peculiar kind of menace: a cheery perviness all too topically evocative of Sir Jimmy Savile. This guy is so weird, he makes The Joker look wholesome.

The film gets off to a terrific start in Istanbul, with a thrilling rooftop chase of a kind you won't have seen before. Quite apart from its ingenuity, it's a valuable reminder that CGI is no match for superb stunts, courageously staged.

By the start of the title sequence, Bond is already missing,

Skyfall 387

believed dead, and M has written him a careful obituary. Needless to say, he has miraculous powers of recuperation, and he's soon helping the head of MI6 track down Bardem, who – like all Bond villains – seems to have endless funds and a limitless supply of henchmen.

The action roams the globe from Turkey to London, then off to Shanghai, before ending up in Scotland for a splendid climax that's like *Home Alone* with an unlimited budget. Here, Mendes pays tribute to earlier writers in the spy genre, particularly John Buchan and Michael Innes, and reveals more of Bond's back story and traumatized childhood than anyone has before.

There are more acting scenes than we're used to in a Bond films, but because of the quality of the cast and gravity of the ideas being discussed they don't drag; they make most action adventure films look rushed and superficial.

Mendes delivers not only some wonderfully exciting scenes but some new, genuinely surprising twists and a welcome element of humour, most of it thanks to Bardem and Dench.

Daniel Craig is superb as a defiantly virile Bond well past the first flush of youth, and not the crack shot or honed athlete he used to be. The film makes more of his patriotism and his resilience than any previous 007 movie, and his relationship with M becomes all the more touching as we realise that she's become the mother he virtually never had.

Mendes steers clear of cheap sentiment, and British upper lips have rarely been stiffer. But this movie has a respect for Bond, and for the secret services, that hasn't always existed in previous adventures of the world's most famous spy.

Longstanding 007 devotees will enjoy the way elements

are brought back from much earlier films, especially a rather well-known car. But the reason *Skyfall* excels is that it builds on our familiarity with the Bond canon and takes it in a new direction, much more relevant to world politics in the twenty-first century.

With this film, Bond enters the age of cyber-terrorism. 007 has been regenerated in such a way that now it is he who makes Jason Bourne look old-fashioned.

The ingenious central idea is to probe the heart of what we demand from our intelligence services in the age of WikiLeaks and public accountability. Is it really that murkiest of concepts, transparency, or something deeper than that? Isn't it really our primeval desire to be safe?

Thanks to *Skyfall*, the future of Bond movies is assured for years to come. Everyone connected with this brave, wholly successful enterprise deserves congratulation. Whether or not it triumphs at the Oscars, I don't see how anyone can deny that this is a cracking story, very well told.

SLEEPLESS IN SEATTLE *(1993)*

Annie (Meg Ryan) is engaged to formal, well-meaning Walter (Bill Pullman), but she hears on the radio a widower, Sam (Tom Hanks), being interviewed – much against his will – about his wife. More and more, Annie finds herself harbouring the screwball idea of meeting this mystery man, whom the Radio Station christens Sleepless in Seattle.

Nauseatingly sentimental, hopelessly predictable, a "women's weepie", Hollywood film-making at its most cynically commercial. *Sleepless in Seattle* was dismissed as all of these by critics. They were wrong: it's one of the great romances of all time, a movie which will be making people laugh and cry fifty years from now.

Any film is a bit sentimental which believes in the possibility of love at first sight – or, in this case, first hearing. But *Sleepless* does not, as so many romances do, ignore painful emotions: Hanks gives a very convincing portrayal of bereavement. The film casts a sceptical eye over the way Hollywood conventionally depicts romance and recognizes some uncomfortable aspects of modern life – notably, that in the age of feminism and Aids dating is difficult, often unrewarding, and potentially lethal.

In some ways, the film is quite subversive, dismissing as a second-best compromise the kind of relationship for which many less fortunate mortals settle – and towards which Annie is heading as the film begins. The movie ends up taking a ruthless stance in favour of the kind of total bonding which Hollywood has always seen as "real" love, and which Annie feels herself drawn to, much against her common sense.

Nor is the outcome as predictable as its detractors think. Right up to the last moment of suspense – will they or won't they meet on top of the Empire State Building? – there is the possibility of a bitter-sweet ending: with the woman settling for second-best (like Judy Davis in *Husbands and Wives*) or learning to live alone (like Jill Clayburgh in *An Unmarried Woman*), or being kept apart from her lover by fate and geography (as in *Manhattan*). That Ephron chooses to end her film differently is, these days, refreshingly unconventional.

Then there's the accusation that this is a "woman's weepie". Well, yes: it's concerned with love and relationships, and most women will love this film. But men may shed the odd tear too, for at least half the film is seen from a male point of view. Ephron and her male co-writers, David S. Ward and Jeff Arch have brilliantly avoided the flaw in so many "women's pictures" of portraying the men as cardboard cut-outs. Sam is a living, breathing character, with faults, responsibilities, and a masculine suspicion of "chick's movies" like this one might have been.

As for the film's supposedly flagrant commercialism, that's wisdom after the event. The premise of the movie was, on the contrary, commercially dangerous: it was about middle-aged people at a time when most moviegoers were below 30, and it went against the format of almost every successful Romantic Comedy: "boy meets girl, boy and girl hate each other, boy and girl fall in love". It's unique in motion picture history, in that the two lovers hardly meet, let alone have a developing relationship.

The premise of the film poses a seemingly intractable problem for a film-maker: how to show two people are ideally suited, when they don't even know each other. Ephron's solution is to build up visual and aural connections between the pair – most obviously through songs and common attitudes, more subtly through shared tastes in decor, clothes and colour (notice how both like the identical shade of blue). In doing this, she is wonderfully served by her designer Jeffrey Townsend and cinematographer, Sven Nykvist. His work for Ingmar Bergman (notably *Cries and Whispers* and *Fanny And Alexander*) may have brought him more critical kudos; but he's never done better work.

SNATCH *(2000)*

A couple of aspiring boxing promoters named Turkish (Jason Statham) and Tommy (Stephen Graham) are unwise enough to employ an Irish gypsy called Mickey (Brad Pitt) to be knocked out in the fourth round of a an illegal boxing match. The fight has been fixed by an East End crime boss Bricktop (Alan Ford), a nasty guy who likes nothing better than dissecting those who displease him and feeding them to his pigs.

Mickey is a hard man to communicate with because of his impenetrable Irish accent and, in any case, he has a mind of his own. He appals his employers by achieving an effortless knockout in the first round. Bricktop agrees not to feed Mickey, Turkish and Tommy to his pigs if they will participate in another rigged fight; but this time the volatile Irishman had better obey orders or else…

Meanwhile, a digitally deficient American jewel-thief called Frankie Four Fingers (Benicio Del Toro) has carried out a daring diamond heist in Antwerp. He stops off in London on his way to deliver a huge diamond to his Mafioso boss in New York (Dennis Farina). He becomes involved with a Hatton Garden dealer (Mike Reid) who's obviously an Anglo-Saxon cockney but so incorrigibly dodgy that he tries to melt into the background by pretending to be Jewish.

Then a dangerously psychopathic Russian called Boris the Blade (Rade Serbedzija) discerns that Frankie has not only appalling taste in gents' outfitting but a gambling compulsion. Boris encourages him to bet on one of Bricktop's illegal boxing matches, but before Frankie can be relieved of his money he is robbed of the diamond by three black crooks (Robbie Gee, Lennie James and Ade) notable for their amateurishness, cowardice and lack of cool.

This cool becomes even more noticeable by its absence when Frankie is accidentally shot and they find themselves pursued by virtually every criminal in London, including the Mafioso Avi, who arrives in England and hires an East End hit-man with the mellifluous name of Bullet-Tooth Tony (Vinnie Jones) to get his diamond back.

Everything goes horribly pear-shaped, numerous other people get shot by design or accident, and by the end of the movie even the hardened Mafioso Avi is happy to escape with his life. On returning to the States, an immigration official asks him "Anything to declare?" And Avi replies with a shudder: "Yeah – don't go to England."

At the turn of the 21st century there was a glut of British gangster films released to cash on the success of *Lock, Stock and Two Smoking Barrels.* There's only one that was worth going to see – and that's *Snatch.*

It's on a far higher level than the competition because it's faster, funnier and superbly produced by Matthew Vaughn. Snatch shows that, though Guy Ritchie is a flashy director, his first success with *Lock, Stock…* was no flash in the pan. For verve, originality and sense of fun there's no British director to touch him.

Ritchie's screenplay is cleverly plotted yet totally unpredictable, and the characters are as colourful and absurd as any in the New York tales of Damon Runyon. The result is like a very superior episode of *Minder,* but directed with the flair of a Quentin Tarantino or Baz Luhrmann.

Like Raymond Chandler, Damon Runyon and Tarantino before him, Ritchie is an intelligent outsider fascinated by the sleazy but colourful world of organised (or, in this film, disorganised) crime. His dialogue is slangy and snappy, and the eccentricity of the characters ensures that the plot constantly careers off in refreshingly unexpected directions.

Good though the British actors are, the movie is stolen by Brad Pitt. Pitt is hugely funny and totally convincing as a wild man that not even the prospect of becoming pigfood can frighten. It's impressive to see a Hollywood superstar taking a small part in a British film, and building it into one of the most memorable supporting performances in years. Pitt is often undervalued as an actor, and this performance is good enough to win him his first Oscar.

As the 18 certificate suggests, this is not a film for everyone. *Snatch* is very violent and full of bad language (though often it's used to uproariously comic effect). It also invites the audience to laugh at extremely callous acts of brutality.

But to take the film at all seriously is a mistake. It's essentially a romp set in a gangster Neverland. To inveigh against it would be a bit like going to *Guys and Dolls* or *Kind Hearts and Coronets* and waxing indignant at their glamorisation of criminality. *Snatch* is a fantastical black comedy, and should be judged as one.

Besides, there is underpinning it a sense of right and wrong, however unconventional. The bad guys get their just desserts, and the less bad guys get off relatively lightly.

I wouldn't argue that *Snatch* is a particularly moral film, or that its content in any way measures up to the brilliance of its style. The justification for its existence is that it's wickedly entertaining and outstandingly directed.

THE SOCIAL NETWORK *(2010)*

The Social Network is a warts-and-all biopic of Mark Zuckerberg, the computer geek who became the world's youngest billionaire thanks to his invention of Facebook.

It is director David Fincher's equivalent to Orson Welles' *Citizen Kane*: the story of a capitalist who is awe-inspiring in some ways but tragic in others, enviably clever and driven but also repellently ruthless and treacherous.

The irony is that a man who was able to make billions out of social networking, never understood how to make friends, let alone keep the few he had. Alternative titles might have been *Revenge of the Nerd*, or *Despicable Me*.

The picture works on three levels. It is an inspiring story of an ambitious young man sticking to his guns and blowing out of the water anyone who gets in his way. It's a cautionary tale about the price of such single-mindedness. And it's a sharply satirical portrait of a new business generation operating without a moral compass.

One of Hollywood's best young actors, Jesse Eisenberg has shown warmth and intelligence in *Roger Dodger*, *The Squid and the Whale* and *Adventureland*. As Mark Zuckerberg, he switches off the warmth but keeps the intelligence.

He is so chillingly arrogant that he becomes exhilarating in his self-belief. He persuades you that his coldness and detachment from conventional morality were central to Facebook's success.

Much of the film takes place as Mark is being attacked in separate lawsuits, both of which lead to flashbacks from varying points of view. One suit is by identical twins Cameron and Tyler Winklevoss (muscular rowers who tower over our diminutive anti-hero and are played with an odious air of entitlement by Armie Hammer) who claim that Zuckerberg stole the idea for Facebook from them.

Screenwriter Aaron Sorkin (*The West Wing*) avoids taking sides, but shows why Zuckerberg resented the Winklevosses' snobbery, and not unreasonably considered himself their creative superior. As he put it, "They came to me with an idea; I had a better one".

The other lawsuit is brought by Eduardo Saverin (British actor Andrew Garfield, nuanced and touching). He's Zuckerberg's only friend and original business partner, suing for what he regards as his rightful share of Facebook – 600 million dollars.

Sorkin has obvious sympathy for the way Eduardo was frozen out, but also recognises that the company outgrew his naivety and needed the contacts of his rival, Napster founder Sean Parker, played by Justin Timberlake with an explosive mixture of confidence and paranoia, magnetism and sleaze.

Most movies have a moral centre, but this one has more of a moral tangent. Well played by Rooney Mara, she's an invented character called Erica, who appears to be an amalgamation of several Zuckerberg girl-friends. We meet her in the opening scene, where she becomes even more annoyed than we are by Mark's fretting about social status, his arrogance and his lack of emotional empathy.

Later on, he makes some attempt to apologise, and she

rounds on him for his misogyny, his thoughtlessness and his obsessiveness. At the end, the movie hints that she is the equivalent to *Citizen Kane*'s Rosebud, the unattainable object of Zuckerberg's desire. It's a rare concession to sentiment.

In most movies, Erica would redeem the leading figure, but here she's condemned to be peripheral. This movie has, quite deliberately, an amoral centre. Zuckerberg doesn't care much if he's redeemed or not. What he minds about is his project.

The nearest thing Mark shows to love is in a restaurant when Parker reveals that he is on the same wavelength as Zuckerberg about the direction Facebook ought to take. There's a meeting of minds, a near-sexual frisson, a touch of hero-worship in Zuckerberg's eyes – and this is the moment when Eduardo first realises he is being left out in the cold.

Not everyone will respond to this very masculine movie. After all, it's asking us to care what happens between a number of rich young American males fighting over percentages. There are few concessions to anyone too slow to follow the whip-smart dialogue. Not everyone is going to understand what's happening, let alone be bothered about who wins.

But even Fincher and Sorkin remain detached from the struggle and its outcome. They're fascinated by the characters, and especially by the way Zuckerberg himself is extraordinary, yet typical.

In a welcome return to form after the skilled but schmaltzy *Benjamin Button*, Fincher directs with the same hard-hitting panache he brought to *Fight Club* and *Se7en*. The technical wizardry that enables him to cast the same actor as identical twins is breathtaking because of its invisibility.

He is also a master at generating suspense and a variety

of moods. You get a feeling for the atmosphere of a dorm at Harvard where no one sleeps, a pitch to a New York businessman going horribly wrong, a rented house in California full of immature geeks. Without unnecessary flashiness, different scenes stylishly reflect Eduardo's helplessness, Parker's paranoia, Zuckerberg's icy indifference to any opinion other than his own.

I was reminded of Budd Schulberg's comic novel about an opportunist, *What Makes Sammy Run?* and F. Scott Fitzgerald's classic parable about the rich, *The Great Gatsby*. Most of all, it's reminiscent of Stephen Sondheim's brilliant commercial failure, *Merrily We Roll Along*, a musical about a Richard Rodgers-like composer who sacrifices personal relationships in pursuit of worldly success.

This is not a film that bothers to dissect the allure and shortcomings of Facebook; it's too busy showing us its vision of the characters involved. But the callous way the anti-hero uses the internet first to bully his former girl-friend and then to inquire if she will be his friend exposes a very interesting and significant dysfunctionality in the Facebook generation.

One thing's for sure. See this movie, which manages the rare feat of being both entertaining and a cultural landmark, and you'll never be able to hear the expression "Facebook friend" without mentally putting inverted commas around it.

SPIDER-MAN 2 *(2004)*

What is happening to Hollywood sequels? You used to be able to rely on them being more poorly crafted than the original movies, cheaply made and frequently not even starring the same actors. The studios could depend on them to make around 60% of the revenue earned by the original, which represented a good, reliable return for minimal effort. The critics could sit back happily with a superior smirk and the word "Typical!" hovering on their lips. The only people disappointed were the audiences.

But now we're in a run of Hollywood sequels that are classier, more spectacular and even better made than the originals. *Toy Story 2*, *Shrek 2* and now *Spider-Man 2* are all improvements upon very good predecessors. And whereas the first *Spider-Man* was so violent it earned a 12 certificate that prevented much of its potential audience from enjoying it in the cinema, this time director Sam Raimi has wisely toned down the brutality to gain a PG certificate – which should ensure that it becomes one of the biggest blockbusters in history.

It is also, within the limitations of a comic-strip action spectacular, an intelligent, well-written film. This is the *Hamlet* of popcorn movies. Alvin Sargent's script burrows into the psyche of a young man who can't decide whether he wants to be normal or a Super-hero. To swing at high speed from skyscrapers and rescue damsels in distress or not to swing at high speed from skyscrapers and rescue damsels in distress, that is the question.

To most of us, the question would have a simple answer: take the glory and swing. But for Peter Parker (Tobey Maguire), the solution is not so straightforward. The life of a Super-hero has grave disadvantages. It leaves little time for his science degree at college, it tires him out, and it's financially unrewarding.

Saving people from certain death is always making him late, which makes his boss angry when he doesn't deliver pizzas on time, and his actress girl-friend Mary-Jane gets upset when he can't even be relied upon to turn up to see her act in *The Importance of Being Earnest*.

Moonlighting as Spider-Man also makes it impossible for him to declare his love to Mary-Jane, because he's afraid that as the girl-friend of a Super-hero she will become an immediate target for all the local Super-villains.

Raimi has great fun illustrating Peter Parker's existential nightmare, cleverly setting his period of freedom from the responsibility of being Spider-Man with a version of *Raindrops Keep Falling On My Head*.

Moviegoers with longish memories will know that the same song was used to show the happiest time of Butch and Sundance's lives as they messed around with Katharine Ross before being hounded to the deaths by the law.

Here, the same song is used ironically, with Peter celebrating the fact that he's getting higher grades at college and wandering round with a goofy grin, trying not to notice as mayhem and muggings go on around him.

It's tempting to ascribe the movie's success to its obvious

entertainment value. It's the first comic-strip movie really to involve the audience with its Super-hero's thought-processes.

All the acting is of superior quality. As the love-interest, Kirsten Dunst is cute without being cloying, and she's curiously sexy as she kisses her new boy-friend on the lips upside-down and wonders why this doesn't give her quite the same thrill as when Spider-Man used to do it.

As our hero's wise. saintly auntie, Rosemary Harris is, as always, a class act. The less reliable Alfred Molina as the super-villain Doc Ock gives one of his best, and most complex, screen performances, helped by tremendous special-effect arms that turn him into a formidable, homicidal octopus.

And J.K.Simmons is funnier than ever as the tabloid editor of the Daily Bugle, alternately denouncing Spider-Man or hailing him as a hero according to whim. He's valuable comic relief whenever the film seems in danger of taking itself too seriously. "A guy called Otto Octavius gets eight limbs," he muses on learning the existence of the new super-villain Doc Ock. "What are the odds?"

Sam Raimi does a terrific job of deepening the subtext of his movie without short-changing us on humour or thrills. There are plenty of exhilarating action sequences to make audiences cheer – he has a cartoonist's eye for an iconic image – and this time the near-seamless integration of live-action with computer-generation makes it far less easy to see where Maguire or Molina ends and the digital effects begin.

But when a movie makes more money in its first six days than any movie in cinematic history, it is clearly tapping into something that's of some cultural significance.

The subject of the movie is, in a word, responsibility. Peter Parker tries to avoid the responsibility that comes with being a super-hero, but comes to realise that it's something you can't back away from. The bad guys will find you anyway, threaten your loved ones and indeed your whole society.

The reason the movie strikes so resonant a chord with Americans at present is that the USA sees itself as the only super-hero, or super-power, on earth, and has been going through a very similar crisis of conscience.

Like Spider-Man, America has discovered that some of its most well-intentioned actions are portrayed in parts of the media as acts of criminal aggression, and there seems to be an inexhaustible supply of bad guys in the world.

In coded form, *Spider-Man 2* asks what America should do: attempt to retreat to normality as it was before 9/11, or accept its responsibilities as a super-power and stand up to be counted.

You won't be surprised to hear that the hero of the movie chooses the latter course, and it's cheering that – even with Michael Moore's dishonest documentary *Fahrenheit 9/11* around to demoralise the masses – the vast majority of the American people appears willing to accept the challenge of responsibility.

The success of *Spider-Man 2* may well provide a more reliable clue to the outcome of November's Presidential elections than Michael Moore's much-touted documentary. Most Americans are clearly convinced by the film's argument that isolationism, passivity and defeatism are simply not an option.

STANDING IN THE SHADOWS OF MOTOWN *(2002)*

Who are the most successful rock musicians of all time? And who had more hits than the Beatles, Rolling Stones, Beach Boys and Elvis put together? The Funk Brothers, that's who.

They played on every Tamla Motown hit, whether it was by the Supremes, Four Tops, Miracles, Martha and the Vandellas, Stevie Wonder or Marvin Gaye, but without any credit (except on Gaye's 1971 *What's Going On* album). Their names were virtually unknown outside a small recording studio in Detroit, called The Snakepit, which was really Motown owner Berry Gordy's garage.

It's the achievement of Paul Justman's documentary that it pays respect to musicians who have been undervalued for four decades. The bass players, especially – James Jamerson and Bob Babbitt – must rank among the very best of all time.

In telling their story and bringing the ageing survivors back together for a concert in 2000 – like those Cuban old-timers who reconvened for *The Buena Vista Social Club* – Justman captures far more than nostalgia for a bygone era. This isn't just a lot of interesting information, it's also fabulous entertainment.

Perhaps the greatest revelation is that, 41 years after they last played together, the Funk Brothers still perform with the same infectious enthusiasm and astonishing precision. Their sound is as fresh and exciting as ever. It's obvious that virtually any decent singer could have had a hit with these sidemen.

As I write this, I'm listening to the CD from the movie, with new versions of old classics such as *Heat Wave* (sung by Joan Osborne), *I Heard It Through The Grapevine* (Ben Harper), *What Becomes of the Brokenhearted* (Joan Osborne again) and *Ain't No Mountain High Enough* (Chaka Khan and Montell Jordan). These are no ordinary cover versions. Thanks to new technology, they sound even better than the originals.

The CD has won two Grammy awards, and the New York Film Critics voted this the best documentary of last year. I can understand their enthusiasm. I don't remember a music documentary that has given me as much enjoyment.

It has minor faults. It doesn't probe deeply into any tensions there might have been within the group, nor does it more than hint at their resentment of Berry Gordy, the record mogul who kept them resolutely in the shadows, never paid them a dime in royalties and abandoned them summarily in 1972, when he believed they were past their sell-by date. Gordy is conspicuous by his absence. And the film doesn't give enough credit to the songwriters or record producers.

But this never attempts to be a critical documentary. It works brilliantly as a celebration of some terrific talents and extremely likeable men. Their pride in their music and joy in each other's company come across with terrific power and charm. The film captures the camaraderie of music-making better than any movie since Alan Parker's *The Commitments*.

These guys still swing (it comes as no surprise that all of them played jazz for their own amusement). They also stand as an inspirational example of blacks and whites working together.

This has to be the most revelatory rockumentary of all time. Anybody who has ever loved a Tamla Motown record should seek it out, and drag along someone who hasn't. It should open a new generation's ears to the greatness of music that makes today's pop records look soulless and manufactured.

There ain't no mountain high enough to keep me from seeing this movie again and again.

STAR WARS
(1977, Special Edition 1997)

One of the most popular and profitable movies of all time, Star Wars was the first big hit to use computer animation; the first big science fiction hit since 2001: A Space Odyssey; and its huge success sparked a revived interest in making films with a strong narrative.

In the mid-Nineties, writer-director-producer George Lucas and Twentieth Century Fox spent millions of pounds improving the sound and special effects of the trilogy, even adding new scenes. Some fans of the original were outraged, claiming that Lucas is tampering with their childhood memories, but the re-released *Star Wars* was a huge commercial success – and no wonder.   One of the best sci-fi films of all time was back, and it really did look and sound better than ever.

The story remains unchanged – of how an unassuming, uncommitted backwoodsman is encouraged by a mysterious old man to join forces with a motley collection from various races to defeat the forces of darkness. It's basically the same plot which Tolkien used in *The Lord of the Rings* , but George Lucas had the wit to see its potential as science fiction.

In 1977, the film flew in the face of cinematic fashion,

not least for its straightforward view of right versus wrong – simplistic, but a breath of fresh air after the moral uncertainties of the Sixties and early Seventies.

Though criticised on release for cartoonish characters and bad acting, Harrison Ford is very much a star as the film's anti-hero, Han Solo, who learns that being handsome and solo isn't everything. Alec Guinness adds necessary authority as Obi-Wan Kenobi. The baddies, led by horror veteran Peter Cushing and James Earl Jones as the voice of Darth Vader, are genuinely menacing.

Carrie Fisher is sparky as the princess, even if her hairstyle does make her look as though she's listening to the dialogue through headphones. Even the much-maligned Mark Hamill is adequate as the Candide-like innocent abroad – and, best of all, there are the robot R2D2 and android C3PO to act as a space-age Laurel and Hardy.

Though a technical trailblazer in its day, *Star Wars* was produced on a shoestring budget, and before recent advances in electronic technology. Compromises were made, and these have now been rectified with considerable skill.

The original *Star Wars* soundtrack wasn't even in stereo. Vastly more impressive sound adds to the excitement of the space battles, and maximises the impact of John Williams's terrific score, a cinematic landmark for the way it brought symphonic film music back into fashion.

For the 1997 Special Edition, there is one wholly new scene (shot in the Seventies, but not included because the special effects let it down) between Han Solo and the character to whom he owes money, Jabba the Hutt. There are new monsters, to make use of technology which was perfected by Lucas's technicians twenty years on, in *Jurassic Park.*

Most of all, there's an enrichment of the visual detail and atmosphere. The space port with its notoriously seedy bar becomes a much more densely populated place which reeks of danger.

Some critics have blamed *Star Wars* for ending a so-called "golden age" of American cinema which created intelligent, politically committed movies like *Nashville* and *Five Easy Pieces*. Oddly enough, though, it is those films – not *Star Wars* – which look dated today.

The more morally conservative, narrative-based movies of Lucas and his colleague Steven Spielberg (who went on to collaborate as producer and director on the Indiana Jones trilogy) are equally intelligent and far more timeless. Most importantly, they reinvigorated mass interest in the cinema, and reversed film's seemingly inevitable decline into being a minority art-form.

Star Wars always was an exciting, uplifting experience. The Special Edition improves it still further, and even critics will find it easier to love.

SUNSHINE STATE *(2002)*

For me to describe the plot would take many thousand words, so I'll just mention the main characters. There's Marly Temple (exquisitely played by Edie Falco, from *The Sopranos*) a drink-sodden, sharp-tongued but still attractive divorcee who's running her retired father's motel and hating every minute of it. Her toyboy (Marc Bluco) is abandoning her to become a pro golfer, and the only other man she fancies (Timothy Hutton) is an itinerant landscape architect who is helping to destroy the only environment she likes, turning it into a rich people's paradise of condominiums and golf courses.

The scenes of romantic sparring between these two actors are funny, realistic and touching, some of the best since the heyday of Spencer Tracy and Katharine Hepburn.

The other central character is the black and upwardly mobile Desiree (the magnificent Angela Bassett, in the most demanding role she has played since the biopic of Tina Turner). She left the area 25 years ago, failed as an actress but is taking her trophy husband, a hospital anaesthetist (James McDaniel), home to visit the apparently sweet, grey-haired mother (Mary Alice) who drummed her out of town as a pregnant 15 year-old but now blames her for never calling or writing.

This is an achingly accurate portrait of a damaged mother-daughter relationship where each woman is more like than the other than either is willing easily to accept.

Meanwhile, the mother's elderly doctor boyfriend (Bill Cobbs) is unsuccessfully battling the property developers who are buying up the mostly black-owned houses along the beach.

The developers are being helped by a dodgy businessman (Gordon Clapp) trying to pay off his gambling debts in between suicide attempts. At the same time, his relentlessly cheery but really very unhappy wife (Mary Steenburgen, excellent as ever) puts on ghastly pageants that are reinventing the area's distinctly chequered racial history.

If *Sunshine State* isn't a commercial hit, that will reflect more on our debased, celebrity-obsessed culture and the dwindling attention span of modern audiences than on any faults in the film itself.

It isn't for everyone. If you found John Sayles's previous masterpiece about the Texan-Mexican border, *Lone Star,* too slow and rambling, or couldn't see the point of Robert Altman's panorama of Los Angeles in *Short Cuts,* you may not get much out of *Sunshine State,* which dissects present-day Florida on a similarly epic scale.

But if, like me, you despair of the dumbing-down embraced by too many American movies, *Sunshine State* is a breath of warm, unpolluted air.

It has a wealth of characters who are fully rounded and unpredictable, seemingly drawn at random from real life but with interrelationships that becomes wonderfully revealing by the end.

John Sayles takes on big, important themes that affect people everywhere – the joys and burdens of family, how far children should go to please their parents, whether we should try to understand or sanitize our history, and how different races and income-groups can live together.

The result is extraordinary – a timely picture of the way ordinary human beings can cope with life under the capitalist system.

Sayles's early film career showed a keen interest in union activism and social protest, but he has matured to an extent that he now recognises the importance of coping with the forces of history and economics, rather than trying to turn the clock back to a kindlier but far less dynamic time.

His core subject is the vital one of how to keep your humanity and sense of caring for others when those around you seem to be losing theirs. And, miraculously, he puts across his highly sensible ideas about family and socials responsibilities without hectoring us.

The plot description above may sound like the set-up for a politically correct, anti-capitalist, anti-racist rant, but it's nothing of the sort. Humanity is found in the unlikeliest of people, as is commercial acumen. Connections and dependencies between characters are revealed in surprising and often very touching ways.

At the centre of the piece are the two leading women – Edie Falco's apparently "white trash" character realising that she has to break free of her family's expectations and leave, and Angela Bassett's black yuppie discovering that her family roots are stronger than she thought, and she may have to stay.

The piece is a triumph of ensemble acting, and Sayles's writing has never been sharper, more truthful or wittier. No wonder top-quality actors want to work for him.

Jane Alexander gives a sensational supporting performance

as an apparently unworldly teacher of community drama – at least the equal of those for which this astonishingly underused actress won Oscar nominations (if you're wondering, these were in *The Great White Hope, All The President's Men, Kramer Vs Kramer* and *Testament*).

Towards the other end of the age scale, a young black actor to watch, Alexander Lewis, is terrific as a troubled adolescent arsonist, whose parents died in violent circumstances and who uses the entire range of teenage grunts and body language to ensure that no one comes close enough to hurt him again.

Without any need for preaching on Sayles's part, this character becomes a microcosm of disaffected, uncommunicative black youth everywhere. He's on a knife-edge, teetering between crime, drugs and pointless resentment on the one hand, and a responsible, constructive life as a carpenter on the other.

Sayles eloquently makes the point that throwing money at this boy won't help, nor will imprisonment. He is desperately, if silently, in need of a father-figure and continuous encouragement to find work that he is good at.

At Sayles's best, as he is here, he is like a modern Dickens. He has a naturally funny writer's eye for the telling irony, a quality journalist's nose for social detail, and a thinking man's conscience that won't let him close his eyes to the consequences of human selfishness and greed.

Sunshine State is a beautifully crafted, complex work of art and a revealing social document. This is a wise, politically and socially sophisticated picture, one of a tiny number that politicians of all parties could learn from.

SUPER 8 *(2011)*

J.J. Abrams' ingenious mixture of charming-rites-of-passage kids' movie with science-fiction-monster-spectacular is super indeed. As a nostalgic rites-of-passage movie, it's more touching than Rob Reiner's *Stand By Me*. As sci-fi action-adventure, it's as thrilling as *Jurassic Park* or Abrams' last hit, *Star Trek*.

In part, it's an inspirational love-letter to the process of film-making. The hero of the picture is mild-mannered 12 year-old Joe Lamb (newcomer Joel Courtney). We're in an Ohio steel town in the 1970s. Joe's just lost his mother in an industrial accident, and his father (Kyle Chandler), the local deputy sheriff, is too busy to cope with his own grief, let alone the needs of his son. He wants Joe to go off to baseball camp and be a normal child.

But Joe wants to make movies, even bad ones. He loves the creative camaraderie of working with friends, and he enjoys model-making and cosmetic effects, especially fake blood. Joe is happy to leave directing duties to his more confident friend Charles (Riley Griffiths). Charles is a junior Orson Welles, in physical stature as well as ambition, and plans to enter a home-made zombie movie in a national competition.

So they assemble a small cast and crew, including their

scarily pyromaniac pal Cary (Ryan Lee) to supervise the special effects, and recruit a leading lady, in the form of the blonde and frighteningly talented Alice (Elle Fanning).

As Joe powders her face for a night shoot at the local deserted railway station, he gazes adoringly at Alice, in a beautiful scene that captures the exact moment innocence tips over into agonised puberty. The tension is broken first by the need for a "take", and then by a moment of horrific (and superbly filmed) spectacle, as a military train crashes into a car that has made its way on to the track.

Only Joe notices that the crash was no accident. In the car is the boys' science teacher (Glynn Turman), badly injured. He issues a terrible warning to the children: "They will kill you. Do not speak of this or else you and your parents will die".

As if this isn't thrilling enough, something huge and dangerous has escaped from the train, and a large section of the US military is out to find it. And then all kinds of things start disappearing from the town: car engines, microwave ovens, all the town's dogs...

I'm not going to spoil the film by telling you any more, but it's essentially a compendium of ideas from all Steven Spielberg's classic hits (and a few non-Spielberg successes, such as the under-rated *Eight-Legged Freaks*), cleverly combined to make something fascinating and new. This is no accident, as Spielberg is the movie's producer and was clearly very personally involved.

Some critics are bound to object that the film is no more than pastiche, but I think they're wrong. Abrams' picture is a very timely reminder about what's important in popular film-making. The idea of movies is not just to bludgeon the audience into submission and turn us into passive consumers, it's to make us feel our humanity, laugh and feel the film is actually about something.

So the special effects are as marvellous as you would expect of a 21st century blockbuster, but the reason this film will endure and inspire is that it makes you care about the characters, believe in their milieu and share in their anxieties and excitement.

It's probably too scary for very small children, but that's another way of saying that it delivers plenty of thrills to satisfy grown-ups as well as the teenagers at whom it's centrally aimed. Though it's a 12A, I would think most children above the age of nine would be able to handle its intensity.

There's even a certain amount of depth. The friendship between the children seems real, and all they all give enjoyable, authentic performances of considerable charm. Elle Fanning, who was also terrific in the far inferior Sofia Coppola film *Somewhere*, is clearly the most exciting female acting talent America has produced since her big sister, Dakota.

The developing relationship between two of the fathers and their respective children feels genuine, too. Kyle Chandler resembles a young Alec Baldwin as Joe's dad (and I do mean that as a compliment), while Ron Eldard neatly avoids making Alice's father the kind of melodramatic villain you normally encounter in children's films.

Other valuable ingredients, which have all too often been missing from 21st century blockbusters, are playfulness and humour. Abrams enjoys toying with the audience's expectations, and he has fun hiding the creature for most of the movie. This is no mean feat, as it is extremely large.

He also has enormous affection for these children playing

at being film-makers, just as he himself did as a teenager, and Spielberg did before him. Stick around for the end credits and you'll see the film within a film, an enjoyably inept, deliberately badly acted zombie movie enthusiastically made by shambolic amateurs.

It's delightful, funny and humane – all epithets which apply equally to the main feature. I really, really loved it.

SWEENEY TODD:THE DEMON BARBER OF FLEET STREET *(2007)*

It's a bleedin' masterpiece. I Lovett. Four people with a touch of genius worked on this: composer-lyricist Stephen Sondheim, director Tim Burton, actor Johnny Depp and orchestrator Jonathan Tunick. So it should be no surprise that they have come up with one of the few great musical films of recent years.

It deserved many more Oscar nominations than the three that it has received (for Depp, costumes and art direction) and is in many ways superior to *Chicago*, which won Best Picture a few years ago. This is a gripping tale, splendidly set to music. Some may object that it should have been sung more operatically, but I adored every exhilarating minute of it.

Bizarrely, some American reviewers have objected that it's gory, stylised and a musical. This strikes me as like accusing Shakespeare's *King Lear* of being visceral, mostly in verse and a tragedy. What on earth did they expect?

Sweeney Todd tells the melodramatic story, inspired by real events, of a nineteenth-century barber, crazed by being transported overseas for a crime he did not commit, who returned after 15 years to be told that his wife was dead, and his daughter had fallen into the hands of the judge who had sentenced him.

Sweeney avenged himself on society by killing his customers and passing them on to his mistress, Mrs Lovett, who baked them into meat pies, which apparently went down well with beer, if not the judiciary.

Director Tim Burton is at home with such gothic material, and visually the film is as much of a treat as his other best-looking films, such as *Edward Scissorhands* and *Sleepy Hollow*. He is a magnificent, visionary director, now at the peak of his powers.

Although much of the movie is dark and menacing, set in a London brimming with corruption and injustice, it's also extremely funny – nowhere more so than when it launches into Mrs Lovett's colourful fantasy sequence, imagining herself and a bathing-costumed, improbably domesticated Sweeney settling down happily beside the seaside.

First staged in 1979, this is one of the finest musicals ever written, with some of Sondheim's wittiest lyrics and most powerful music. It's brilliantly orchestrated on a magnificent scale, and most of the theatrical score is mercifully intact, although the opening number (*The Ballad of Sweeney Todd*) has been cut, depriving us of the joy of hearing Christopher Lee sing it, in his eerie, sepulchral bass. I gather it has been recorded, and I would like it to have been played over the end credits – perhaps we'll be able to enjoy it on the DVD.

Sondheim is often accused of writing unmemorable tunes. All I would reply is: listen to *Not While I'm Around* and *Johanna*, two of his most melodic ballads.

As usual with Sondheim, there is a certain amount of

camp cynicism along with the wit; but there's also a strength and passion, both musically and lyrically, which elevate this to being a major work of art.

And it's thoroughly dramatic. I defy anyone to experience Depp serenading his long-lost razors, holding one out and announcing "At last my arm is complete again!" without feeling a shiver down their spine.

Depp has given many great performances, but never has he been this smoulderingly volcanic. And he reveals an unexpectedly strong and flexible singing voice – not operatic, but with feeling and resonance. It's like David Bowie in his maturity, which is all right by me. And Depp's diction, so often a weakness in American screen actors, is terrific. I've never heard so many of Sondheim's words before.

Helena Bonham Carter's soprano voice is more fragile, and lacks the earthiness that the score demands. But, with her big, black, marmoset eyes, she brings a sexiness and pathos to Mrs Lovett that I haven't seen in any of the four stage productions I have witnessed.

The supporting cast is superb. Alan Rickman and Timothy Spall are marvellously repellent as the lecherous Judge and porcine Beadle. Sacha Baron Cohen sings and cavorts surprisingly well as Pirelli, the rival, quasi-Italian barber. As the young, gin-sodden orphan Toby, Ed Sanders is tremendous, and sings the beautiful (though savagely ironic) *Not While I'm Around* extremely affectingly. Even the potentially wet lovers Johanna and Anthony are engagingly played by newcomers Jayne Wisener and Jamie Campbell.

Be warned that the film includes some extremely grisly throat-cuttings. But despite the necessarily gruesome subject-matter, the breathtaking talent on display here should be enough to send anyone home euphoric.

THELMA AND LOUISE *(1991)*

Thelma, a downtrodden wife (Geena Davis), and world-weary waitress Louise (Susan Sarandon) go on a weekend which turns sour. Louise shoots a man who tries to rape Thelma, and decides to go on the run to Mexico. Robbed of their money, they hold up a convenience store and are pursued by the FBI.

Ignore the solemn socio-sexual analysts: this is no feminist tract, but an exhilarating female riposte to the buddy-buddy movie. Some of the world's silliest feminists criticized the film for being insufficiently militant: neither Thelma nor Louise displays even a hint of lesbianism, and their first impulse when in trouble is to phone up their men (a perfectly natural reaction, but not one which will endear them to radical feminists). Surprisingly soon after nearly being raped, Thelma picks up a male hitch-hiker and goes to bed with him – not very likely, I admit, but Geena Davis's enthusiasm is enough to make you believe it at the time.

The movie isn't perfect. Like many of its male characters, it sags in the middle; there's something slightly depressing about any film where guns and cars are used to confer independence and strength on the leading characters; and the fate of the truck-driver's tanker smacks of escapist fantasy. But why shouldn't one action movie in ten thousand respond to women's fantasies, rather than men's?

Like most big commercial successes, it contains at least one timely social insight: namely, that feminism can be sexy. Geena Davis transforms herself from submissive child-woman to resilient adult so attractively that she will undoubtedly influence more women to re-evaluate their lives than the entire works of Andrea Dworkin.

Susan Sarandon has to make a less positive transformation and is lumbered with the only laboured scenes in the film, as she decides whether to accept her boyfriend's clumsy proposal of marriage; but hers too is a performance of taste, intelligence and warmth.

The screenplay, a first-time effort by Callie Khouri, wittily inverts the audience's expectations all the way along, and is the first since *Alien* to harness Ridley Scott's visual talent to an involving story. Scott's flair for using landscape to arouse emotion (a memorable aspect of *Blade Runner* and *Black Rain*) gives the film more than just surface gloss: it lends it a mythic, allegorical clarity. Adrian Biddle's photography was Oscar-nominated, as was Thom Noble's editing.

Some commentators have found the end nihilistic, or a blatant rip-off of *Butch Cassidy*; but for the audience it's inevitable and emotionally satisfying. It contains a central truth about feminism: there is no return to dependency on men, any more than a child can regain innocence.

The whole film is an exhilarating celebration of popular cinema's ability to turn stories of ordinary people into myths with a social resonance; and the final frames are a signal that, whatever the fate of *Thelma and Louise* themselves, their story will survive. This is more than an entertaining movie: it's a great one.

THERE WILL BE BLOOD (2007)

There will be superlatives – and why not? Here is the most profoundly ironic, rags-to-riches story since *Citizen Kane*. In every way except technical innovation, it surpasses Orson Welles' classic.

When we first meet Daniel Plainview (played in one of his too rare screen appearances by Daniel Day Lewis) it's 1898, and he's digging for precious metals. By luck, he discovers oil, which sets him on the path to becoming an oil man.

A mining accident leaves Daniel with an orphan to care for, and he raises the boy, whom he calls HW, as his own. In 1912, he follows a promising lead to California, where he defeats the opposition of local preacher Eli Sunday (played with wonderful subtlety and a hint of oiliness by Paul Dano, the sullen teenager in *Little Miss Sunshine*). The devious Plainview presents himself to the locals as a straight-talking philanthropist, buys up land and starts drilling.

When he strikes oil, bigger concerns try to buy him out, but he won't sell. He becomes the model of a ruthless, self-made businessman: outwardly charming, gentle and kindly, yet capable of deceit, cruelty and even murder.

The film looks magnificent – a credit to Robert Elswit's cinematography and Jack Fisk's production design. The faces seem to have stepped out of Walker Evans' photographs. Towering over everyone and everything, however, is Daniel Day Lewis. His performance is one of the finest ever captured on film.

Like a one-man combination of Macbeth and Lady Macbeth, Plainview makes you see things from his driven perspective, and you share in his tragedy. In many ways, he's the nastiest character in the movie. Yet, he is also curiously admirable.

Adopting a gruff voice reminiscent of John Huston, Day Lewis makes him complex and contradictory: satanic but benevolent, a personification of Mammon but also a man capable of paternal feelings and old-fashioned courtesy. There's a grandeur to his greed, a style to his cynicism, a verve to his vengefulness towards those he thinks have betrayed him.

No other actor would attempt some of the eccentric line-readings Day Lewis gives here, let alone carry them off so triumphantly. For example, late on he fixes one such "traitor" with his eyes and drawls "That makes you my competiTORRRR" with such eccentric emphasis on the final syllable that his madness is funny yet utterly chilling.

If Day Lewis does not win this year's Oscar for Best Actor, the Academy Awards electorate may as well give up. This is a thrillingly real, powerful, charismatic performance that no other actor of his generation – or any generation – could have achieved. In the context of other starring performances this year, he's like a racing car zooming past underpowered family saloons.

He achieves the apparently impossible by being both epic and minutely detailed, full of meaning but enigmatic, larger than life yet unmistakably lifelike. His Plainview is not an horrific monster, as some critics are mistakenly claiming, but a profoundly human being whose desire to become a kind of God on earth leads with sickening inevitability to his disintegration and defeat.

He also represents an extraordinary, discomforting personification of America itself, revelling in wealth yet dependent on a commodity – oil – that it can't control, affecting a religious, family-friendly façade, yet deeply materialistic and murderous. In its oblique way, the film contains a powerful critique of America drunk on its own power and achievement.

As for writer-director Paul Thomas Anderson, this is a class up from all his previous work. *Hard Eight, Boogie Nights, Magnolia* and *Punch-Drunk Love* all had flashes of inspiration; but his adaptation of Upton Sinclair's 1927 novel *Oil!* shows a fierce intelligence, maturity and instinct for cinema that denote the flowering of a major talent.

Not everyone will like the modernist score by Jonny Greenwood of Radiohead, but I did. Occasionally, it's a little too intrusive, but much of it is extraordinarily inspired and atmospheric. In the opening, wordless twenty minutes of the movie, it's like metallic insects rubbing their legs together in demonic dissonance. This is the most revolutionary soundtrack of the year, and certain to prove the most influential.

Be warned that this is an extremely long, gruelling film, and not without its challenges. Plainview's behaviour is sometimes puzzling, and the film serves up its ideas obliquely, rather than spoonfeeding the audience; but such complexity does not seriously detract from a film that deserves the overused accolade "masterpiece".

The landscapes are reminiscent of *Giant* and *Days of*

Heaven. The themes owe something to *The Treasure of Sierra Madre* and Erich von Stroheim's *Greed*. Daniel Plainview's cinematic ancestors include such obsessives as Charles Foster Kane, Captain Ahab and Noah Cross from *Chinatown*.

But there's nothing tired or derivative about this film. And even though it's based on an 80 year-old novel, it serves as a memorably bleak parable for our times, with a coruscatingly savage view of religious hypocrisy and the American Dream.

There are many marvellous sequences, but one of the finest shows Plainview reluctantly consenting to become a Baptist convert in order to finalise an important business deal. It's a scene which shows Plainview incandescent with rage at having to demean himself, yet also crying out to a God he doesn't believe in to give him some kind of redemption for his sins.

The final scene of the film, which echoes that agonised baptism in an even more disturbing, psychotic and vengeful fashion, will stay with me forever.

TO LIVE/ HUOZHE *(1994)*

To Live is a brave indictment of the idiocies of Chinese Communism, Mao-worship and the Cultural Revolution through its story of an ordinary family from the 40s through to the present day. By the end, the dream of a just, Communist society has dissipated, until it has the status of a fairy story – or a Father Christmas that grown-ups only pretend to believe in.

In the west, a magnificent film like this can win awards, such as the Grand Jury Prize and Best Actor at the Cannes Film Festival. In its country of origin, China, *To Live* earned its brilliant director, Zhang Yimou, nothing but trouble. He and his leading lady, Gong Li, were confined within the borders of the country; his next production was closed down by the authorities; and he was forced to apologize publicly for his political incorrectness.

It is Zhang's achievement that he tells a tale which is essentially tragic with humour, warmth and compassion even for the misguided authorities. The old men who run China should have been grateful to him.

To Live is closer in style to drama-documentary than Zhang's most famous films: *Red Sorghum, Ju Dou* and *Raise the Red Lantern.* Even so, it is beautifully framed and lit. Zhang marshals his imagery – puppets, water, food, putting on a show – with the precision of a master film-maker.

Unfortunately for its commercial prospects, *To Live* follows too soon after two Chinese films on a similar scale and theme, *Farewell My Concubine* and *The Blue Kite*. But it is more accessible and moving than either; and, if it lacks the anger which made *The Blue Kite* so powerful, it also manages to be less depressing, by finding something positive in the indomitable spirit of its central family. As the mother and father, Gong Li and Ge You give two of the most moving performances of this, or any, year.

THE TOURIST *(2010)*

Have you ever watched an old Hitchcock caper starring Cary Grant and murmured "they don't make them like that any more"? If so, *The Tourist* is the picture for you. It's a glossy, sophisticated, gloriously improbable romp – escapist fun for these austere times.

A shy, unassuming American tourist on a train to Venice (Johnny Depp in the Cary Grant role) is lured by an absurdly glamorous Englishwoman (Angelina Jolie, never more sensually enigmatic) into a devilish web of dangerous intrigue. First the British police (under a grumpy Timothy Dalton and a fanatical Paul Bettany) and then Russian gangsters (led by a Bond-villainish Steven Berkoff) wrongly identify him as an elusive master-criminal. He's also being followed by a dark, handsome, mystery man (Rufus Sewell at his most laconic). Who on earth could that be?

The Tourist is a luxurious trifle with nothing serious to say – a vastly superior version of the Tom Cruise – Cameron Diaz misfire, *Knight and Day*. The good news is that there are twists and chases a-plenty, and it juggles its hoary old clichés with supreme confidence.

A remake of an obscure 2005 French thriller called *Anthony Zimmer* (which starred Yvan Attal and Sophie Marceau), it's written with tongues firmly in cheek by the director, Florian Henckel von Donnersmarck, who gave us the much more critically respectable *The Lives of Others*, that consummate professional Julian Fellowes (*Gosford Park*) and Christopher McQuarrie, whose best work this is since *The Usual Suspects*.

At least three other scribes were involved – Jeffrey Nachmanoff, William Wheeler and Jerome Salle, but their names appear to have dropped off the credits, along with any mention of *Anthony Zimmer*.

The film's had more than its share of production difficulties, with a couple of directors (Lasse Hallstrom and Bharat Nalluri), two male stars (Tom Cruise and Sam Worthington) and one leading lady (Charlize Theron) all falling by the wayside. Fortunately, those problems aren't visible onscreen. It may be significant that none of those who have dropped out has ever been noted for his or her sense of humour.

The end product is extremely silly, bordering on high camp – so much so that it might easily have been directed by Baz Luhrmann. I guessed what it was up to from reel one, but that didn't stop me from being thoroughly entertained all the way to its joyously barmy conclusion. Not to be taken even half-way seriously, this is – if you're on the right, ironic wavelength – the most nostalgic of escapist pleasures.

An afterword: the overwhelmingly hostile critical reception did not surprise me in the slightest. This is the same kind of movie as *Love Actually* or Baz Luhrmann's *Australia* – a film that plays with cliches and needs the viewer to be on the same wavelength as the people making it. All that most critics saw was some failed attempt at realism, not a highly sophisticated deconstruction of glamour, stardom and this kind of romantic escapism in the movies. I hope that my review enabled a few more people to appreciate it for what it actually was. Interestingly, both stars were nominated for Golden Globes, as was the movie – so clearly a lot of film journalists enjoyed it, even if they weren't prepared to admit so in print.

TOY STORY *(1995)*

Toys come to life as soon as their six year-old owner, Andy, leaves the room. They are the kind of playthings which suggest that Andy's mother (as in so many American "family" films, there's no evidence of a father) has exceedingly retro tastes. Many date from the Fifties or Sixties and they include a cowboy called Woody (with voice by Tom Hanks) who is head toy by virtue of his nice, shiny Sheriff's badge, and the fact that he goes to bed with the boss.

But then Andy has a birthday, with a new influx of presents, and Woody's dominance is threatened by Andy's latest passion, a plastic space ranger called Buzz Lightyear (voice by Tim Allen). Buzz has ideas above his space station – he refuses even to acknowledge that he is a toy, and insists that he has been sent to save the universe, or at any rate Andy's bed, from the evil Emperor Zurg.

The rest of the story is about how Woody is cured of his jealousy and Buzz's delusions turn into realism. They join forces to escape the clutches of Sid, the boy next door, a vicious heavy-metal fan who delights in destroying toys and re-assembling them in devilish combinations – shades here of Tim Burton's *The Nightmare Before Christmas*: very small children may find Sid's mutant creations frightening.

Toy Story was the first movie to be generated entirely by

computer. Fortunately, humans – under the skilful direction of John Lasseter – were still needed to programme those computers. And new technology has been harnessed to an equally inventive script and old-fashioned flair. The result is state-of-the-art fun – not just a children's hit but a landmark in movie entertainment.

Of course, there's nothing new about the idea of toys coming to life. It lies behind nursery tales from Hans Andersen to *Rosie and Jim*. But never before has it been managed with such wit and wizardry.

Even so, digital technology has not reached the point where computer-generated humans can't be distinguished from the real thing. It is at its best evoking hard, plastic, waxy or rubbery surfaces – far less accurate with flesh, so that even the would-be sympathetic human beings in *Toy Story* look so artificial as to be creepy.

Although the screenplay is full of humour and invention, this remains essentially a buddy-buddy action story with no sub-plots, and only just sustains itself for its full 81 minutes.

It is also more likely to appeal to boys than girls. The original intention of the six (male) screenwriters was to have had a Barbie doll help rescue Woody and Buzz from Sid, but Mattel executives vetoed the idea (something they may regret – sales of all toys featured in the movie have rocketed), and there is no sign of Barbie in the finished product – except a set of suspiciously feminine legs forming the bottom half of one of Sid's mutant toys.

The film-makers' introduction of sex (via a docile but man-hungry Bo-Peep, who looks out of place in Andy's bedroom) will elicit cheap laughs from some adults and adolescents, but is unwise since it introduces irrelevant speculations as to what toys get up to in the darker recesses of their toybox. Walt Disney would have excised it, and rightly.

Despite these defects, *Toy Story* was rightly a huge success, and not only with children. It recovered its costs within two days of opening in America, and is among the most profitable films ever made.

The explanation does not lie in electronics. The history of movies is littered with technologically adventurous flops such as *Tron*, *Dune* and the critically acclaimed *Blade Runner*, which failed to tap into the spirit of their age – whereas anyone who cares to probe beneath the surface of *Toy Story* will notice that it tells us more about the Nineties than most supposedly "serious" films.

For the toys in this movie are recognizably grown-ups, and *Toy Story* is essentially a parable about adult male insecurity. The characters inhabit a world where each birthday is a time not for celebration, but for new anxieties about the inevitability of being kicked out of work, in favour of new, technically sophisticated replacements.

The toys may take considerable trouble to gain advance warning of whether their jobs are under threat, but they have no power to protect themselves and certainly no thoughts of unions. Woody, the one toy who does take direct action against the new technology, is immediately sent to Coventry by his colleagues. *Toy Story* is the Nervous Nineties' answer to *The Angry Silence*.

Children watching these toys are, in fact, being invited to sympathise with their own parents – especially their fathers – and the actors do a great job of investing the toys with humanity. Tim Allen (from *Home Improvement* and *The Santa Clause*) makes the egotistical Buzz touching in his naivety. Tom Hanks covers a wider emotional range than in many of the movies which have made him a star.

Other delights include Don Rickles (as Mr Potato Head, understandably grouchy about the way his facial characteristics have of coming unstuck in a crisis) and Wallace Shawn (as a Woody Allenesque Tyrannosaurus Rex neurotic about his macho image).

The world of *Toy Story* reflects a universe in which we are all ageing toys – powerless playthings of employers, technological trends, whimsical Gods. The Satanic Sid, especially, calls to mind that line in King Lear: "As flies are to wanton boys, are we to the gods; They kill us for their sport".

There's an underlying bleakness which is common to many of the great children's films, from *Bambi*, *Dumbo* and *The Wizard of Oz* right through to *Babe*. It helps to make *Toy Story* more than just a technical achievement or a commercial blockbuster, but a children's classic.

TOY STORY 2
(1999)

In this superior sequel, Woody the cowboy doll (voiced with all the charm and subtlety you would expect from Tom Hanks) is having intimations of mortality.

One of his arms gets broken during play and his boy-owner, Andy, doesn't take him camping because of it. He is left to gather dust on an upper shelf. Then Woody, with his ingrained belief in all-American heroism, attempts a daring, one-armed rescue of another endangered toy – a penguin that has lost its squeak – from that ultimate toy nightmare, a yard sale.

Marooned in the yard, Woody gets picked up and stolen by an obsessive toy collector (Wayne Knight) who recognises him as a valuable rarity, one of a set of toys merchandised to cash in on an old, Fifties TV show which featured old-fashioned marionettes (the excerpts we see recreated affectionately in scratchy black and white are reminiscent of our own *Thunderbirds* or *Four Feather Falls*).

Will Woody be sentenced to a life of insulated stardom behind glass in a toy museum, or will he be rescued by his old friends, spaceman Buzz Lightyear (Tim Allen), the irritable Mr Potato Head (Don Rickles), Hamm the pig-headed Piggy Bank (John Ratzenberger), Rex the neurotic

Tyrannosaurus (Wallace Shawn) and Slinky Dog (Jim Varney)?

The answer isn't as clear as you might think, for Woody must consider the rival charms of Jessie the Cowgirl (Joan Cusack) and Stinky Pete the Prospector (Kelsey Grammer), to say nothing of Woody's enthusiastic horse, Bullseye. And, as these new chums point out, if Woody does go back to his boy-owner Andy, he is only going to be outgrown.

"Do you really think," Stinky Pete inquires sarcastically, "Andy is taking you to college? or on honeymoon?" Whereas, if Woody chooses life in a museum, Pete reminds him "you'll be adored by children for generations."

Those are the bare bones of a plot which carries the action far away from Andy's playroom. Oh, did I mention the sub-plot where Buzz Lightyear encounters a new, improved version of himself and is stalked by his deadliest foe, the Emperor Zurg? Or the moment when the chums are tempted from the straight and narrow by go-go dancing Barbie dolls (all voiced with a wicked lack of innocence by the little mermaid herself, Jodi Benson)?

Toy Story was very good, but the sequel is better. It is sweeter, funnier, wittier and more imaginative, with a cleverer story, more exciting adventure and unsurpassed animation. The results on screen are striking: a far greater range of visual expression, especially in the humans (who are starting to look much less like plastic), and some stunning perspectives which exceed even the producing studio Pixar's last offering, *A Bug's Life.*

There's a thrilling chase in an airport baggage-handling area, but that is only one visual highlight (another involves our toy heroes trying to cross a busy main road disguised as traffic cones). And the camera, which even five years ago was limited to simple movements, is able to move as freely as in any live-action picture.

With this movie, animation achieves new heights of visual brilliance. The really encouraging aspect of *Toy Story 2*, however, is the way it marries new technology to time-honoured story-telling skills. This delivers everything you would expect after the first movie – it's basically another chase-and-rescue story – but it is far more than a routine reworking of a familiar formula.

There are numerous riches along the way, including witty jokes about frustrating computer games and the *Star Wars* trilogy; and, refreshingly, the jokes aren't only for grown-ups. There's even a selection of out-takes at the end, just like the ones after *A Bug's Life* (and nearly as funny).

Director and co-writer John Lasseter has five boys of his own, ranging in age from 2 to 18, and it shows. He understands the tastes of modern children (girls included, but especially boys); and I can't imagine any child, from tiny toddler to torpid teenager, whom this film won't entertain and delight.

Adults and children alike will be impressed by the state-of-the-art digital technology. This is the first film to bypass celluloid altogether, and will be shown in certain cinemas via digital projection. The visual and aural clarity are stunning.

Intelligent children should also be able to appreciate the movie's hidden depths. *Toy Story 2* is one of the most thoughtful films there has been about growing up.

There is a surprising degree of universality in the idea of toys being outgrown. After all, it happens to people when they are fired from a job or left by a loved one, or when their children leave home. This film finds something in toys that is not only human and sad, but also noble and uplifting.

Toy Story 2 will remind adults and children alike of toys they once loved but "grew out of". And, in only 95 fast-moving minutes, it makes time to express, emotionally but unsentimentally, some truths about the passing of time that are too often left unsaid.

It's a movie that raises profound issues in a positive way. See it with or without a child, and you'll be talking about it long afterwards. It is a peculiar irony that if you've been waiting for a film with a mature outlook and something valuable to say about love, commitment, morality and mortality, the movie you should be beating a path to is *Toy Story 2*. But it wouldn't do to get too pompous or serious: the bottom line is that this picture is terrific fun.

TOY STORY 3D *(2010)*

Films with 3 in the title don't exactly inspire confidence. Remember *Spider Man 3? Rush Hour 3? Shrek The Third?* However, I am happy to report that the third Toy Story is more like Peter Jackson's *The Return of the King*, a triumphant complement to two great films that preceded it.

Really, it didn't need the gimmickry of 3D. It succeeds because of classic virtues: an exciting story, endearing characters and visual flair.

It's not the usual Hollywood conveyor-belt product. Made with love and intelligence, this adventure has enough thrills, laughs and emotion to satisfy any adult or child. Indeed, there are moments of terror so intense that very small children may find this a tougher experience than they – or their parents – might expect.

It begins mischievously, with a 6-year-old boy's idea of an action adventure – illogical, preposterously overblown and full of thrill-ride pyrotechnics. It's both an introduction to the central toy characters, and a tongue-in-cheek parody of the Michael Bay-Jerry Bruckheimer-Joel Silver school of wham-bam filmmaking. It sums up the energy but limited range of a childish imagination.

But then the movie cuts to 11 years later. Former child-dreamer Andy (voiced by John Morris) is now 17. His mother is nagging him to clear up his room, and get rid of all those toys he hasn't played with for years. Nostalgically, Andy decides to take his favourite, Woody, the noble, heroic, endlessly loyal cowboy (voiced as ever by Tom Hanks), with him to college. The rest, Andy puts in a bin-liner for storage in the attic.

A mix-up with the bin-bags leads to the toys being dispatched, along with a discarded Barbie doll, to Sunnyside, a children's play centre. At first, this seems like paradise, as they are welcomed by a soft-talking, strawberry-scented teddy bear called Lots-o'-Huggin' (Ned Beatty).

Lotso says children will play with them every day, and when these kids become too old they will be replaced. The toys need never worry again about being abandoned.

Unfortunately, this new heaven turns out to be more of a hell. The children turn out to be vicious little savages, too young and uncaring to play with toys this breakable.

Lotso turns out to be a malevolent dictator who hates the young and runs Sunnyside as a police state. He even re-programmes Buzz Lightyear (Tim Allen) to be one of his henchmen.

Meanwhile, Woody has landed up in the toy collection of a shy, imaginative little girl called Bonnie (Emily Hahn), where he discovers that his friends are in danger. So he breaks into Sunnyside and finds his chums behind bars. Together, they plan a jail break.

That bald summary leaves out a good deal that's inessential to the plot, but a lot of fun: the on-off relationship between Barbie (Jodi Benson), ever in search of love, and her new beau Ken (Michael Keaton), besotted with Barbie but a slave to fashion accessories; the tender relationship between Mr and Mrs Potato Head (Don Rickles and Estelle

Harris); the sinister, screaming, cymbal-crashing toy monkey that warns Lotso whenever one of his prisoners tries to escape.

The third script may not be quite as witty as the first two, but it exploits the familiar characters in their unfamiliar settings very effectively, for sentiment as well as laughter.

There is menace, suspense and surprisingly profound emotion, especially towards the end as the toys find themselves on a conveyor belt heading for destruction and they join hands in what may well be their last moments.

Here and throughout the movie, there is a sense of the fragility of existence, as the previously loved but now damaged toys struggle not just for dignity, but also for survival.

The first two Toy Stories explored issues of ageing, change and obsolescence. The third movie takes this further. It even dares to examine the very grown-up idea that some day our lives will have run their course.

Intelligent adults may notice that the movie is, at heart, about letting go and facing death. The fact that it can cover such a weighty topic, and do so with sympathy and humour, is no small miracle.

Another extraordinary achievement of *Toy Story 3* is that it makes us forget that we haven't played with these toys ourselves, that we don't know these characters personally.

Furthermore, the whole film has a very Dickensian feeling for the importance to the human spirit of play and imagination, especially in a lovely scene where an actorish toy hedgehog (voiced by Timothy Dalton) reminds Woody of the pleasures of performing. There are echoes here of the actor-manager Vincent Crummles in *Nicholas Nickleby* and the circus-master Samuel Sleary in *Hard Times*.

Dickens himself would have admired the ingenious

plotting and the ending, which feels sensitive and right. It certainly brought tears to my eyes.

The director is Lee Unkrich, who co-directed *Toy Story 2, Monsters Inc.* and *Finding Nemo.* He and Pixar veterans John Lasseter and Andrew Stanton are credited with the story, though the screenplay is by the admirable Michael Arndt, who rightly won an Oscar for *Little Miss Sunshine.*

They have come up with a masterpiece of animation: a sweet, moving, humane story with heartfelt ideas about the importance of imagination, loyalty and responsibility.

Other films, plays and ballets have captured how toys move. Only the *Toy Story* movies have conveyed the way toys might think. This is one of Pixar's finest, and proof yet again that there's no need to dismiss the best family films as kids' stuff. This is a proper, grown-up film.

UNITED 93 *(2006)*

Can any of us not remember where we were when we saw the first pictures of 9/11? And who among us on the night of 9/11 did not have the nightmare of being on one of those terrorist-controlled airliners – especially on United 93, the fourth plane to be hijacked and therefore the only one on which the passengers knew what had happened to the others? I certainly did, and I wasn't sure whether or not I wanted to live that experience again in the cinema. If I were related to someone who had died, I would have looked forward to this movie even less. But watch it, I did; and *United 93* turns out to be one of the most powerful, visceral films I've ever seen.

Ethically, it's a tribute to director Paul Greengrass that in researching his film he has involved the relatives of those who died, and been sensitive to their wishes.

The film is upsetting, but it's also inspiring to see the human spirit responding to terrorism. Even though this is "only" a movie, it does what only movies can do: make you truly feel as if you were there, but simultaneously give you an overview of what was going on.

United 93 is immaculately researched, expertly shot in a cinema verite way at Pinewood Studios, and makes marvellous use of an unknown cast, some of them actors but a few of them – mostly in the various control-rooms that were trying to make sense of unprecedented events unfolding at terrifying speed – real people who took part in the events, recreating their actions and reactions with astonishing authenticity.

Some critics might argue that Greengrass could have done more to analyse the causes of 9/11 and the grievances of the terrorists; but that is for another film. I'm sure he was right to narrow his focus and make the film that he has achieved so perfectly.

He captures how it must have felt to be intimately involved in the day's shocking events, and he does so to devastating emotional effect. He doesn't sensationalise or sentimentalise. He tells it how it was – and utterly gripping and involving it is, too.

So much has been written about events of that day that we may feel we know all there is to know, every conclusion there is to be drawn. But I was surprised at the almost complete lack of preparedness of the authorities, and the tragi-comic failure to lead by the President and Vice-President when hard decisions had to be made in a hurry.

Horrific as the attacks were that day, they might easily have been worse; and the authorities were at best ineffectual and at worst incompetent. For me, the most unexpected and disturbing aspect of the movie is the total lack of forward planning or procedures by the military to click into place when the nature of the attacks was known.

Disaster movies come in every shape and size, and are generally used to inspire us with tales of heroism. There is heroism in *United 93*, but it's of a non-Hollywood, realistic kind. Greengrass celebrates not only the heroism of the ordinary passengers who tried to overpower the terrorists, but just as importantly the humanity and innocence of those who did not.

This is a great thriller, but it's more than a thriller. It tells a story that needs to be told, and remembered. For those in any position of any power or influence, it should be an inspiration and a warning: to ensure that nothing similar can happen again.

Watching it is much less grim than you might imagine. It will make you treasure your own life and loved ones all the more. There hasn't been a more superbly realized drama-documentary, or one that will etch itself so deep in the memory. It cries out to be seen.

UP *(2009)*

Pixar's tenth film is one of the most uplifting ever made. It's an instant classic and one of those rare movies which will appeal to all ages and intellects. It has heart and intelligence, beauty and excitement, plus loads and loads of imagination.

Pixar has already given us some of the best animated films of all time, in the form of *The Incredibles, Toy Story* and *Ratatouille*. This is on that same exalted level, and it has such originality and so infectious a sense of fun – not to mention some extremely good jokes – that it will bear re-seeing many times.

It's the first Pixar film to have been made in 3D, and that adds something to the experience, with its dizzying heights and balloons so plump you feel you can reach out and pop them, but it's the quality of the storytelling that makes it a masterpiece. It would be just as unmissable on a small, black and white TV.

I don't have any serious criticisms of it as art or entertainment, so consider this an appreciation instead.

It's the tale of Carl Frederickson (brilliantly voiced by Ed Asner), a grumpy septuagenarian who once dreamed of being an explorer – as did his beloved wife Ellie. Together, they saved up to follow in the footsteps of Charles F. Muntz (Christopher Plummer) and visit Paradise Falls in South America, home to a lost world of curious creatures.

But everyday considerations – such as burst tyres and a leaking roof – meant they never followed their dream, and their marriage, though loving, was childless. All this is told in a marvellous montage, as perfect as any the cinema has produced. It's a throwback to the heart-rending emotionalism of the great silent movies, and beautifully scored by Michael Giacchino.

After Ellie's death, Carl decides to escape the developers who are building all round his house by attaching helium balloons to it, and floating off to Venezuela. He accomplishes lift-off with surprising ease, but is annoyed to find himself accompanied by a spherical eight year-old Asian-American called Russell (Jordan Nagal) who is determined to get his last scouting badge by "assisting the elderly", even if Carl patently doesn't wish to be assisted.

I won't tell you any of their adventures, except to say they involve a pack of talking dogs and a large, multi-coloured bird called Kevin. The story becomes extraordinarily bizarre and whimsical, but writer-directors Pete Docter and Bob Peterson somehow keep us amused, excited and aware that there is an underlying point.

For Russell needs a father-figure in his life, and Carl has to learn that parenthood – or, in his case, surrogate grandparenthood – is, in some ways, the ultimate adventure, even if the kid is Asian-American. It's *Gran Torino* with balloons.

Up also has an interesting take on the old Hollywood cliché "Follow your dream". This movie points out that following your dream may take you to a very unexpected reality. Childhood heroes may end up disappointing you. And in order to achieve your full potential you may have to let go of one dream and follow another, which you might previous have dismissed as too prosaic. It's a not dissimilar message to another movie classic, *It's A Wonderful Life.*

This is not a finger-wagging, moralistic film, but it's firmly on the side of conservation, family life and responsible dog ownership, all of which are fine by me.

It wears its profundity lightly and makes all its points with great economy. Would that all Oscar contenders were like this.

Children will enjoy the film, but I'd advise parents to see it with them (don't worry – it's no chore). It raises questions about childlessness and mortality which some may find disturbing, especially if they're clever and/or sensitive. This is not a criticism of the movie – more a sign that some of it, especially the opening montage, may involve children more deeply than the average family film.

Grown-ups may enjoy spotting references to *The Lost World, The Wizard of Oz, Howl's Moving Castle* and even Werner Herzog's *Fitzcarraldo.* The wonderful use of dogs as both threatening characters and light relief evokes fond memories of the Disney masterpiece *Lady and the Tramp.*

It's easy to see that Carl Frederick's square, irascible face was inspired by Spencer Tracy, and the dashing but unreliable Muntz has more than a look of Kirk Douglas.

But *Up* is much more than the sum of its cinematic influences. I especially admired the way it marries the workaday – such as financial worries, creaking, elderly bones and the need of small children to go to the lavatory at inopportune moments – to the most outlandish flights of imagination and adventure.

There are things the characters get up to in the action climax that would have even Indiana Jones scratching his head and taking early retirement.

One minor quibble is that the chronology doesn't make sense, unless Muntz has somehow located a fountain of eternal youth. Another is that the film rarely obeys the laws of physics. But, to be quite honest, I didn't care.

That's mainly because, along with its other virtues, *Up* is funny. I especially liked the way the characters got out of scrapes by using their knowledge that dogs like chasing balls and are easily distracted by squirrels.

There are moments when even a notorious curmudgeon such as myself has to throw up his hands and admit that he was entertained and delighted. Family films as stunning as this don't come along more than once or twice a decade.

UP IN THE AIR *(2009)*

George Clooney revels in the role of his life in this unique and often brilliant mixture of topical drama, romantic comedy and corporate satire.

Ryan Bingham (Clooney at his most charmingly insincere) is an executive whose job is flying round America to do the unpleasant job of "career transition counselling" – in other words, firing people. He shields cowardly bosses from having to tell long-serving employees that they are being "let go".

Ryan is great at his job. Urbane, professional and seemingly caring, he makes his victims feel that there's no shame in getting the sack, indeed that it may open up for them a new world of opportunities. He is as generous with vacuous promises as an air-brushed politician.

Three events make him re-evaluate his predatory lifestyle. His younger sister (played by Melanie Lynskey with a delightful, homely innocence) is about to marry – a reminder that he is semi-detached from his family, at best.

He meets another frequent flyer, Alex (Vera Farmiga) who's as slick, materialistic and keen to avoid "that whole responsibility thing" as he is. They manage a casual coupling whenever their schedules permit. Ryan even finds himself becoming interested in turning their non-relationship into something more permanent.

Thirdly, Ryan's own employer (Jason Bateman) – a sleazebag who greets the global downturn with a delighted "This is our moment!" – becomes worryingly intent on streamlining his own business. He takes on a thrusting young graduate Natalie (Anna Kendrick), who reckons she can do Ryan's job more efficiently by firing people over the internet.

There is, in fact, a gigantic plot hole here. Since Bateman's company is used by employers who can't stomach sacking their own employees in person, why would they hire Bateman's company to do something they could just as easily do themselves? You might think someone as smart and calculating as Ryan would point this out, but hey, it's only a movie...

Anyway, this rickety plot mechanism leads to scary little Natalie accompanying Ryan on his final tour, as a kind of trainee Angel of Death.

Against both their expectations, she is to some extent humanised by her experiences, and Ryan discovers within himself some of his previously repressed paternal instincts.

All of this is funny, well observed and beautifully acted. Kendrick excels as the thawing ice-maiden. Clooney has never been subtler, as he takes his character on a giddyingly steep ascent from callous anti-hero to just-about-feasible redemption.

As two people so glossy and well groomed they seem to have stepped out of a corporate infomercial, Farmiga and Clooney have a sexual chemistry unseen since Pierce Brosnan and Rene Russo struck sparks off each other in *The Thomas Crown Affair.*

Clooney is bound to remind older viewers of Cary Grant in his prime, and Farmiga resembles Barbara Stanwyck at her most fascinatingly impenetrable. Together, they're terrific.

Director and co-writer Jason Reitman, still only 32, has a fine ear for corporate cynicism, as he showed in *Thank You For Smoking*, and an equally great eye for soulless modern hotels and airport architecture. There are, I think, deliberate echoes of Bertolucci's *The Conformist*.

Meanwhile, to increase the fun element, Anna Kendrick's childlike tactlessness towards her elders has the same cutting edge that was evident in Mr Reitman's last hit, *Juno*.

The plot skilfully avoids taking too easy a trajectory. Some unexpected turbulence towards the end delivers a nasty jolt to the audience, just when we think the movie's heading towards Richard Curtis-style cosiness.

The trailer hints at straightforward romantic comedy, with Clooney caught between two women; but really *Up In The Air* is an acerbic morality tale, with a big debt to the tougher, darker side of Hollywood comedy, personified by those near-forgotten greats, Preston Sturges and Billy Wilder.

Clooney's character becomes an iconic figure of the screen – a Gordon Gekko for the 21st century – as he learns belatedly, and painfully, what he has been missing. Refreshingly, too, the women in his life come across as rounded characters, not mere satellites around a dominant alpha male.

Reitman's movie, co-written with Sheldon Turner, is inspired by a novel written by Walter Kirn in 2001, before the present recession, but could hardly be more timely.

Despite his comparative youth, Reitman understands the pain of unemployment and cleverly includes testimony from ordinary people who have lost their jobs – their reactions range from resignation to rage, panic to misery.

Along with the underlying melancholy of recessionary times, *Up In The Air* captures superbly the airlessness of lives lived in the impersonal luxury of hotels and executive lounges.

In essence, the film has something pretty simple to say, which is that careers aren't everything, or even the most important thing, in life. But just because a message is simple doesn't meant that it's false, or shouldn't be stated. Few movies have come out more persuasively in favour of family values.

Hollywood hasn't come up with many mature, intelligent films recently, but this is a film that is much more than the glib comedy that it initially appears. It captures something important and disturbing about our times.

THE VANISHING *(1988)*

A young couple, Saskia (Johanna Ter Steege) and Rex (Gene Bervoets), are driving to the south of France on holiday, when they stop at a service station. Bafflingly, Saskia disappears without trace. Three years later, Rex – taunted by postcards from someone claiming to be Saskia's kidnapper – is still trying to find out what happened to her, via an expensive poster campaign and appeals on television. Eventually, Rex and the villain come face to face.

George Sluizer's first version of his frightening thriller is far superior to his Hollywood re-make, which lost everything that was unusual and truly scary from the original.

This is not a whodunit. We are never in doubt as to the identity of the kidnapper: an apparently ordinary, middle-aged family man, whom we see preparing for the kidnapping with obsessive precision but no great competence. The absorbing questions which remain unanswered until the end are: why did he do it? and what on earth did he do?

As Hitchcock always appreciated, one of the most important things in a thriller is to establish the underlying normality of the protagonists. Sluizer is wonderfully served by all his principals. Johanna Ter Steege is delightful as Saskia, every centimetre the girl next door. Gene Bervoets is a complex, flawed hero (early on in the picture he leaves

Saskia alone in a tunnel: a petty cruelty which finds an echo in the eventual denouement).

Bernard-Pierre Donnadieu is no less complicated a villain: capable of good acts as well as bad, curious to know the extent of his capacities.

Even more skilfully than such acknowledged classics as *Psycho, The Vanishing* plays with the familiar conventions of the thriller, to reveal the sickness, perversity and horror that can lie below the surface of normal life. This is one of the finest, and grimmest, thrillers ever made.

WALLACE & GROMIT: THE CURSE OF THE WERE-RABBIT *(2005)*

Shame on those of you who wondered if Britain's most eccentric auteur Nick Park might cave in to Hollywood pressure and turn out to have feet, as well as characters, of clay. If ever you doubted whether Wallace and Gromit, his most captivating creations, could make the tricky transition from short films to feature-length blockbuster, you can relax. In fact, you can pop the champagne corks and start celebrating. *The Curse of the Were-Rabbit* is pure, 24-carrot gold.

Only recently, Aardman Productions suffered the disaster of having their warehouse burn down. Now they can rejoice in their greatest triumph. The creators of three of the most inventive, funny, animated shorts in history – *A Grand Day Out, The Wrong Trousers* and *A Close Shave* (all starring Wallace and Gromit) – have made an even funnier full-length one. And two of our most cherishable national treasures are about to conquer the world.

Entertaining though Aardman's first full-length feature *Chicken Run* was, Park's second, made by a team of 250 over five painstaking years, is classier and cleverer.

It clocks in at a ceaselessly inspired 85 minutes – you'll need to sit right through the end credits or you'll miss the final joke. The sophistication of its technique is marvellous, mingling claymation with computer animation so miraculously that you can't see the join. Yet it always remains true to its roots in low-tech plasticine-modelling. Park's team has even left in the thumb and finger-marks that give the models such a personal touch.

Their sense of humour is unsurpassed. The addition of *Madagascar* writer Mark Burton to the writing team has not inhibited the whimsical absurdism of director/ producer Nick Park and his usual co-writers Bob Baker and Steve Box (who also co-directs). Although the film is financed by a Hollywood company, Dreamworks, it remains defiantly, eccentrically, refreshingly English.

The story is gentle but not sentimental, child-friendly without being childish, simple enough for tiny tots to follow, yet richly humorous enough to reward the most sophisticated adult (although there are a few seaside-postcard-style, naughty jokes, these are funny rather than gross, and will sail over the heads of children).

The movie has at its centre surely the two most charming characters in animation history. The incorrigibly optimistic inventor Wallace (immaculately voiced, as ever, by Peter Sallis) and his more cautious canine chum Gromit (who has no voice and no mouth, yet still manages to be hilariously expressive) have formed a civilised vermin-removal company for the humane protection of vegetables, called Anti-Pesto.

On the eve of the annual Giant Vegetable Competition in their idyllic village, a sort of north-country Market Blandings, they seem at first to have eradicated the menace of ravenous rabbits by means of Wallace's amazing, dafter-than-Dyson invention, the Bun-Vac 6000. But then a buck-toothed bunny of enormous proportions starts marauding the local vegetable patches by moonlight.

Desperate to avert carrot-crunching catastrophe, the super-aristocratic organiser of the contest, Lady Campanula Tottington (delightfully voiced by Helena Bonham Carter) commissions Anti-Pesto to save the day and ensure that the buck stops here.

Wallace and Gromit's rival bunny-exterminator is Lady Tottington's snobbish and avaricious suitor Victor Quartermaine (Ralph Fiennes at his most splendidly maniacal) who fancies himself as a hunter and wants to shoot the beast – and any other furry creature who gets in his way, including Gromit – with his elephant gun.

Who will succeed in destroying the voracious veggie before it can masticate Gromit's massive marrow? Can Lady Tottington reconcile her need to protect the local fruit and veg with her insistence that "I believe the killing of fluffy creatures is never justified"? Can Wallace and Gromit tempt the monstrous mammal to its doom with a gigantic female rabbit that can flutter its eyelashes, and even bump and grind to David Rose's *The Stripper*?

Will the appalling Victor or the love-smitten Wallace win the hand of the fair and flirtatious Lady ("Call me Tottie") Tottington?

And what is the true identity of the hopping horror that appears by night? What, above all, is its symbolic significance? Can the vicar be right to claim, when he can be torn away from furtively perusing his favourite magazine "Wrestling Nuns", that the Were-Rabbit is an act of God – that by raising vegetables of unnatural size, the village has brought a terrible retribution on itself?

Last but not least, with a rabbit on the rampage that's

the size of King Kong, isn't it a trifle incautious of Lady Tottington to turn up to the Annual Vegetable Competition dressed as a giant carrot?

Don't be deterred if you have never seen any of the Wallace and Gromit film shorts (though I would strongly advise you to do so). Don't worry even if you haven't seen the old films that Nick Park and his pals lovingly lampoon – including such classics as *Frankenstein, Dracula* and *The Wolf-Man*. As Wallace would say, you'll still have a cracking time.

Be warned that this film contains groan-inducing puns. Wallace's obsession with cheese even extends to his library, which includes *East of Edam, Grated Expectations* and *Fromage to Eternity*. And guess where Gromit went to college? Yes: Dogwarts. But so frantic is the rate of great visual as well as verbal gags – I would estimate, at least five or six per minute – that whatever your sense of humour, you should be laughing out loud throughout.

With this film, which builds domestic absurdity to new, surreal and spectacular heights without sacrificing the quaint, homely charm of the original shorts, the endearingly naïve, sweet-natured Wallace and the endlessly resourceful Gromit join the pantheon of great cinematic double-acts.

Fred Astaire and Ginger Rogers themselves would envy the couple's effortless camaraderie, their grace – and, most of all, their scripts.

Like many classic double-acts, not excluding Don Quixote and Sancho Panza, Steptoe & Son, and *Minder*'s Arthur Daley and Terry McCann, Wallace and Gromit are a disguised marriage.

Wallace considers himself the clever, masculine, visionary one, while the more practical, wifely partner (in this film,

Gromit even gets to knit) watches over his excesses with an anxious expression, tries to control the master's intake of Wensleydale (which is giving him middle-age cheese spread), and comes speeding to his rescue whenever he gets into life-threatening scrapes.

The Curse of the Were-Rabbit is uproariously funny, witty and sweet, with many moments of sheer genius. I'm not ashamed to admit that it made me cry, first with laughter, then with joy. You don't often see perfection in a movie, but this is it.

WALL-E *(2008)*

Here's a hero for our time in a masterpiece of futuristic animation. Pixar have brought us some of the most charming and memorable movie icons of the past two decades: from Woody the cowboy and Buzz Lightyear in *Toy Story* through to Remy the ratty restaurateur in *Ratatouille*.

They've created their most appealing character yet in *WALL-E*, pronounced Wally, whose name stands for Waste Allocation Load Lifter – Earth Class. Though essentially a pair of binoculars on a battered metal box, he deserves to stand alongside Babe and ET as representatives of family film at its finest.

WALL-E is the last robot left on earth, because he's solar-powered and nobody bothered to switch him off. He's a game but grimy little chap roaming the planet – not that much of the planet is visible beneath piles of garbage. Mankind has trashed the place and left.

WALL-E spends his time compacting debris into bricks, and piling them up as skyscrapers of scrap. WALL-E's only source of entertainment – a reminder of human contact and better days – is an old VHS tape of the Musical *Hello Dolly*, starring a very young Michael Crawford.

Like Will Smith in *I Am Legend*, WALL-E is lonely. His only friend is a cockroach, and he isn't much of a conversationalist, still less a love object.

WALL-E's robotic routine is disrupted by the arrival of EVE, an egg-shaped reconnaissance device from outer space. He's understandably wary at first of her temper, which is on a short fuse, but falls head-over-caterpillar-tracks in love with her smooth, hi-tech curves. He plucks up the confidence to woo her. He even takes her back to his place, where he introduces her to the delights of bursting bubble wrap.

As part of his attempt to thaw EVE's distinctly mechanical lack of emotion, WALL-E presents her with an old boot, containing the green shoot of a plant he has spotted growing among the debris – at which point she closes down altogether, and awaits the arrival of a rocket to take her back to her mother ship.

WALL-E overcomes his fear of the unknown and tendency to fall apart in moments of stress, and hitches a ride with her into space.

The mother ship is a computerised dystopia, now in the 700th year of a five-year cruise. The human passengers have grown obese, lost the use of their legs and become couch potatoes on their perpetual holiday. WALL-E upsets their cosseted but empty existence, just like Charlie Chaplin innocently sabotaging the company production line in *Modern Times*.

The captain, alerted by the plant to the possibility of life on earth, decides to recolonise the planet, but his on-board computer – like the sinister HAL in 2001: A Space Odyssey – has other ideas. Can the captain, WALL-E and EVE save, or rather re-occupy, the planet?

Writer-director Andrew Stanton's first film for Pixar was the child-friendly *Finding Nemo*. *WALL-E* is more sophisticated, but I did worry whether it was too complex for children to follow.

The pace sags when WALL-E and EVE reach the mother ship, and the Pixar animators fall a little too much in love with their own sci-fi imagery. The film's most enthusiastic admirers may be artists, film-school students and critics. That's not necessarily a good thing. The core audience for this kind of film should surely be children.

Storywise, I would have liked to see more interaction between WALL-E and the captain. The film is least involving when the captain becomes the protagonist, and WALL-E is sidelined. However, the little robot makes a touching comeback in the final reel, and he is so cute during the first 40 minutes that he will keep most children entertained through the bits they don't fully understand.

Despite its imperfections, *WALL-E* deserves the acclaim it will undoubtedly receive. It is superbly animated, full of witty sight and sound gags, and achieves a visual poetry rarely seen in today's action-oriented cinema. I especially liked the way it takes time to be lyrical about things we take for granted, such as dancing or simply holding hands.

The depth of detail, splendid imagery and timelessness of its message mean that it will bear reseeing.

Fans of science fiction will note its numerous allusions to previous high achievers in the genre, including *Star Wars* – in which the mini-robot R2D2 is clearly an ancestor of this movie's hero – and the little-known 1971 film *Silent Running*, which was the first major sci-fi film to have a "green" agenda.

Without seeming to preach, *WALL-E* carries pertinent warnings about the consequences not only of our pursuing an unsustainable level of consumerism, but also of our dumbing down our culture to the point where we become luxury-obsessed simpletons.

WILD BILL *(2011)*

Just when many of us wanted never to suffer through another British gangster film, along comes the best of the lot – a picture that sums up everything that's good about British movie-making. It's quirky, warm and charming. It's also well acted, beautifully written and superbly directed.

Like *Billy Elliot* before it, it inventively recycles dozens of tired clichés to come up with something fresh and exciting.

Charlie Creed-Miles gives the performance of his life as "Wild Bill", a once violent, now befuddled criminal just released after eight years in prison. He drops in on his old council flat in East London, and discovers that his wife has gone on permanent vacation to Spain with her new squeeze.

They've abandoned Bill's understandably angry fifteen year-old son Dean (Will Poulter, the outstanding young actor from *Son of Rambow* and *Voyage of the Dawn Treader*) and his wayward kid brother Jimmy (Sammy Williams, a diminutive urchin who made brief but memorable contributions to *Attack The Block*).

Dean has taken on the burdens of single fatherhood, doing a cash-in-hand labouring job at the Olympic velodrome and cooking to lower than *Masterchef* standards. When Jimmy asks what's for dinner, Dean tells him "toast".

Dean wants nothing to do with the dad who deserted

them. This doesn't bother Bill, as he's planning to go up north and work on the oil rigs. Children are a nuisance, right?

The trouble is that, once Bill has shown up, the social services – in the form of Olivia Williams, Jason Flemyng and Jaime Winston – start trying to put the family together again. This gives the plot comic impetus, with the authorities' keenness to help contrasting with their clients' extreme reluctance to help themselves, but it adds to the realism as well. Too many British films act as though the welfare state doesn't exist.

So Dean blackmails dad into staying on a week or two, long enough to ensure the two boys aren't taken into care.

The big problem is that Bill hasn't got a clue about fatherhood or family. Creed-Miles' face is a study in misery as he puts himself through the hell of trying to be "normal".

Creed-Miles is funny as a transparently hopeless loser – stupid, selfish and feckless – forced by events to undergo a process of redemption. He's helped by a script, by Dexter Fletcher and Danny King, that crackles with cockney wit and has its heart firmly in the right place. It reminded me of the best episodes of *Minder*.

There's a serious side to the film, too. The picture shows the redevelopment of Stratford while making clear that not much has changed below the surface. Without preaching, it's a more effective social document than many films that wear their agenda on their sleeves.

This is a male-dominated picture that doesn't avoid cliché – there's even a tart with a heart – but Liz White manages to endow that potentially stereotypical role with an attractive quirkiness, as does Charlotte Spencer playing a teenage femme fatale and single mother.

Wild Bill has the energy that made Guy Ritchie's first

two films stand out, but doesn't fall prey to the kind of heartless flippancy that ran through *Lock Stock and Two Smoking Barrels* and *Snatch*.

Too many British films, before and after Ritchie, have been seduced by the camaraderie of gangsterism. They trivialise its effects and glamorise its violence.

Wild Bill has its share of swear-words and crudities, but it's moral. This picture has no doubt at all who are the bad guys, though it's happy to acknowledge that some cops are a little too in love with being menacing (Sean Pertwee has an effective cameo as one) and criminals aren't always as tough as they pretend to be – there's a lovely, de-glamorised punch-up towards the end, where one of the bad guys makes his apologies and leaves, explaining that violence isn't really his cup of tea.

This debut film deserves to make 46 year-old Dexter Fletcher a bankable director, especially if next time he can step outside his comfort zone and try something more innovative. His is a familiar face. He starred as a child in *Bugsy Malone*, and as a teenager in TV's *Press Gang*. His career as an adult actor has seen highs and lows, and his misfortune has been to give his best performances in mediocre films, notably *The Rachel Papers* and *The Raggedy Rawney*, which were not widely seen.

Behind the camera, he shows real star quality. His biggest asset is *War Horse* cinematographer George Richmond, who does an excellent job within the budgetary limits, and ensures this never looks like telly.

The title hints that the East End is the new Wild West, and some framings deliberately echo Sergio Leone's spaghetti westerns. As the camera tracks past the tower blocks of east London, they are like a shambolic parody of Utah's Monument Valley in John Ford westerns.

Thematically, the film owes its greatest debt to the classic *Shane*, for it's essentially the story of a father-son relationship. Creed-Miles and Poulter are great in their scenes together. Please don't miss this refreshingly talented new film.

WILLIAM SHAKESPEARE'S ROMEO + JULIET (1996)

Foolishly overlooked at the Oscars, where it received only one nomination – for art direction – this is, I firmly believe (and I've seen it four times), the best Shakespeare picture ever made, and one of the few truly revolutionary films of recent years.

But first, a few warnings. It is loud and crude – deliberately so. The film contains only Shakespeare's text, but this has been pared down to half its length, and some of the dialogue is yelled or drowned out by effects and music – intentionally.

The Australian director Baz Luhrmann (whose first film was the equally entertaining, but more modestly scaled, *Strictly Ballroom*) has noticed, as the makers of *West Side Story* did before him, that there is a strong element of violence and vulgarity in Shakespeare's greatest love story.

Luhrmann, almost alone of those who have approached Shakespeare in the west, has spotted that Shakespeare did not write a play about polite, English people from the professional classes – in other words, the sort of people who have supported Shakespearean theatre since the Victorian era.

He has transported the action to a modern-day equivalent of Verona – a Hispanic-American Verona Beach (the film was shot in Mexico City and Veracruz), where corporations are at loggerheads, gangs carry guns openly, and religious piety exists side-by-side with rampant commercialism. Surprisingly, the Shakespearean verse seems at home here. Iambic pentameters are curiously akin to rapping, which imposes rhythm, structure and metaphors on a way of life that might otherwise fly into fragments.

I am usually suspicious of updated Shakespeare, but here it is carried through with an endearing sense of fun, and sustained over two hours with breathtaking imagination. It may seem, at first sight, to be gimmicky – the prologue is delivered by a TV newscaster, Mercutio is a black drag-queen and drug-pusher, Romeo swallows a tab of Queen Mab (Ecstasy) before going to the Capulets' party; but there's method in this madness, and it springs from a highly intelligent reading of the text.

The Capulet-Montague riots of the play are big acts of public disorder, the kind which would be reported nowadays on television; Mercutio is a show-off, a spinner of dreams, and more than a little infatuated with Romeo; long before he meets Juliet, Romeo is in love with the idea of love – he's in a state of near-perpetual ecstasy.

Inevitably, some will take exception to the flashy style of shooting, which is more MTV than RSC. But whereas the MTV style is often used to disguise second-rate product, here it illustrates first-rate art, generates genuine excitement and reflects a dangerously psychotic society spinning out of control, a hideously vulgar older generation and a horribly violent younger one.

When it's time to slow down and focus on the two starcross'd lovers and revel in Shakespeare's lyricism, the film does just that. There are scenes here of great tenderness and beauty, and we really do come to care about this Romeo and Juliet.

A good deal of snobbery remains in critical circles on both sides of the Atlantic about Americans speaking Shakespeare's verse – for no good reason, since there is no evidence that modern English is any closer to the Elizabethan accent than present-day American. The actors here have been accused of being unintelligible and unprofessional. Not by me. Some of the verse isn't instantly comprehensible to modern ears and repays closer study; but these actors know precisely the meaning of what they are saying, and communicate it with verve, great sensitivity to rhythm, and emotional intensity.

At the head of a terrific cast, Leonardo DiCaprio and Claire Daines are touchingly youthful and inhabit the roles with painful sincerity. Miriam Margolyes exploits her wicked sense of humour as the Nurse, with an outrageous but accurate Hispanic accent; Pete Postlethwaite provides an anguished moral centre as Father Laurence; and Diane Venora is one of the best Lady Capulets I have seen.

Some older people dismissed the film as a lively but flawed introduction to Shakespeare, aimed at those too immature to appreciate the real thing. I disagree profoundly. This is the real thing. It's as fresh, exciting and visually imaginative as *Pulp Fiction*, but with better dialogue and more heart. Of all the American movies released last year, it's the only one which could – and perhaps should – have beaten *The English Patient* to Best Picture.

The fact that it wasn't even nominated says a good deal about cultural conservatism in the USA, but it is no reflection on the talent and daring which went into its making. In the future, when its radical influence will have been felt on the next generation of film-makers, this will be seen as a high point in movies, and a revolution in the treatment of Shakespeare.

THE WINGS OF THE DOVE *(1997)*

It's the decade before the First World War. The heroine is a penniless aristocrat called Kate (Helena Bonham Carter). Her mother is dead, and her father (Michael Gambon) is an alcoholic opium-addict. She is under the wing – and thumb – of a socially ambitious aunt (Charlotte Rampling) who plots her marriage to the young aristocrat Lord Mark (Alex Jennings). Auntie poisons the burgeoning love affair between Kate and an impoverished young journalist called Merton (Linus Roache). Kate gives Merton up, out of family obligation and financial desperation. But Lord Mark has it in mind to marry not our heroine (whom he does love, after his fashion) but Milly (Alison Elliott), a dying American heiress whom he doesn't love at all, but whose money he fancies considerably.

Our heroine notices that rich Milly fancies Merton, the penniless journo, rather than Lord Mark, the scavenging aristo, so she concocts a neat, if cruel, plan: become best friends with Milly, and engineer a romance between Milly and Merton in Venice, so that she will leave him her wealth, thus enabling Kate and Merton to marry...

Movies of Henry James' novels are usually long-winded, fusty and sexless. This is the exception: a glorious film – beautiful, moving and fearsomely truthful about human nature. It has humanity, intelligence and sensitivity.

It creates a world where financial security is all-important, and love is a poor loser. The film presents a chilling portrait of social and sexual mores, but one that most of us can recognise. The ignoble choices that the leading characters take are credible and curiously sympathetic. These characters know they are doing wrong, and it causes them pain. In most movies today, characters do wrong without even knowing it, and the film-makers don't seem to know it either.

The two conspirators are far more sympathetic in the film than they are in the novel – highly necessary, if we are to care what happens to them – yet they haven't been softened.

Where Hossein Amini's script is brilliant – far superior to his work on the critically acclaimed *Jude* – is that he makes James's book relevant to the present day without losing a sense of period. He updates the language with great subtlety, then wisely reduces it to a minimum. The most common fault of literary adaptations is wordiness. Here, words and looks speak volumes. Hardly anyone says what he means, anyway, or means what he says.

Nothing in Iain Softley's directing career – he made *Backbeat*, the movie about the Beatles in Hamburg, and the teen thriller *Hackers* – would suggest he was the right man for this material, but he does a good job. The film is as handsome as anything by Merchant Ivory, and has the lethal perception of Scorsese's *The Age of Innocence*. Unlike Scorsese's film, it is easy to follow and has narrative drive, so it can be enjoyed by a far wider audience.

The Wings of the Dove compares with the very best costume dramas, such as *Sense and Sensibility*. This is partly down to Sandy Powell's lovely costumes, and to Venice, beautiful and threatening thanks to Edouard Serra's masterly cinematography.

It is immaculately cast and acted. Linus Roache works miracles with Merton, who could easily have seemed weak. Alison Elliott – as Milly – radiates the same, natural goodness and wisdom that she showed in *The Spitfire Grill*. Alex Jennings manages the difficult leap from stage to screen far more successfully than he did in Adrian Noble's *A Midsummer Night's Dream*; he is excellent as Lord Mark – no aristocratic buffoon, this, but a deeply troubled man.

However, this is Helena Bonham Carter's show, and she dominates with her dark eyes, strange beauty and sly humour. She deserved to win an Oscar.

She has lost that gawky immaturity which made some of her earlier performances hit-and-miss, and blossomed into a far more controlled actress, capable of replacing a page of dialogue with a single glance, able – like only the very best – to communicate two or three things at once, none of them necessarily the same as the words she is saying.

Her role could easily have been cheapened into the kind of camp villainess that Joan Crawford used to play; Bonham Carter adds sex appeal, intelligence and understanding. This Kate is more than the devious vixen of Henry James's novel; she is a moral being who doesn't always choose the most moral course – which, tragically, makes her like most of us.

THE WRESTLER *(2008)*

In *The Wrestler*, Mickey Rourke delivers the performance of his life, and one of the finest I have ever seen on film.

Rourke's beefy physique more than hints at his other career as a boxer. His swollen, ugly mug makes him look as if a hundred doors have slammed in his face. He's the ideal actor to play Randy "The Ram" Robinson, a wrestler on the skids who's a self-confessed "useless, broken-down piece of meat".

Rent arrears mean that one night, returning from glorious victory, he can't get into his own, squalid trailer, so he has to sleep in his van. The fact that he keeps bedding in there suggests this may not be the first time.

Years of performance-enhancing drugs have taken their toll. His eyes and ears are starting to fail. His long, bleached hair isn't getting any more fashionable.

He hasn't been on speaking terms for years with his daughter (Evan Taylor Wood), and his glaring, masculine defects may have contributed to her becoming a lesbian.

He has bleary eyes for a local lap-dancer (Marisa Tomei) but she isn't allowed to date customers, and anyway her priority is her young son. The Ram's one true love has been his fan base. But even they are deserting him.

The Ram's heyday was twenty years ago. Now, after

collapsing in the dressing room and being given a heart by-pass, doctors warn him that any attempt to re-enter the ring will result in heart failure and death.

So, for once in his life, he does the sensible thing. He retires, gets a job serving at the deli counter of a New Jersey supermarket, and gets back in touch with his daughter. But he is what he is, and that doesn't include being an unselfish family man. Offer him the temptation of a coke-sniffing slut, and he'll forget everything else. He's part lovable lug, part self-destructive loser; and there's never much doubt which side is going to come out tops in that particular wrestling match.

Robert D. Siegel's screenplay is spare, elegant and beautifully structured. I liked the way that Tomei's main supporting character parallels The Ram's emotional journey. She and he are good at only one thing, pleasing an audience, and both are aware that their powers and earning ability are waning fast.

Tomei's role seems at first like a cliched tart with a heart, but she's not only real, she's moving. She still looks extremely fit for her age, which is 44, and Oscars have been won for much less than she achieves here.

As for Rourke, his recent turn in *Sin City* suggested he was ripe for a comeback, and this is it. He shows total commitment to The Ram, finding in him a rueful humour and even a tragic grandeur.

Director Darren Aronofsky was guilty of pretentiousness in both his debut *Pi* and his last movie, the disastrous *The Fountain*. Not here.

Although *The Wrestler* is more conventional than anything he's attempted before, it's more than just a throwback to other great fight movies, like *Rocky* or *Body and Soul*. And It's more warm-hearted than the film it superficially resembles, Scorsese's *Raging Bull*.

Where Aronofsky's previous best film, *Requiem for a Dream*, evoked the horror of drug addiction, *The Wrestler* is equally clear-eyed about the danger of other addictions: to performing, success, and most of all the fickle adulation of fans.

There are two classic scenes at the deli counter: one where The Ram uses his showmanship to make the job work for him, and then a second, when he realises that the public wants him only for what he was, and will always regard the older him as a loser.

Aronofsky takes an unsentimental view of wrestling, seeing it as a degrading modern equivalent to gladiatorial combat. But he also has the sense to see its practitioners as showmen risking all for their "art" and giving each other respect. It's not wrestling but the crowd's applause that's the dangerous drug.

You could see The Ram as some kind of Christ figure, but the movie has fun with that possibility early on, when Tomei looks at his injuries and says they remind her of *The Passion of the Christ*. She tells him about some of the trials experienced by Jesus in Mel Gibson's movie. "Tough dude," he comments, admiringly. "Sacrificial lamb," she replies.

Note the hero's nickname. He is a sacrificial Ram. Although he's the "good guy" in the ring and therefore must triumph to satisfy the mob, convention means that first he has to suffer bloodily at the hands of the "bad guy".

That's why Aronofsky is right to show The Ram's physical suffering in detail. The after-effects of in-the-ring brutality with razor blades, barbed wire and staple guns, are shot with unflinching candour. This is The Passion of The Ram.

And we understand why he's willing to suffer such torments. It's for love of his audience's adulation – for their sins, if you like, which include voyeurism, sadism, gullibility and sheer bad taste.

This is strong meat, and the exact opposite of a feelgood chick flick. You end up with a visceral sense of a brutalised, brutalising celebrity culture, its attractions for adoring and adored alike.

Most films take a benevolent view of the masses – hardly surprising, really, since they are trying to make money out of them. This movie isn't afraid to show the cruelty of the public, and that's virtually unique in a Hollywood film. It's also the reason why, although it's the bravest and best picture of the past twelve months, it probably won't be Oscar-nominated for Best Film.

I watch very few movies which couldn't have been improved upon, but this is one of them. I loved every mythic moment of it.

ABOUT CHRISTOPHER TOOKEY

For 20 years, from 1993 to 2013, Chris was sole film critic for the Daily Mail and the world's most popular online newspaper, Mail Online. In 2013, he won the award Arts Reviewer of the Year from the London Press Club.

Before the Mail, from 1985-93, Chris was TV and Film Critic for the Sunday Telegraph, with other features and reviews (film, TV, theatre and book) for the Sunday Times, Observer, Daily Telegraph, Mail on Sunday, European, Prospect, Books & Bookmen, Literary Review and (in America) National Review.

As a broadcaster, he has frequently presented Back Row and the Film Programme for BBC Radio 4, and appeared as Film Critic for the Radio 2 Arts Programme, BskyB and BSB, Meridian (BBC World Service) and Front Row (Radio 4), along with numerous other radio and TV programmes.

From 1994 to 1998, he was Chairman of the British Film Critics' Circle, producing and presenting its annual awards ceremony in London, in aid of the NSPCC (National Society for the Prevention of Cruelty to Children).

Online, Chris is writer and creator of www.movie-film-review.com, the biggest collection of film criticism in the world, which includes over 10,000 movies from 1902 to the present. He is also the author of the non-fiction books *The*

Critics' Film Guide (1994); Named & Shamed: The World's Worst and Wittiest Film Reviews From Affleck to Zeta-Jones (2010); Tookey's Turkeys: The Most Annoying 144 Films From the Last 25 Years (2014); and *Tookey's Talkies: 144 Great Films from the Last 25 Years (2014).* He is a visiting lecturer on journalism on the City University journalism MA course.

As a composer of musicals, Chris has composed and arranged theme music for several long-running television series and composed 11 stage musicals, produced at the Theatre Royal, Windsor, Haymarket and Phoenix Theatres Leicester, Arts Cambridge, Belgrade Theatre Coventry, Bush and Gate Theatres on the London fringe, and Theatre Royal, Haymarket. In the West End, he has produced and directed shows at the Theatre Royal Haymarket, May Fair, Piccadilly and Fortune Theatres.

The hundreds of TV programmes Chris directed between 1975 and 1986 include the award-winning rock series *Revolver* (ATV), the acclaimed Channel 4 series *After Dark*, the Emmy-winning *Network 7*, the ratings successes *Showtime, Luna* and *Celebrity Squares* (Central), and international chart-topping rock videos including the Katrina and the Waves classic, *Walking On Sunshine.*

Chris was educated at Tonbridge School, where he won a scholarship in History to Exeter College, Oxford. He was President of the Union, Editor of Isis, President of the Etceteras and Musical Director of Oxford Theatre Group. He also directed the winning new play in the Sunday Times-NUS Drama Competition, Tina Brown's *Under the Bamboo Tree.*

REACTIONS TO

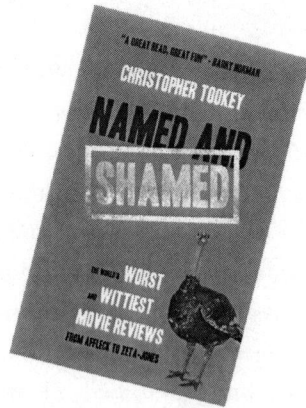

"A great read, great fun. It shows, delightfully, what thoroughly nasty, spiteful people movie critics can be."
(Barry Norman)

"Deriving pleasure from others' misery is not an elevating pastime, and I am not proud of how much I enjoyed this book. But I could not put it down."
(Julian Fellowes)

"I was amused."
(Philip French, *Observer*)

"A comprehensive tribute to the neglected heroism of film critics, who watch awful performances so that public doesn't have to, warning them off with dark savage wit."
(David Gritten, *Daily Telegraph*)